Regine Pe...
1/1988

W9-AJO-109

#9055

(ANTHRO)

THE
GREAT
JOURNEY

THE GREAT JOURNEY

THE PEOPLING OF ANCIENT AMERICA

BRIAN M. FAGAN

with 126 illustrations

THAMES AND HUDSON

To John Desmond Clark and Marie Wormington
with affection and gratitude

© 1987 Thames and Hudson Ltd,
London

First published in the United States
in 1987 by Thames and Hudson Inc.,
500 Fifth Avenue,
New York, New York 10110

Library of Congress Catalog Card
Number 87-50196

Printed and bound in the German
Democratic Republic

Contents

INTRODUCTION

An Archaeological Drama

This book tells the story of the search for the first Americans. The tale is a complicated, sometimes dramatic one, a quest for early artifacts and human fossils, for indisputable proof of the antiquity of humankind in the Americas. It resembles a detective story, but with scientific heroes and villains instead of murderers, sinister butlers, and gifted sleuths. Above all, it is a chronicle of changing ideas about the very beginnings of American history, theories that began as soon as the first conquistadors set foot in the New World.

Even after five centuries of sporadic, and sometimes frenzied, inquiry, the subject is fraught with unresolved enigmas and widely differing theoretical viewpoints. Anyone studying the first Americans sets sail in hazardous academic seas, beset on every side by passionate emotions and contradictory scientific information. So our journey takes us through a maze of controversy. It begins, however, with a quest common to all humanity: the search for our past.

The Quest for the Human Past

All human beings are interested in their origins. They try to account for their existence through complex legends and rituals. European Neanderthals more than 100,000 years ago may have been the first people to ponder the supernatural and the afterlife. Their successors, *Homo sapiens sapiens*, evolved much more complex myths to explain and organize the natural world, myths found in every corner of the globe in the form of chants, poems, songs, and recitations.

One of Western civilization's more marked characteristics is a desire to put myths to the test, to explore not just our immediate surroundings but the world beyond the next horizon. This curiosity led Alexander the Great to the Indus, the Greeks to speculate about the barbarians of the far north, the Romans to explore the Sahara Desert. The Venetian merchant Marco Polo ventured to China in about 1271. Not only fabulous profits, but a deep-seated curiosity, drove him and his father along the Silk Route to the east. When the Age of Discovery dawned in the fifteenth century, Prince Henry the Navigator and his successors sent expedition after expedition down the west coast of Africa and beyond, in search of new markets, in the service of God, and in response to a quiet, almost irrational, urge to explore new places, perhaps the mythical Golden Land, Paradise on Earth. The Age of Discovery did not reveal Paradise, but it led to the most startling find of all, that of the Americas.

It is difficult for us, living as we do in a familiar world of jet aircraft and instant communication, to imagine what it would be like to encounter a wholly new continent, not only with unfamiliar plants and animals, but also with a startling variety of human inhabitants. Today, our frontiers lie in the unpeopled wilderness of space, but 500 years ago the frontier was on earth – a land inhabited by people so exotic that those who discovered them were tempted to wonder whether they were human at all. These were the American Indians, a people of such cultural diversity that there were at least 2,000 different societies among them.

Centuries passed before Europeans adjusted to the very existence of the American Indians and ventured beyond the bounds of raw exploitation, casual curiosity, and romantic illusion. But from the very earliest days of European settlement, sheer curiosity impelled cleric and scholar alike to puzzle over the

From the very first days of contact, Europeans were intrigued by the native Americans and their customs. Cortés brought back a group of Indians from Mexico and they were displayed at the Spanish court, among them a man in a brilliant feathered cape (left), a juggler (center), and a warrior holding a parrot and what may be an Aztec battle insignia (right).

origins of the native Americans. The early Spanish friars listened to Indians talking of their symbolic world. "It is told that when all was in darkness, when yet no sun had shone and no dawn had broken – it is said – the gods gathered themselves together and took counsel among themselves . . ." began one Aztec legend. Their philosophies of life and attitudes to their own history were very different from those of Christian people. The Aztec traditions did not go far to satisfy European scholarly curiosity. Who were these exotic people? Where had they come from, and how long ago had they settled in their vast homelands? The Spanish theologians and historians of the day looked beyond the tribal lore of the Indians themselves into a timeless historical vacuum, as featureless and unknown as space.

Five centuries ago scholars turned to the only known historical sources that might yield clues about the Indians – the scriptures, and the classical writings of ancient Greece and Rome. It was hardly surprising that the first theories about Indians spoke of Phoenicians, Tartars, and other exotic peoples mentioned in the Old Testament. These speculations persisted for more than three centuries. It was not until the nineteenth century that archaeological discoveries in North America and Mexico were to replace theological supposition with hard, scientific facts. And for generations, until the 1840s, the priceless historical information collected by sixteenth-century Catholic friars among the Aztecs, Incas, and other Indian peoples languished in ecclesiastical archives, suppressed by a bureaucracy obsessed with vanquishing idolatry and heresy.

Lost Civilizations and Brave Adventurers

While early scholars pored over their documents, the myth-makers stepped into the breach – and have never fully been dislodged. Like the ancient Egyptian pyramids, Stonehenge, and the Dead Sea Scrolls, the first Americans attracted every variety of mystic, crackpot, and religious cultist. Such wild theorizing would not be surprising in the eighteenth and nineteenth centuries, when so little was known of American Indian society. However, as so often happens, many people have now changed these theories into articles of faith, into pseudo-scientific dogma that brooks no opposition. The Phoenicians, who never ventured this far from the Mediterranean, and the lost continent of Atlantis are alive and well in twentieth-century America!

Why do such lunatic ravings persist? Perhaps it is the subject matter, the mystery of the unexplained peopling of an entire continent. Many cultists have philosophical axes to grind, often based on racist assumptions that American Indians were incapable of much more than the simplest of tasks. This fringe literature is rich in obscure Biblical quotations and stirring tales. There are vicious wars between competing hosts, epic voyages across Atlantic and Pacific, as well as survivors of sunken continents peopling the New World.

To read the crank literature on the first Americans is to enter a fantasy world of strange, often obsessed, writers with a complex jargon of catchwords and "scientific" data to support their ideas. Some of them even form new religious cults, with themselves in the role of the ultimate prophet, or the Supreme Deity himself . . .

Few would deny that these topics are entertaining byways. But archaeologists believe that the scientific search for the first Americans is much more engrossing.

Caution and Controversy

Scientists, by the very nature of their work, are concerned with ideas, just as pseudo-scientists are, but with a difference. Their ideas are hypotheses, propositions based on scientifically collected data, then tested and modified by more data. Such hypotheses can thus change, sometimes slightly, sometimes dramatically, every time the scientist ventures into the field or examines another colleague's work. However, beyond agreeing that science is quite different from pseudo-science, there is little unanimity among American archaeologists about the origins or dating of the first Americans.

A small group of archaeologists is devoting their careers to the search. Many are cautious scholars. Others are gripped by profound convictions that cause them to espouse extravagant viewpoints in the face of overwhelming evidence to the contrary. A gathering of scholars studying the first Americans is never dull, for controversy invariably erupts, sometimes veiled in carefully studied politeness and firm dogma, sometimes dissolving into academic shouting matches. Very often the arguments are more remarkable for their vehemence than their scientific substance.

This passion is hardly surprising, for the peopling of the Americas was an event – or series of events – unique in world history. How did humans, essentially tropical animals, free themselves from their primeval African environments and journey from Asia into a vast, seemingly unpopulated landmass? This momentous journey ranks among the greatest adventures in human experience, far more exciting to analyze than the lost tribes or sunken continents of the lunatic fringe.

The earliest claims made by scientists date first settlement to 100,000 or 200,000 years ago, perhaps even earlier. This school of thought was once led by the late Louis Leakey, world famous for his early fossil discoveries at Olduvai Gorge in East Africa. In his later years, Leakey believed that very early human fossils and artifacts would be found in the Americas. "Americans don't know what these things look like," he told me many years ago. "Anyone from Africa is qualified to look over there. We know what early tools look like." I was a young African archaeologist at the time. He urged me to search in North America for chopping tools and artifacts like those from Olduvai

Gorge. At Calico Hills in southern California, Leakey later believed he had found his proof, stone tools up to 200,000 years old.

Leakey's claims for Calico Hills would imply that the toolmakers there were a pre-modern species – since modern humans did not appear until 40,000 years ago – probably *Homo erectus* or early *Homo sapiens*, people with much more limited intellectual capabilities than ourselves.

But if not 200,000–100,000 years ago, could people have settled in America between 100,000 and 40,000? This was the time of the Neanderthals in the Old World. Neanderthals have been popularized in Jean Auel's bestselling novels, such as *Clan of the Cave Bear* and *The Mammoth Hunters*. They were skilled hunters and food gatherers, as we shall see, who adapted to a very wide range of tropical, temperate, and cold environments. On the face of it, there is no theoretical reason why they could not have settled in the New World. Some scholars believe that they did.

The last great Ice Age glaciation climaxed after 35,000 years ago, reaching its icy peak between 25,000 and 15,000 years ago. Many isolated stone artifacts and rockshelter finds are claimed to document first settlement during the cold millennia after 25,000 years ago, perhaps even somewhere between 35,000 and 25,000. By this time, Neanderthals had died out. Scientists of this persuasion thus believe that the first settlement coincided with the emergence of fully modern humans – *Homo sapiens sapiens* – in the Old World, and with a rapid colonization of hitherto unoccupied lands, including both Australia and the Americas. Hunters and gatherers would therefore have lived in the New World during the last millennia of the Ice Age. Recent claims for 32,000-year-old settlement in a rockshelter in northeast Brazil have been greeted with great enthusiasm by archaeologists who argue for a relatively early date for the first Americans.

The most conservative viewpoint argues that no humans lived in the Americas before the end of the Ice Age. Tiny numbers of big-game hunters moved south of the great North American ice sheets as the glaciers retreated after 14,000 years ago. The newcomers followed large Ice Age animals into more temperate latitudes. They expanded rapidly over vast tracts of virgin hunting territory, their immediate descendants the famous Clovis people, whose distinctive stone spearpoints have been found over much of North and Central America.

This hypothesis implies that cultural or environmental barriers prevented people from entering the temperate heart of the New World until the climate warmed up in post-glacial times. Ice sheets, severity of climate, rugged terrain, perhaps inadequate arctic clothing or tools, even the lack of suitable watercraft, may have inhibited earlier settlement.

This book is both a narrative and a detective story, the marshaling of archaeological and other scientific evidence against at least four contrasting viewpoints. The story is a challenging one to piece together, largely because the evidence for the first Americans is still incomplete, a script of archaeological shreds and patches.

The word "script" is appropriate, for archaeology has been compared to an unperformed play – a set of separate scenarios that await the actors to link them into a coherent whole. Our journey into America's past is like such a play, a sequence of interconnected scenes that themselves also stand on their own. It is not so much from the detail, but from the *overall* picture of world prehistory that emerges, that we find the clues that support, or undermine, the archaeologists' competing hypotheses. So the narrative is written in the form of a drama with several acts, the sum of the whole providing a cumulative hypothesis as our solution of the mystery.

The first act begins not in the Americas, but deep in the Old World, where hunting and gathering societies flourished hundreds of thousands of years before human beings set foot in the New World. An understanding of what happened in Old World prehistory is vital, for one of the main contentions is that inhabitants of the Americas must have come from elsewhere. Their cultural and biological roots, it is argued, grew thousands of miles away from the North American heartland, from Mexican lowland forests, or Andean deserts. They lay in the Old World. So the events of the first act have a critical bearing on later scenes set in the Americas themselves.

Once in the New World ever-changing climatic conditions, rising and falling sea levels, massive ice sheets, and the habits of game animals, large and small, all feature prominently in the story, both in what is now Alaska and the Yukon Territory and in more southern latitudes. The narrative reaches its climax with the appearance of the Clovis people about 11,500 years ago, the moment at which a continuous record of human achievement in the New World begins. The last act recreates their opportunistic, highly mobile existence, living off not only now-extinct mammoth and other big game, but all manner of smaller animals and plant foods as well.

The drama may have resolved the main enigma of first settlement, but it has revealed further puzzling and fascinating mysteries. Why did the great big-game animals of America die out at the end of the Ice Age? Were human hunters the culprits or was it a natural catastrophe? How did the Folsom people of the Great Plains – successors to Clovis – adapt to life without the mammoth as prey? And were there successive waves of immigrants from Asia, or did the societies Renaissance Europeans discovered all evolve from those very first Ice Age bands? Our final three chapters explore these enigmas and the great diversity that was the native American achievement.

But our story begins in the fifteenth century, when scholars had little more than the scriptures and classical literature as sources on world history. Nearly four centuries were to pass before archaeology became a science and the archaeologists of the 1850s to 1880s posed the basic questions that still concern us today.

PART ONE

IDEAS

"After the discovery of America, the minds of the learned and ingenious were much exercised to account for its habitation by men and animals."

Samuel Haven, 1856

Frontispiece to an astronomical text of 1537, by which time America had been correctly identified as a separate continent, even if its exact location remained in doubt.

CHAPTER ONE

Friars, Antiquarians, and Moundbuilders

On 12 October 1492, Christopher Columbus, Admiral of the Ocean Sea, sailing under the Spanish flag, set foot on the tiny island of San Salvador in what is now the Bahamas. There he found naked people, "very well made, of very handsome bodies and very good faces." The Admiral's first inclination was to clothe the men and set them to work. "They ought to be good servants and of good skill," people "that would easily be made Christians." Columbus claimed speciously to his Spanish backers that the islanders wanted nothing more than to become Christians and good subjects of the Crown. Within a generation the exotic island populations were decimated by disease and mistreatment, enslaved, and viciously exploited to the point of virtual extinction. Few paused to wonder where they had come from, or how long they had lived in their homelands.

Columbus himself believed that he had reached the outlying islands of east Asia. So he called the inhabitants of the new lands "Indians." At the time, "India" referred to all of Asia that lay east of India's Indus River. So it was entirely logical for him to call the lands he claimed for Spain "the Indies," and its people *Indios*. The name has persisted to this day. But only seven years after Columbus' death in 1506, Vasco Nuñez de Balboa trekked across Central America and gazed on the Pacific. The Indies were not part of China at all, but what "we may rightly call a New World more densely peopled and abounding in animals than Europe, or Asia, or Africa." The discovery of this world was an intellectual watershed in Western history that raised fascinating, and fundamental, questions about the origins of the indigenous Americans.

Lost Tribes, Sunken Continents

The debate over the American Indians began when Columbus paraded some of his captives before the Spanish court. Who were these strange people? Were they rational human beings, who could be converted to the True Faith? Pope Alexander VI himself issued a proclamation declaring the Indians were "people well disposed to embrace the Christian faith." This opened the way for a floodtide of exploration and European settlement. Most Spaniards

The King of Spain observes Columbus's landing in the Indies – a woodcut of 1493.

thought of the Indians as primitive savages living on the fringes of Asia. As such they might make excellent slaves. But in the event the Indians proved an unprofitable investment in the slave trade since they tended to succumb quickly to European diseases. Their importation was soon forbidden.

At first, all Indians were assumed to be simple, unsophisticated people. Then, in 1521, Hernando Cortés conquered Mexico and revealed the dazzling and exotic world of the Aztecs. Thunderstruck, his conquistadors gazed on the Aztec capital, Tenochtitlan. "These great towns . . . and buildings rising from the water, all made of stone, seemed like an enchanted vision," wrote conquistador Bernal Diaz. The Spaniards wandered through an Indian metropolis of more than 200,000 people, and marveled at a great market that rivaled those of Seville and Constantinople. The Aztecs, polished warriors and diplomats, people of grace and manners, were a far cry from the Bahamian Indians, even if they did engage in human sacrifice.

Soon stay-at-homes in Europe could see a surprisingly wide variety of native Americans, shipped back by explorers, missionaries, and slavers. The Aztec nobles and acrobats who spellbound the Spanish court in the 1520s were by far the most sophisticated captives to reach European shores. Others were much simpler people of a "sooty colour." Bristol merchants brought back some North Americans "clothid in beastys skinnys," who ate raw meat and had the manners of "bruyt bestis." And when King Henri II of France visited Rouen in 1550, no fewer than fifty Brazilian Indians danced, fought, and hunted in a specially constructed jungle village on the banks of the Seine.

2 **The World: A Modern View** North America, with Siberia (top left), the arctic polar ice cap (top center), and northern Europe (top right), as they might be photographed from an orbiting satellite. Today the frontiers of exploration lie in the wilderness of space, from where we can see the world for the first time as a single, fragile entity. But modern science also enables us to explore further back into the past than has ever been possible before. When and where did humanity evolve? Who were the first Americans? New discoveries in archaeology in recent decades have revolutionized our knowledge of human origins. The peopling of America can be understood only as part of the process of the peopling of the globe.

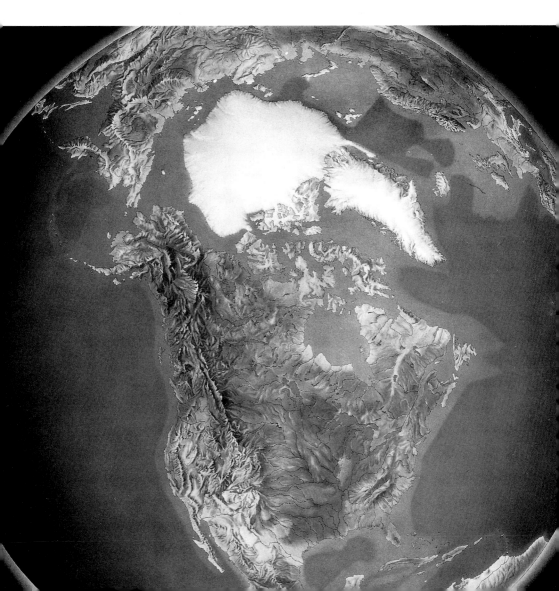

1 **Nebraska Sioux Indian** Hollow Horn Bear, photographed in 1907, a proud descendant of America's first colonists. His straight hair, dark eyes, and beardless chin are hallmarks of the American Indian. Despite many physical similarities, American Indians became a very diverse people.

3 **The World: An Aztec View** In contrast, the Aztecs dwelt in a more narrowly circumscribed world. Although they controlled the destinies of over 5 million people, the Aztecs had only a limited geographical knowledge, confined to Central America. They knew that other civilizations had preceded them in a symbolic world that was destined to end one day. Their world view was based on ancient cosmic myths, some of them commemorated on the famous Stone of the Sun, a sacrificial altar dedicated in about 1470. It depicts Tonatiuh, the Sun God. His countenance is surrounded by paneled reliefs depicting the dates when four earlier worlds ended. The Fifth Sun, the Aztec world, the world of the stone, will also end. The Aztecs believed they could ensure the continuity of life by nourishing the sun with the magic elixir of human hearts. But all they could do was to postpone the end of the Fifth Sun. For many Aztecs the Fifth Sun ended with the Spanish conquest.

4 **Tenochtitlan**, the Aztec capital, an impressive metropolis that housed more than 200,000 people. The huge central Plaza, here reconstructed by artist Ignacio Marquina, could hold "8,600 men, dancing in a circle." The Great Temple, dedicated to the national war-god Huitzilopochtli and the rain-god Tlaloc, dominated the north side. Moctezuma lived in a palace on the east side. The Plaza was a bustling place, ablaze with bright colors and brilliant uniforms.

5 **Jan Mostaert's "An Episode in the Conquest of America"** (*c.* 1542) may depict the attack by the Spaniard Coronado and his men on the Zuñi Indians of the Southwest in 1540. Mostaert's fantasy landscape shows a simple, pastoral people confronted by strange invaders. Images like this inspired subsequent exploration by competing European powers.

White's drawings of Eskimos from Baffin Land in 1577 (*right*) show the sewn clothing that enabled them to adapt to the extremes of the arctic. The man carries a simple bow. Both the man and his wife wear anoraks with closely fitting hoods (a child peers out of hers). Eskimo garments were much more effective than contemporary European cold-weather clothing, and caused considerable interest in exploring circles.

10 **The French in Florida** French artist-cartographer Jacques Le Moyne painted explorer René de Laudonnière with Chief Athore in 1564. Despite the peaceful image, mutiny and disease soon destroyed the French expedition.

6–9 **John White's America** Elizabethan artist John White depicted Virginia Indians of the Carolina Sounds and their lives in a charming, romantic style that was to influence European views of the Indians for generations. In about 1585 he painted a stockaded settlement with thatched houses (*below*), complete with families sitting around a fire and storehouse. The bow-carrying warrior (*right*) bears intricate body tattoos and a feather in his hair. A chief's wife (*near right*) carries a gourd, accompanied by her daughter "of the age of 8 or 10 years." Similar male and female figures were depicted taking part in a ceremonial dance (*opposite below*), stepping "with all the antick postures they can invent" around wooden posts carved with human faces.

Even the most unsophisticated observers began to realize there were not just "Indians," but dozens of different tribes, bands, and civilizations, many of them at odds with one another. But how is it, scholars asked, that there are such contrasts in Indian societies, between simple hunting bands and complex civilizations only a few hundred miles apart? The only historical precedent came from the scriptures. The Old Testament showed that all humans were descended from Adam and Eve, and from the eight survivors of Noah's Flood. Their descendants had peopled not only Europe, Africa, and Asia – but the New World as well. How had the Indians reached the Americas? By land or sea from Asia? Or, alternatively, had some "unknown pilot" crossed the Atlantic from the Mediterranean long before Columbus? Had Europeans discovered the New World centuries earlier, and then simply forgotten about it?

In the sixteenth century, the Atlantic school held sway, arguing that ancient Carthaginians had settled the Americas in epic voyages more than 2,000 years before Columbus. This hypothesis gave way to the legend of the Lost Continent of Atlantis. In 1535, the Spanish writer Fernandez de Oviedo read the Greek philosopher Plato's *Timaeus* and *Kritias*, in which the Athenian wrote of the lost civilization of Atlantis from the western ocean, which mastered the world. "Afterwards there occurred violent earthquakes and floods; and in a single day and night of misfortune . . . the island of Atlantis . . . disappeared in the depths of the sea." Oviedo and his successors were captivated by the story, but they modified it to conform with religious dogma. They believed Atlantis was a vast, flooded continent that had once extended from Cadiz in Spain to the Americas. This had allegedly been colonized by the descendants of Noah after the great inundation. When disaster struck, only the American Indians survived to greet the conquistadors centuries later. The Atlantis legend is perhaps the most persistent of the early theories. Even today, constant rumors of sunken temples in the Bahamas and off the coasts of Spain spark "scientific" expeditions and titillate the imaginations of the romantically inclined.

Then there were the ideas of an obscure Dutch theologian named Joannes Fredericus Lumnius. He argued in 1567 that the ten tribes of Hebrews exiled by Assyrian King Shalmaneser in 721 BC, and mentioned in II Kings 17:6, had escaped to spread all over the world, even across Asia to the New World. He, and many of his successors, were more than ready to relegate the American Indians to the same miserable status as that enjoyed by many European Jews. The Lost Tribes theory has been closely tied to religious beliefs ever since the sixteenth century. It forms a central part of the *Book of Mormon*, which declares that the American Indians are descendants of the Hebrews. The voluminous literature on the Ten Tribes traces cultural parallels all over the world. It treats of sun worship, physical features like long noses, and exotic burial customs – all traits said to link the Indians with the Hebrews.

Even as Lumnius' theory took hold, however, a handful of serious scholars in New Spain (Mexico) and Peru were delving into American Indian history.

"Short Stretches of Navigation"

Spanish friars, ardent missionaries of the True Faith, were the first serious students of the American Indians. Bartolomé de Las Casas had been a landowner in Cuba in the 1500s before suffering a crisis of conscience about the treatment of the Indians. He became a Dominican friar and spent the rest of his life advocating the Indian cause. Although with little time to study or speculate about their origins, he did observe some traces of early occupation in Mexico covered by more recent soil: "Because this could not happen except by the passage of many years and most ancient time," he wrote presciently, "there is not a great argument that the people of these islands and continent are very ancient."

Another, somewhat younger, Dominican friar, Bernadino de Sahagun, devoted his life to chronicling Aztec history and customs preserved in their fast-vanishing oral traditions. He learnt their language, Nahuatl, and spent years talking to survivors of the Spanish Conquest. Sahagun heard about the intensely symbolic Aztec world, a world known as the Fifth Sun that was destined to end in cataclysm, about the Aztecs' rapid rise to power in the Valley of Mexico, and about their sophisticated religious beliefs and philosophies. Sahagun's research was controversial with his superiors. His great twelve-volume work, *A General History of the Things of New Spain* (compiled 1547-1569), was considered so pro-Indian and potentially subversive that it was filed away by the church authorities. Publication could well have advanced the cause of idolatry, so the *General History* languished in Catholic archives until the more tolerant nineteenth century.

Sahagun's contemporary, the fanatical Bishop Diego de Landa, worked among the Maya Indians of Mexico's Yucatan. He spoke the local dialect so fluently he could preach to the Indians in their own tongue. De Landa visited long-abandoned Maya temples and ceremonial centers. He admired "many beautiful buildings . . . all of stone very well hewn" and examined prized Maya codices (bark-paper documents), even deciphering some of their elaborate hieroglyphs. Then he calmly turned round and burned the priceless records, as "they contained nothing in which there were not to be seen superstitions and lies of the devil." The wholesale burning "caused them [the Maya] much affliction," he wrote with glee. Modern archaeologists have also bitterly regretted his cavalier act.

With no other historical sources to turn to other than the scriptures, the friars believed, like everyone else, that all American Indians, even the Aztecs and Maya, were ultimately related to familiar ancient societies in the Old Testament, like the Tartars, Scythians, and biblical Hebrews.

In the sixteenth and seventeenth centuries, North American Indians were thought of by Europeans as simple people, scantily clothed and leading a primitive existence, as in this Florida hunting scene of 1590.

The less sophisticated Indians to the north of Mexico were even more confusingly diverse. The personal qualities attributed to them reflected the biases of their observers. For instance, the promoters of Elizabethan Virginia depicted their Indian neighbors as friendly, noble-minded people who did not abuse nature. The more northern tribes were apparently hardier, like explorer Martin Frobisher's Baffin Land Eskimos. He brought a man and a woman back to England in 1576. The hunter obligingly paddled his skin canoe on the Avon River near Bristol and shot ducks with his bow and arrow.

The few North American Indians known in Europe during the sixteenth and seventeenth centuries were thought of as simple people, many of them wearing few clothes and using the most primitive of artifacts. They contrasted dramatically with the Aztecs and the Inca of Peru. Given Christian belief in the Fall of Mankind, most observers thought of all Indians, even the most civilized, as degenerate, irreligious people who had migrated from the Garden of Eden and not been in the New World for long. The philosopher Francis Bacon summed up prevailing feelings well: "Marvel you not at the thin population of America, nor at the rudeness and ignorance of the people," he wrote, "for you must accept your inhabitants of America as a young people: younger a thousand years, at least, than the rest of the world."

If the Indians had indeed come from the Garden of Eden, how, then, had they got to the New World? Siberia was still a geographical blank on sixteenth-century maps, but there were a few scholars who wondered if the American Indians had walked rather than sailed to their homeland. The Jesuit missionary José de Acosta served among the Indians of Mexico and Peru during the 1570s and 1580s. His famous *Historia Natural y Moral de las Indias*, which appeared in 1589, was remarkable for its speculations on the subject. It was entirely possible, he wrote, that "men came to the Indies driven unwittingly by the wind." However, he felt that most of the Indians had reached the New World in the same manner as the unfamiliar wild beasts that abounded in the Americas – by land. He theorized that small groups of "savage hunters driven from their homelands by starvation or some other hardship" had taken an overland route through Asia to their present homeland. There were, he speculated, "only short stretches of navigation." At first, Acosta continued, only a few Indians lived in the Americas. But they settled down and their descendants developed not only agriculture, but elaborate states such as those of the Aztecs and Inca. Acosta calculated that the first migrations had occurred as early as a couple of thousand years before the Conquest of Mexico. He wrote all this a century and a half before Vitus Bering sailed through the Bering Strait in 1728.

Mounds and Moundbuilders

In 1856, just over two-and-a-half centuries after José de Acosta wrote of "only short stretches of navigation," a wise and sober antiquarian named Samuel Haven sat down in his comfortable Massachusetts study to compose an essay on the archaeology of the United States. Haven had served as Librarian of the American Antiquarian Society for nineteen eventful scientific years. Every significant monograph or article on American archaeology had passed through his hands. He had been at the center of research into the ancient Americans for a generation. This bluff, reserved scholar was well qualified for the onerous task that lay in front of him.

With cool and dispassionate skepticism, Haven cut through the centuries of speculation. He started with the accounts penned by early travelers like Robert Beverley, a Virginia-born Englishman, whose *History and Present State of Virginia* appeared in 1705. Beverley was deeply intrigued by the Algonquin Indians, who were his neighbors. He admired their physique: "They are straight and well proportion'd, having the cleanest and most exact limbs in the world. . . ." He described their dwellings, fortified settlements, and daily life. The honest Beverley looked at the Indians through somewhat romantic eyes, as was fashionable in intellectual circles in Europe at the time.

John Lawson was a contemporary of Beverley, who traveled deep into what is now the Carolinas. His account of the Indians there appeared in 1709. He admired the Waxhaw Indians with their flattened heads shaped by binding during infancy. They showed him how to stalk deer with a decoy mask, and he lamented the rapid passing of their ways. Lawson was no romantic, but was favorably disposed to the local people, who were under severe cultural stress. "We look on them with Scorn and Disdain," he wrote. "For all our Religion and Education, we possess more Moral Deformities and Evils than these Savages do." He accused the settlers of making way for a Christian colony "through a Field of Blood."

Haven also read accounts of Indian life compiled by travelers into the far interior of the unknown country west of the Appalachians. There was Dutchman Antoine Simon Le Page du Pratz, who explored the Mississippi in the service of the French-financed Company of the West for sixteen years from 1718. His *History of Louisiana* (1758) summarized not only his experiences among the Natchez and other Mississippi peoples, but the travels of other French explorers along fur trade routes, even as far afield as western Kansas. Le Page du Pratz theorized that " the natives of North America derive their origin from the same country, since at bottom they all have the same manners and usages, as also the same manner of speaking and thinking." He believed they were descended from the Tartars of Asia, except for his favorite Natchez, who were of Phoenician origin.

The Age of Enlightenment made science fashionable in eighteenth-century intellectual circles. Informal associations of gentlemen botanists and zoologists in London and other European capitals corresponded with travelers and fellow enthusiasts in America. In time, an equivalent closely knit natural history circle came into being in Philadelphia. The circle included many famous men, among them Benjamin Franklin, Benjamin Smith Barton, and Thomas Jefferson, as well as members of the Bartram family, probably the most famous botanists ever to work in North America.

The Bartrams, father John and son William, were brilliant collectors, whose botanical garden near Philadelphia, America's first, was stocked with thousands of plant species from all over the southeast and elsewhere. William Bartram traveled widely in the 1770s, among the Seminoles of central Florida, also the Cherokee and Creek peoples further north. A deep believer in the nobility of humanity, he viewed the Indians as "generous and true sons of Liberty." His *Travels* set the Indians in a tropical summer paradise, the Cherokee living in villages built on, and around, ancient artificial mounds. Hundreds of these earthworks dotted the landscape, but the Cherokee could only tell him they had been there when their ancestors settled in the area.

Bartram's *Travels* appeared in 1791, and proved a disappointment in America, where few people thought of the Indians in a romantic light. But European scientists and intellectuals embraced the book with enthusiasm. It became a source of inspiration for Coleridge, Wordsworth, and other English poets. The occasional Indian chief brought to London was no longer a curiosity, but living proof that "noble savages" were dignified and uncomplicated people.

Thomas Jefferson was a friend of the Bartram family and, untypically for his time, a serious scientist with a deep interest in, and respect for, American Indians. Jefferson had collected Indian artifacts, and was an authority on their languages. He urged collection of vocabularies that would "furnish opportunities to those skilled in the languages of the old world to compare them with these . . . and hence to construct the best evidence of the derivation of this part of the human race." Not without justification has Jefferson been named the "father of American ethnology." While armchair antiquarians sat in Philadelphia's coffee-houses and puzzled over Bartram's mysterious earthworks, the tireless Jefferson dug into a prehistoric mound near his Virginia estate in about 1780. In America's first proper excavation, he observed layers of bones and concluded that this mound at least was an ancient Indian burial place.

Samuel Haven recognized that Thomas Jefferson was the first man to bring science to bear on the ancient Americans. Not that Jefferson's conclusions had much impact, for even more exciting discoveries were being made further west. The 1780s and 1790s saw a torrent of colonists pouring over the Allegheny Mountains into the unknown west. There they were astounded to find hundreds of elaborate earthworks and large earthen mounds. "Treasure, treasure," cried the impoverished farmers. But they found no gold and silver, only dozens of human skeletons, all sorts of strange copper and mica ornaments, and weapons quite unlike those used by surviving Midwestern tribes. By the 1850s, abandoned earthworks had been discovered over an enormous area from Nebraska and the Great Lakes, through the Midwest, and far southeast into Florida.

Who had built these silent mounds? Most people, whether intellectuals or just common folk, assumed that the Indians could never have done so. If they had not, who, then, was responsible? Haven was familiar with the bestselling works of the mythmakers and popular writers, men like Josiah Priest, whose *American Antiquities and Discoveries in the West* sold over 20,000 copies in the early 1830s. Priest wrote lyrically of great armies of white, warrior moundbuilders rivaling those of Alexander the Great, that "might have flourished their trumpets, and marched to battle, over these extensive plains." Battles to the death, valiant generals, even great warrior elephants and mythical heroes peppered the pages of dozens of literary fantasies that were devoured not only by armchair enthusiasts, but around innumerable camp fires in unfamiliar lands as well.

Only a few investigators examined the mounds at all systematically. Caleb Atwater, the postmaster of Circleville, Ohio, surveyed and excavated large numbers of them early in the nineteenth century. He found hundreds of burials and numerous finely crafted artifacts, including mica sheets in the shapes of bird claws and humans. Atwater refused to believe they were of Indian manufacture. He insisted that the moundbuilders were non-Indians, shepherds and farmers from Asia, who had crossed the Bering Strait soon after the Flood. As for the Indians, he felt they might also have crossed from Asia, but long after the earthworks were abandoned.

Haven then turned to the research of Ephraim Squier, an intelligent and sensitive man with a deep and abiding interest in the past. Small-town Ohio journalist, traveler, and later a successful diplomat, Squier was one of the first people to describe Inca archaeological sites in Peru during the 1870s. In 1845, the American Ethnological Society commissioned him to examine the mounds of the Ohio Valley. He teamed up with a local physician, Edwin Davis, and they spent two years surveying, excavating, and pondering earthworks throughout the valley. Some of their site plans are so accurate that they still

The Grave Creek Mound in West Virginia, an illustration from the mound survey by Squier and Davis published in 1848, in which they argued erroneously that American Indians were not the Moundbuilders.

guide visitors round Ohio mound groups! In 1848, the newly founded Smithsonian Institution published their 300-page monograph, *Ancient Monuments of the Mississippi Valley*. Samuel Haven read it from cover to cover and was chagrined to discover that the authors were intellectual prisoners of their times. They refused to believe that the Indians had built the earthworks. Instead, the mounds had been constructed by defensive experts, who had been attacked from the northeast by "hostile savage hordes." As for the Indians, they were "hunters averse to labor," and quite incapable of building a single earthwork.

"The Archaeology of the United States"

Samuel Haven violently disagreed with Atwater and Squier. Unlike almost everyone else interested in American archaeology, Haven knew that knowledge of the past was changing rapidly. He had followed a whole series of sensational discoveries in Europe, Mesopotamia, and Mexico. The 1840s saw French antiquarian Boucher de Perthes finding primitive stone axes and the bones of extinct animals in the gravels of the Somme River – the archaeological evidence that with Darwin's *Origin of Species* (1859) was to establish the great antiquity of humankind. These were the years of high adventure and archaeological diplomacy along the Tigris, too, when Paul Émile Botta and Austen Henry Layard uncovered the Assyrian civilization of the second book of Kings. Above all, the 1840s was the decade when the Aztec and Maya civilizations emerged from centuries of deep historical obscurity.

Between 1839 and 1843, John Lloyd Stephens and Frederick Catherwood revealed the Maya civilization of Mexico and Guatemala to an astonished world. Stephens was a brilliant travel writer, his partner an artist of outstanding ability. Their bestselling books took the reader to an exotic world of abandoned pyramids and temples deep in wild rainforest, at times clothed in moonlight so brilliant it was possible to read a newspaper at midnight. While Catherwood sketched furiously, Stephens wandered entranced through the richly decorated plazas of Copan, Palenque, Uxmal, and Chichen Itza, plazas adorned with figures and hieroglyphs quite unlike those on the Nile. He was convinced the Maya civilization had been forged from purely Indian roots by the ancestors of people still living in the Yucatan in the 1840s. "We are not warranted in going back to any ancient nation of the Old World for the builders of these cities," he wrote in 1843, just as Squier and Davis started work in Ohio.

Haven had met not only Stephens and Catherwood, but the Boston historian William Prescott as well. For five years, Prescott had labored over Spanish documents from archives in Seville and Mexico City, weaving the story of the Spanish Conquest of the Aztecs against a rich and hitherto unknown historical tapestry. In romantic, flowery terms, he described how

A stela from Copan,
Honduras, drawn by
Frederick Catherwood on one
of his pioneering journeys
with John Lloyd Stephens in
Central America that revealed
the lost world of the ancient
Maya.

the Aztecs had created a great empire in a few short centuries, rising from obscurity after the fall of the even earlier Toltec civilization. *The History of the Conquest of Mexico* became an immediate bestseller in 1843. For the first time, American readers learned of indigenous Indian civilizations that had flourished for centuries before the Spanish Conquest, civilizations with well-founded roots in prehistoric times.

His study piled high with dozens of monographs and learned papers, Haven culled through a vast body of unintegrated information. "We desire to stop where evidence ceases," he wrote firmly. No Prescott this, but a sober scholar. Haven had many more lines of evidence than Squier and Davis – not only Stephens and Prescott, but a growing body of travelers' descriptions of modern Midwestern Indian tribes. A few historians had also begun to realize the potential of Spanish archives for studying seventeenth-century North America. There was valuable biological evidence, too. Seventeen years earlier, in 1839, the celebrated physical anthropologist Samuel Morton had measured a series of eight "moundbuilder" skulls from Ohio as well as modern Indian crania. He concluded that the ancient and modern specimens all belonged to a single "Mongolian" race, even if they were separated on purely cultural grounds. In other words, the first Americans were of Asian origin, and their descendants still lived in the New World.

For months, Haven read and analyzed, examined artifacts, and corresponded with colleagues. Then he drafted *The Archaeology of the United States*, the first essay ever written on the origins of the American Indians. He was in no doubt that the first Americans had arrived from Asia. "All their [the Indians'] characteristic affinities are found in the early conditions of Asiatic races," he wrote. Almost certainly, the first Americans had arrived from across the Bering Strait. How long ago was still a mystery, but he suspected they were of far greater antiquity than most people believed. Their stone artifacts were easily found, and their descendants were living American Indians.

Scientifically speaking, Haven stuck his neck out, for there was precious little evidence to support his hypothesis of high antiquity. Yet, ironically, the evidence was already to hand. In 1839, fossil hunter and showman Albert Koch had come across the bones of a mastodon, a long extinct elephant, in Missouri. Along with the bones he dug out some stone artifacts. Koch looked at his finds from a strictly commercial standpoint. He exhibited the mastodon in a traveling show, then sold the bones to the British Museum and the artifacts to a German collector. The thought that the two were contemporary was ludicrous! No one, except perhaps Samuel Haven, seriously believed that human beings had lived in North America at the same time as extinct elephants.

CHAPTER TWO

Palaeoliths and Extinct Animals

In 1856, as momentous new biological and geological theories were freeing science from the shackles of Holy Writ that had confined it since medieval times, the Smithsonian Institution published Samuel Haven's *The Archaeology of the United States*. Darwin's *Origin of Species* was to appear three years later, in 1859, but the intellectual revolution in science had begun long before that. Scholars such as Descartes and Newton in the seventeenth century had argued that science dealt with subjects of matter (the profane), the scriptures with humanity (the sacred). Thus science was distinct from theology and devout scientists could practice their craft without threatening their faith. Eventually science expanded to new frontiers. In the 1820s and 1830s, European geologists pushed back the age of the earth farther and farther into the remote past. But, partly because of the all-embracing power of the church, they left the thorny problem of the antiquity of humankind on one side. The world still lacked scientific proof of the contemporaneity of humans and extinct animals. Any suggestion that humanity was older than the 6,000-odd years of the Biblical creation was still considered dangerously close to heresy, a challenge to the historical veracity of the scriptures. Many years later, the great Victorian biologist Thomas Huxley affectionately remembered the days of his youth, when any attempt to question orthodox views was met by an unspoken barrier that read: "No thoroughfare. By Order. Moses."

Stone Tools and "Glacial Man"

That barrier began to crumble fast during the 1840s and 1850s, when amateur fossil hunters tunneled into the earthen layers of prehistoric caves throughout western Europe. Time and again, they found the bones of extinct animals associated with obvious stone artifacts. The scientific establishment refused to accept these claims. But the tide turned at last in 1859, when a group of English geologists visited Jacques Boucher de Perthes and his excavations in the Somme River gravels near Abbeville in northern France. The eccentric and flamboyant Boucher de Perthes was a customs officer and antiquarian who claimed that he had found finely manufactured ancient stone axes, but no

Darwin's "Origin of Species," first published in 1859, provided the evolutionary framework for many of the scientific discoveries made in the first half of the nineteenth century. The implications for the evolution of man were lampooned in this "Punch" magazine cartoon of 1881, with Darwin himself at the center.

human fossils, in the same layers as the bones of extinct animals like the hippopotamus and elephant. At first de Perthes was ignored, but the British visitors were astounded to see humanly-made stone axes being excavated from fossil-bearing strata. They were convinced and soon publicly embraced a high antiquity for humankind. A few months later Darwin's *Origin* provided a theoretical framework for tens of thousands of years of unknown prehistory that could encompass everything from the first humans to moundbuilders, Aztecs – and the as-yet-undiscovered first Americans.

But how old were these first Americans? Were they as ancient as the Somme people, or much more recent arrivals? News of the Somme excavations reached the United States during the uneasy years of the Civil

War. Among those who read of them was Joseph Henry, Secretary of the Smithsonian Institution and a scholar with a deep interest in archaeology. It was he who had authorized publication of Haven's essay. He was profoundly excited by the implications of de Perthes' finds and the new antiquity of humankind. Henry's lively mind formulated all kinds of unanswered questions. Had people lived in the Americas for tens of thousands of years, just like they had in Europe? Had they hunted long-extinct animals? Would their artifacts be found in the same levels as vanished big-game species? Henry mustered the slender resources of official science to search for such finds. For its part, the Smithsonian prepared *Instructions for Archaeological Investigations in the United States*, a publication aimed at travelers and residents of the "Indian country" out west. It taught them what to look for – not only relatively modern artifacts and skulls, but more ancient finds from caves and shell mounds as well, sites like those found in Europe. Joseph Henry and his contemporaries assumed that the geological beds of the New World would parallel those of the Old. Alas, as a new generation of scientists was soon to discover, they did not.

During the 1860s and 1870s, American scientists, amateur and professional alike, searched everywhere – in caves, shell mounds, river gravels, even swamps – for associations between human artifacts and extinct animals. Few, if any, finds withstood even the most rudimentary expert scrutiny. The deep alluvial gravels and ancient Stone Age caves so common in western Europe were not to be found in North America. Not only that, the stone tools found in American archaeological sites were either associated with what one observer called "more advanced" artifacts, or were clearly similar to modern Indian specimens. So it was almost impossible to tell an ancient artifact from a recent tool.

Nor did any stone tools come from American glacial deposits. The Swiss geologist Louis Agassiz accepted an appointment at Harvard University in 1846 specifically to study the Ice Age geology of North America. A rigorous scientist, Agassiz had spent his early career unraveling the glacial geology of the Swiss Alps. He had shown that a "Great Ice Age," with alternating periods of bitter, arctic cold and almost tropical climate, had mantled much of Europe with huge ice sheets for thousands of years. Stone Age people had lived through these dramatic climatic changes. Agassiz soon found extensive traces of Ice Age glaciation in Canada and as far south as Saint Louis. But neither he, nor any archaeologist, found any signs of stone axes or other human artifacts in Ice Age deposits.

Despite the seeming lack of Stone Age finds, a fierce controversy erupted, one that was to last for a half century, until the 1920s. This dispute pitted believers in Stone Age Americans against an impressive band of government scientists, who argued that the first Americans arrived much later, long after the Ice Age.

The advocates of Palaeolithic (Old Stone Age) occupation were led by Charles Abbott, a New Jersey physician with a passion for natural history and stone tools. During the 1860s, he haunted river gravels on the family farm near Trenton, New Jersey, collecting flaked stone tools by the dozen. At first he thought they were relatively recent Indian artifacts, but he changed his mind in 1876 after meeting Frederick Putnam, the curator of Harvard's Peabody Museum of Archaeology and Ethnology. Abbott claimed his tools dated from the Ice Age, even though the Harvard geologists sent down by Putnam were carefully non-committal. "These traces of men must possess a very great antiquity," Abbott wrote. Abbott and Putnam laid out the Trenton "axes" alongside specimens collected by Boucher de Perthes on the Somme. Altogether about 400 stone tools seemed to resemble those from France. Carried along by his own enthusiasm, Abbott began lecturing about "American River-Drift Men," primitive people who had lived in North America at the same time as their European cousins along the Somme. In Europe, some people called Abbott a scientific prophet and compared him to Boucher de Perthes.

As people learned of Abbott's discovery, inevitably "palaeoliths" turned up all over the place – in Ohio, the District of Columbia, and as far west as Minnesota. No one stopped to define a "palaeolith." It did not matter how old they were, just that the finds looked like European ones. To Abbott and his fellow believers, the American Indians were merely the latest arrivals in a whole series of unrelated immigrants, who had settled in the Americas long before – at an unknown date. In their minds, all the magnificent Indian artifacts in the Smithsonian and other museums were totally irrelevant to the wider question of Stone Age settlement in the New World, the issue of "glacial man."

These theories brought the advocates for Stone Age occupation into direct conflict with many of the talented scientists who were rapidly turning geology, and indeed anthropology, into professional disciplines rather than amateur avocations. Many of these scholars had learned their geology and anthropology the hard way, in the mountains and plains of the Far West. By the 1880s, men like John Wesley Powell of Colorado River fame occupied positions of scientific responsibility back in Washington. Geologist, explorer, and ethnographer, Powell was Director of the Bureau of Ethnology at the Smithsonian when Congress appropriated funds to study the moundbuilders in 1882. "Mound-building tribes were known in the early history of discovery of this continent," he wrote boldly, hiring a minister turned entomologist-and-archaeologist named Cyrus Thomas to prove that " the moundbuilders and the historic [Indian] tribes were part of the same fabric of unbroken cultural development." After seven years of fieldwork and hundreds of excavations between Florida and Nebraska, Thomas and a battery of talented experts proved beyond all doubt that the moundbuilders were Indians.

Powell, Thomas, and many of their contemporaries were experts in a science that taught them to work back from modern strata into ever-remoter levels of geological time. What more logical way to study archaeology than by the same approach? Their observations were accurate, painstaking, and analytical.

The same men carried careful logic into their theoretical readings. Many government scientists had read the works of the pioneer anthropologist Henry Lewis Morgan. His brilliant work *Ancient Society* (1877) argued that humanity had evolved through a series of stages, starting with savagery and ending with a "state of civilization." Powell and others had picked up on Morgan's evolutionary theories, calling American Indians representatives of "savagery." Under Morgan's theories, it was logical to think of a gradual progress from the earliest inhabitants of the Americas up to their living descendants in the 1880s.

From the very beginning, most government scientists rejected Abbott's ideas entirely. To have accepted them would have meant accepting a vast chasm in the archaeological record, between the Stone Age occupation of earlier millennia and more recent Indian sites. And that was an unacceptable notion to any good stratigraphic geologist, especially scientists who believed the Indians were a modern race, whose culture had changed but little in the few centuries since they had arrived in their homeland. In other words, they were certain the first Americans had arrived only a short time before Europeans.

"Dangerous to the Cause of Science"

John Wesley Powell was first and foremost a man of action. His response to any academic problem was to hire people to work on it. He hired William Henry Holmes to study the Palaeolithic problem. Holmes had started his career as a geological illustrator in the west during the 1870s. He spent months sketching convoluted geological strata in the Colorado River Valley. Even today, his panoramas rival the best photographs, capturing the plastic structure of the rock, freezing once-molten lava in artistic motion. From geology he turned to archaeology. At Powell's behest, he produced a series of brilliant monographs on the "aboriginal pottery" of the eastern United States between 1882 and 1898, a foundation of all later research. These were systematic works of classification. Hardly had he begun this research when Powell diverted him to the Palaeolithic controversy in 1887.

The issue of "glacial man" had caught fire in earnest that year, when Thomas Wilson, the Curator of Archaeology at the National Museum, returned from five years working in the Somme gravels and in the Dordogne caves of southwestern France. Wilson embarked on a campaign to find Stone Age occupation in North America. He persuaded the Smithsonian to send out a questionnaire asking people to send in "Palaeolithic" implements or any "rudely shaped" stones. More than 800 poorly documented specimens poured into the Smithsonian from all over the country. Soon Wilson was publishing papers on these "artifacts," basing his arguments on the Abbott and Putnam assumption – if an artifact resembled a European palaeolith, it was a Stone Age tool and evidence for "glacial man."

Wilson was joined by the Oberlin geologist G. Frederick Wright, a great champion of evolution. His two books on the American Ice Age and "glacial man" published in 1889 and 1892 enjoyed a wide readership. Almost to a man, government scientists rose in protest against Wright, and Powell sent Holmes on a five-year study of "glacial man."

It was hard for Holmes to know where to begin. Powell suggested he examined a quarry near Washington, D.C., where Wilson had found "palaeoliths." Holmes sat down among the flaked stones and collected series of them that showed conclusively that all were in fact crude blanks left over from the manufacture of Indian arrowheads. Not only that, he actually made some identical "turtle-back" "palaeoliths" himself. This dramatic experiment effectively demolished Wilson's comparisons with Somme hand-axes.

Holmes now turned his attention to the geological context of American "palaeoliths" elsewhere. He traveled as far afield as Kansas and Minnesota, examining every alleged Stone Age find he could track down, including Abbott's cherished Trenton gravels. For a month, Holmes' assistant watched as city workmen dug a drainage trench through the very bluff where the "artifacts" had been found. Not a single tool came from the actual diggings. Abbott's Stone Age implements were nothing but modern Indian quarry refuse that had settled into the surface deposits. His 10,000 years of Indian occupation were but a day's work by an Indian quarry-worker, wrote Holmes in disgust.

The argument over "glacial man" was waged in print and in the lecture hall. Whenever the two sides gathered, Holmes was always calm and judicious, always ready with a piece of carefully gathered evidence that undermined his opponent's positions. Charles Abbott fumed impotently and talked of a government conspiracy. The absence of "glacial man" in America was "something that must be *proved* at all hazards," he wrote of Powell's scientists in 1893, "Or if not demonstrated, foisted on the unthinking to secure the scientific prominence of a few archaeological mugwumps." Bitter words, but Holmes was unmoved. For years, right through to the 1920s, he continued to examine each new find with dispassionate care. Holmes was like a scientific monolith, who considered the archaeology of the first Americans a matter for scientifically trained scientists, not amateur enthusiasts. So pervasive did his views become that it proved difficult for the young archaeologists of the 1920s to challenge what had developed into dogma: that the human settlement of the Americas was at most only a few thousand years old.

11, 12 Incidents of Travel in Maya Lands
John Lloyd Stephens (*left*) was a founder of
Maya archaeology. He and the artist
Frederick Catherwood explored forest-
shrouded sites like Copan and Palenque in
the years around 1840. Catherwood's
painting of the Castillo at Tulum in
northern Yucatan (*below*) shows the
extraordinary detail of this gifted artist's
work. Stephens believed the ruins to be the
"creations of the same races who inhabited
the country at the time of the Spanish
conquest."

13, 14 The Moundbuilder Controversy
Ephraim Squier (*left*) was one of the first
archaeologists to describe the mounds and
earthworks of the Ohio Valley in the late
1840s. However, he believed they were the
work of non-Indians. The Great Serpent
Mound in Ohio (*below*) was saved from
destruction by Harvard archaeologist
Frederick Putnam in 1887. It is nearly a
quarter-mile long and averages 20 feet
(6.7 m) across, depicting a coiling serpent
with a small mound in its jaws.

15, 16 The Archaeology of the United States Samuel Haven (*left*) wrote his immortal essay on American archaeology in 1856. A painstaking archaeological scholar, he dismissed fantasies about ancient moundbuilders with reasoned argument. Dr Munro Dickeson, a nineteenth-century collector and lecturer, boasted he had opened more than 1,000 mounds. He used a 348-foot long painting on muslin (*below*) as a backdrop for his lectures all over the Midwest. The artist shows excavations in progress and the layers of the mound.

17–20 **Dispelling the Moundbuilder Myth**
Three scientists, Cyrus Thomas (*right*), John
Wesley Powell (*below left*, with Indian
guide), and Frederick Putnam (*below right*),
played major roles in the debunking of the
moundbuilder myth. Powell, of Grand
Canyon fame, was Director of the Bureau
of Ethnology, where he directed efforts to
preserve Indian languages and material
culture. When Congress appropriated funds
for mound excavations, he appointed Cyrus
Thomas to survey and excavate mounds
throughout the Midwest and East. He
showed that the artifacts from them were of
Indian manufacture.

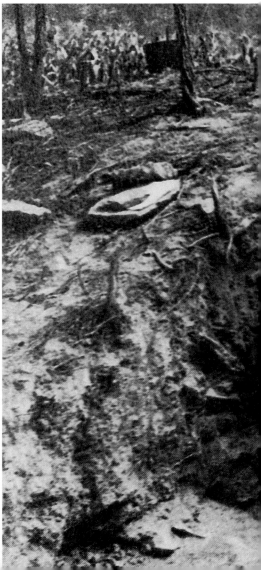

Frederick Putnam also excavated mounds and recovered Indian artifacts. Seen here (*below*) working at a site in the Little Miami Valley, Ohio, Putnam was also a major figure in the controversies over Palaeolithic humans in North America. He made the mistake of comparing prehistoric stone axes from the Somme Valley in northern France (*near right*) with Charles Abbott's "palaeoliths" from the Trenton River gravels (*far right*) by laying them alongside one another without regard to the geological age of the Trenton specimens.

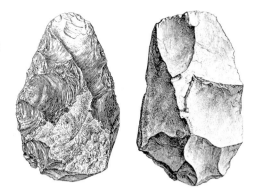

21 **Ales Hrdlička** of the Smithsonian Institution (*above*) was a rigorous, dogmatic scholar, who believed that human beings had lived in North America for no more than about 4,000 years. He laid out basic criteria for establishing the antiquity of fossil skulls found in the Americas. Seen here late in his career in 1931 examining a skull *in situ*, Hrdlička was one of the first American scientists to study the morphology of fossil skulls and teeth and to compare them with modern Indian specimens.

22 **William Henry Holmes** (*right*) was Hrdlička's archaeological counterpart, a scholar who insisted on careful observation of stratification, and of the natural geological processes that could have formed "artifacts." A calm, dispassionate man, Holmes is seen here around 1890 – in his own words – "in an ocean of the *paleoliths* of Abbott, Putnam, Wilson and the rest of the early enthusiasts of American antiquities. All are merely refuse of Indian implement making."

23–26 **Progress in the Twentieth Century**
The first breakthrough in the study of the
earliest Americans came with the discovery
of stone projectile points in association with
extinct bison bones at Folsom in the 1920s
(*below right*). Soon afterwards, Clovis
points (*below far left*) were found stratified
under Folsom points (*below center*) at
another Paleo-Indian site. Preliminary
estimates for Folsom were about 10,000
years, a date vindicated by the radiocarbon
samples processed by physicist Willard
Libby in the early 1950s (*above left*).
Palaeoanthropologist Louis Leakey (*above
right*) revolutionized the study of very early
humans with his discoveries in East Africa
between the 1920s and 1960s. He believed
that equally early humans had lived in the
Americas.

While Holmes concentrated on stone artifacts, other scientists searched for the physical remains of Stone Age man. Ever since the discovery of a human skull in the Calaveras mine in California in 1866, people were on the lookout for ancient skeletons. Most of the finds, including Calaveras, proved to be modern. By the 1890s, only a handful of highly suspect fossil bones were considered even possible Stone Age Americans. These came under the scrutiny of a young Czech-born physical anthropologist named Aleš Hrdlička, a brilliant scholar who joined the staff of the Smithsonian in 1903. Like Holmes, Hrdlička was a sophisticated scientist, and he had a first-hand knowledge of European human fossil finds. Between 1899 and 1912, Hrdlička studied all the available evidence claimed to prove the existence of glacial humans in the New World. He soon realized that his archaeological contemporaries were using excavation techniques half a century out of date. These crude methods were responsible for the plethora of unsubstantiated early man claims. Hrdlička mounted a long campaign to bring more rigorous scientific methods to the subject, enlisting the help of palaeontology and geology as well. His criteria for "glacial man" were rigorous: "indisputable stratigraphical evidence," some fossilization of the bones, and marked anatomical differences from modern skeletal remains.

Hrdlička applied these criteria to every alleged human fossil site he could visit. Without exception, all the locations he examined were much later than the Ice Age. Not only that, all the skeletal remains fell within the range of normal variation of American Indians. From his detailed knowledge of fossil finds in the Old World, Hrdlička was certain that humans had first evolved there. In 1907 he wrote his great report *Skeletal remains suggesting or attributed to early man in North America*. He concluded that "America was peopled by immigration . . . [from Asia], which could not have taken place until after great multiplication and wide distribution of the human species and the development of some degree of culture." Hrdlička also stated that population movements into the Americas had probably taken place toward the close of the Ice Age or early in post-glacial times.

Aleš Hrdlička was an obdurate, imperious man, with a low tolerance of wild theorizing. He actively discouraged consideration of the possibility that humans had settled in the Americas any earlier than his own estimate of 4,000 years ago. Few scholars dared challenge his unshaken belief in this chronology. Meanwhile, Hrdlička himself continued his researches on the peopling of the New World. He concentrated on the "shovel-shaped" incisor teeth* so common among American Indians. The highest frequencies of these occurred among the aboriginal populations of the New World and Asia, while the phenomenon was much rarer in Europe and Africa. Hrdlička believed that

* The shovel-shape of incisors (the forward biting teeth) refers to the scooped-out shape on the side facing the tongue.

shovel-shaped incisors were an adaptive response to a need to strengthen the teeth for eating. He argued that the trait disappeared as improved methods of food preparation and superior tool technology replaced the simple artifacts of earlier times. He also found a high frequency of shovel-shaped incisors among the Neanderthals, and argued that the common incidence of the trait among American Indians was proof that the "Upper Palaeolithic" way of life had survived far longer in the Americas.

Hrdlička believed Europe was the cradle of humankind, and that *Homo sapiens* populations with a way of life that owed much to the earlier Neanderthals had first settled Siberia and northeast Asia before penetrating the New World. This was part of a much wider scheme for peopling the world that had "western Palaeolithic man" separating into a number of discrete geographical breeding units. These ultimately resulted in the racial types of today. While many of Hrdlička's ideas have been outmoded by a mass of new data, it is interesting to note that the modern researcher Christy Turner and other scholars are still using shovel-shaped incisors to study the first Americans.

For more than twenty years, the austere personalities of Holmes and Hrdlička loomed over the study of the first Americans. Hrdlička was particularly unyielding, insisting right until his death in 1943 that it was the morphological features of human bones rather than geological evidence that were the clues to the antiquity of the first Americans. In some ways, it is hard to blame the two men for their dogmatism. They had seen far too many wild and spurious claims of the type that Holmes once called "dangerous to the cause of science" to feel otherwise. It took a chance find by a New Mexico cowboy to loosen the shackles of their scientific dictatorship, even if Hrdlička himself was never fully convinced.

"In My Hand I Hold the Answer . . ."

One fine spring morning in 1908, a black cowboy named George McJunkin was riding slowly along the edge of a dry gully near the small town of Folsom, New Mexico. McJunkin had ridden along hundreds, if not thousands, of such arroyos, dry creeks that meandered for miles over the countryside. There was nothing special about this particular arroyo, so he was casting over the range in search of a lost cow. But when he looked down, he saw some sun-bleached bones projecting from the soil. McJunkin dismounted and prised at the bones with his knife. A sharp stone fragment came loose in his hands, a stone spearpoint somewhat like the ones he had seen lying on the surface elsewhere on the ranch. The bones were much more of a puzzle – much larger and more massive than those of a cow. McJunkin took his finds back to the ranch house, where they lay around for seventeen years. But in 1925 they ended up on the desk of Jesse Figgins, Director of the Colorado Museum of Natural History.

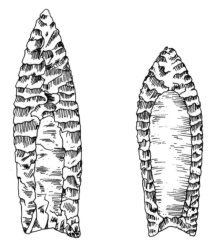

Typical Clovis (left) and Folsom projectile points, whose correct stratigraphic isolation revolutionized the study of the first Americans. Clovis point $2\frac{3}{4}$ in. (7 cm) tall.

Figgins was one of the few fossil bone experts in the west. He identified the Folsom bones at once. They came from a long-extinct form of bison that had roamed the plains at the end of the Ice Age thousands of years before. But the projectile point was another matter. Was it associated with the bison bones, or a more recent artifact? Had prehistoric hunters killed the extinct beast? To find out, Figgins dug into the Folsom site in 1926. He found more stone tools and bones, including a flint point associated with bison fragments. This association was so convincing that Figgins had it cut out in a block of earth and transported back to the museum in one piece. But, to his disappointment, his colleagues were skeptical. They warned him not to jump to any conclusions. Had not the points been introduced into the strata at a later date? The monolithic dogma of Holmes and Hrdlička enveloped the unfortunate Figgins as he journeyed from museum to museum with his finds. Only colleagues at the American Museum of Natural History in New York encouraged him to continue the work.

With weary patience, Figgins returned to Folsom in 1927. When he found more tools and bones, he sent telegrams to various institutions inviting them to verify the association in the field. Two distinguished scientists responded: the palaeontologist Barnum Brown of the American Museum of Natural History, and Frank Roberts, an archaeologist at the Bureau of American Ethnology. Roberts arrived to find Brown brushing the soil away from a projectile point "still embedded between two of the ribs of the animal skeleton." Roberts realized this was *the* discovery that everyone had been waiting for. Mindful of Holmes' potential wrath, his fellow archaeologists sniffed cautiously at the find. But many were convinced by the association, and by the finely made projectile heads. While the archaeologists were favorably disposed, some geologists still shook their heads. As for the physical anthropologists, Hrdlička said little, even when Barnum Brown held up some projectile points at a New York seminar. "In my hand I hold the answer to the antiquity of man in America," Brown cried. "It is simply a matter of interpretation."

1928's field season brought a veritable avalanche of scientists to Folsom. They went away convinced that human beings had indeed lived in North America at a time when Ice Age animals still roamed the continent. But they were surprised by the sophistication of the artifacts found with the bones. The Folsom points – named after McJunkin's site – were a far cry from the "rude tools" diligently sought by Charles Abbott and his contemporaries.

10,000 Years or Older . . . ?

Folsom was far more than merely a landmark discovery. It opened up a new chapter in American archaeology. After generations of Holmes and Hrdlička's short, 4,000-year chronology, the archaeologists now confronted a much longer timescale. At the bottom lay the Folsom finds – soon referred to as "Paleo-Indian" – estimated by Brown and Roberts on the basis of the extinct bison bones to be about 10,000 years old, but perhaps even older. At the top were the modern native American tribes of North America, who were but a few centuries old. In the middle lay a chronological chasm, where, presumably, the immediate and more remote ancestors of the contemporary Indians were to be found.

In some ways the Folsom discovery was like the publication of Darwin's *Origin of Species* in Europe three-quarters-of-a-century before. It led to a minor explosion of scientific research. Soon Folsom had company, sites like Lone Wolf Creek, Texas, where extinct bison bones and stone tools had been found just before Figgins started work in New Mexico. Far from being just one bison-hunting culture, there were soon dozens, which were identified by different projectile-head designs. But which was the oldest? How long ago had the bison hunters lived?

A big breakthrough came at Clovis, New Mexico, in 1932. Two amateur collectors found projectile heads and extinct mammal bones lying along the shores of long-dried-up shallow lakes. Two-to-five-inch-long spearpoints lay between the ribs of some of the animals. These formidable points were far longer than the short Folsom heads. Were these artifacts older or more recent than Folsom? World War II intervened, and the controversy was finally resolved by three seasons of excavations between 1949 and 1951. The two uppermost layers of the site contained Folsom points, but below were the skeletons of four Ice Age mammoths associated with characteristic Clovis points. So Clovis was older than Folsom.

While some archaeologists labored on the plains uncovering a plethora of Paleo-Indian cultures, their colleagues elsewhere began to fill the chronological lacuna that separated Folsom from more recent prehistory. At first the research was somewhat sporadic, but the Great Depression ushered in public-works projects that included large-scale river-basin surveys in many parts of the country. The thousands of sites and artifacts from these surveys and other investigations produced jigsaw-like chronological sequences that linked river valley to river valley, county to county, and entire regions to their neighbors. By the late 1940s, a tentative prehistoric framework had been drawn up.

First came the Paleo-Indians, represented by Clovis and Folsom, then a whole spectrum of hunting-and-gathering cultures that extended from coast to coast. Some relied on big game, others, like the desert people of the Southwest and some Midwestern societies, predominantly on wild vegetable foods. The descendants of the latter developed the moundbuilder cultures that reached their climax just before Europeans arrived on the scene. The great civilizations of Mexico and Peru emerged to the south well over 1,000 years before Columbus landed in the New World.

Yet, despite this relative precision, until the 1950s there was no accurate means of dating archaeological sites much earlier than about 2,000 years before the present. Beyond a vague estimate of about 10,000 years, no one had any idea how old the Paleo-Indians were.

Then, in 1949, a University of Chicago scientist named Willard Libby developed the "radiocarbon dating" method for determining the age of organic materials like charcoal and bone up to about 50,000 years ago. This revolutionary time-clock measured the decay rates of the radioactive isotope of carbon (carbon-14 or C14) found in living things like tree trunks, also animals and humans – decay that began the moment an organism died. Having tested the method against objects of known historical age like ancient Egyptian boats, Libby turned his attention to prehistoric samples. Soon his laboratory resembled an old-fashioned museum of curiosities, where ancient Egyptian mummies lay alongside carbonized wood from Stone Age swamps, samples of prehistoric human hair next to 30,000-year-old wooden artifacts. This confused collection of tools, charcoal samples, and other organic specimens created the first prehistoric timescale, one that had an extraordinary international impact on archaeology. For the first time, major developments like the first settlement of the Americas could be dated by an independent test and the results compared with other samples from areas thousands of miles away.

American archaeologists were quick to realize the potential of the new method. Frank Roberts sent Libby some specially collected samples from

Folsom as soon as he could excavate them. The final readings dated the site to about 10,800 years, astoundingly close to the original estimate of 10,000 years ago. Dates from other Folsom locations soon confirmed Libby's original readings. They fell between 11,000 and 10,000 years ago, with Clovis samples dating to between 11,500 and 11,000 years ago. (Recent calibrations of radiocarbon dates with the aid of tree rings may one day push these dates back even earlier.) So the chronology of the first (known) Americans had come full circle, from a hypothetical few thousand years down to a few centuries, then back out again to 4,000 years ago, and then to 11,000 years ago.

But were the Clovis people the very first Americans? Despite the new radiocarbon dates, the Paleo-Indians remained shadowy and ill-defined figures, almost phantoms on the outer edge of the prehistoric world. For a while, the new radiocarbon dates brought a fresh wave of chronological conservatism in their wake. At conferences where archaeologists gathered, "12,000 years ago at the outside" was the rubric. Eventually, however, there was a reaction and excavators began to announce associations between stone artifacts and the bones of extinct animals claimed to be as much as 15,000, 20,000, even 200,000 years old. These discoveries, most of them from the 1960s, 1970s, and the present decade, have divided American archaeologists into the factions of today.

The new finds came from all over the Americas, from the Yukon Territory in the far north, from the Midwest, the California desert, and from the Andes. Many were scatters of stone artifacts, others associations of fragmentary animal bones and tools, or even isolated human skulls dated by newly developed techniques. Some of these claims were extravagant at best; few were easy to validate. Indeed, as archaeological excavation and analysis became ever more sophisticated, the task of validation became that much harder, even (perhaps especially) when well-known scientists put their reputations and careers behind controversial discoveries.

One internationally known figure to enter the search was Louis Leakey, who lectured regularly on his fossil finds in East Africa all over North America in the 1960s and early 1970s. He lost no opportunity to declare his conviction that very early human occupation would come to light in the New World, far older than anything yet discovered. At the very end of his life, Leakey focussed attention on a site at Calico Hills, near Yermo, California, a location claimed to be more than 200,000 years old. He himself pronounced some of the stone artifacts from this location to be truly ancient, an announcement that caused widespread scientific consternation, except among a few bolder enthusiasts.

Many of the claims for early settlement foundered on geological or chronological grounds. For example, one 1970s controversy revolved around a series of human skulls from southern California. Jeffrey Bada of the Scripps Institute of Oceanography used radiocarbon dating and a technique called amino-acid racemization to date them in 1975. The new method measured the slow processes of racemization (change) in L-amino acids, which produce collagen in bone, to D-amino acids, racemization that occurs over long periods of time, as much as 100,000 years. Bada used one radiocarbon-dated skull from Laguna Beach as a reference point to convert his amino-acid readings into actual dates. Amino-acid racemization could be applied directly to fossil bones, even old finds that were devoid of any geological context. None of the southern California skulls came from well-documented geological horizons, nor were any associated with stone artifacts or occupation sites. To everyone's surprise, the tests produced a range of dates between 70,000 and 15,000 years ago, most of the finds dating to somewhere between 20,000 and 50,000 years ago.

The new dates were a complete puzzle, for the skulls were anatomically modern. Strong emotions swirled around the crania. Many scholars rejected the new dates on the grounds they came from isolated finds. But some archaeologists enthusiastically claimed the crania were evidence for much earlier Stone Age occupation than Clovis or Folsom. "Psychological archaeologist" Jeffrey Goodman went even further. He proclaimed that these were the earliest *Homo sapiens sapiens* skulls in the world. Thus, modern humanity had originated in the Americas and spread from there into the Old World. Whatever their feelings about the first Americans, few if any other archaeologists agreed with him!

Unaccompanied by artifacts and wrenched long ago from their original sites, the California skulls, and one from Ecuador and another from Canada, remained a strange anomaly. Then experts at the University of California, Riverside, radiocarbon-dated the same finds using accelerator mass spectrometric techniques on organic fractions of the bone, an extremely refined carbon-14 dating method. They came up with readings not in the 15,000-to-70,000-year range, but ones that never exceeded 6,300 years ago. "The number of human skeletons in the Western Hemisphere with suggested Pleistocene [Ice Age] age has now been dramatically reduced," the Riverside scientists remarked. There is now general agreement that none of the amino-acid-dated skulls are more than a few thousand years old. Bada himself has recalculated his amino-acid dates using the new carbon-14 readings for the Laguna skull of 5,100 years (as opposed to 17,150), and announced that they now agree with the Riverside radiocarbon dates.

The redating of the California skulls has not dampened enthusiasm for early settlement. The focus of research has now shifted to Central and South America, where excavations in both rockshelters and open sites have yielded a plethora of claims for human occupation before 14,000 years ago. The most recent are a series of radiocarbon dates for hearths found in the lower levels of a large rockshelter in northeast Brazil, some of them as early as 32,000 years old.

Despite the uncertainties and competing claims, however, enough has now been learned to provide the framework for an account of the peopling of the New World. Piece by piece, scientific evidence can be used to construct an archaeological drama, which begins not in America, but in Asia and Africa at the dawn of human existence.

PART TWO

ANCESTRY

---

*"Modern city-dwellers find it
difficult to imagine the possibility
of hunting large adult elephants
with simple weapons of wood, stone
or bone."*

Hans Müller-Beck, 1982

- Torralba
- Monte Circeo
- Neander Valley
- Lehringen
- Lebenstedt
- Ehringsdorf
- Dolni Vestonice/Pavlov
- Mezhirich
- Mezin
- Olduvai Gorge
- Teshik-Tash
- Calico Hills

ARCTIC

ATLANTIC OCEAN

SIBERIA

Black Sea

CHINA

AFRICA

PACIFIC OCEAN

AUSTRALIA

The world between 2 million and 35,000 years ago, together with place-names mentioned in the text. The earliest tool-users, the Australopithecines (bottom left figure), evolved in Africa. Their successors, "Homo erectus" (bottom right), were the first to colonize parts of Europe and Asia, a process of expansion continued by the Neanderthals (top left). But it was not until modern humans appeared (top right) that people adapted fully to the extremes of the arctic.

CHAPTER THREE

In the Beginning

ACT 1, SCENE 1

Africa, Europe, and Asia from about 2 million to 35,000 years ago

The mammoth hunters' hide-covered dwellings squat on a low promontory overlooking the broad river valley. Thin plumes of smoke rise from the houses into the still, cold air this late spring day 25,000 years ago. A group of skin-clad men scrape meat off a large leg bone. Children play nearby, while an adolescent watches the valley below. Suddenly, he calls out softly. The men stop work and gaze intently into the distance. They see a small herd of woolly mammoth making their way to the river. The hunters grab their weapons and descend into the valley. The children halt their play and watch as the mammoth lumber on unsuspectingly. The senior cow stops, as if sniffing danger. Reassured, she moves on to the river, and the others follow. One young beast lags behind. The hunters concentrate their efforts on this one animal.

The spear-wielding hunters stalk their quarry from downwind, slipping from willow thicket to willow thicket at the water's edge, their eyes on the swampy pond upwind, between the mammoth and the river. Meanwhile, two men move away in the opposite direction. They move ever closer to the laggard, who scents them and turns away upwind. The hunters signal, stand up and shout. The solitary animal is now away from the rest of the herd and breaks into a gallop straight for the swamp. The soft mud traps the struggling mammoth, which sinks ever deeper into the mire. The spearmen close in, thrusting stone-tipped weapons into the heart of their prey, and watch as the helpless elephant perishes.

The hunters call out in triumph to the watching families above. The women gather up stone choppers and hides and bring them to the swamp's edge. The butchers work in pairs with stone tools, cutting and pulling back the hide and flesh, dismembering the carcass bone by bone. Everyone stops work and feasts on the edible intestines and soft tongue. They pile the fresh meat on the hides and carry it back to camp. By nightfall, little remains of the hunters' quarry. While predators such as wolves and arctic foxes gather quietly at the carcass to eat their fill, the people feast off fresh meat. The surplus flesh is hung up to dry. The women have already pegged out the mammoth hide to cure on the ground.

How were these West Russian hunters of the late Ice Age connected with the story of the first Americans? To find out, we need to travel even farther back in time, to the world of our earliest ancestors several million years ago.

The First Humans

We begin in Africa because – as Charles Darwin predicted over a century ago – all the evidence suggests that humans first evolved in that continent. The peopling of the New World can therefore only be understood in the context of a much wider phenomenon: the colonization of the entire globe.

But what makes scholars today so certain that human origins lay in the Old World and not the New? Is it inconceivable that our distant forebears might one day be found in Brazil, Mexico or the USA? Quite apart from the total absence so far of very early fossils from the Americas, there is a strong biological basis for the traditionally accepted view. It stems from the distribution throughout the world of potential ancestral populations for humanity. We humans are members of the Order Primates, an order divided taxonomically into the Anthropoidea ("man-like" higher primates), including apes, humans, and monkeys; and lower primates, including lemurs and tarsiers. A number of evolutionary trends separate primates from other mammals, mostly ones related to primates' primary adaptation to life in trees. Primates share a generalized limb structure, more mobile fingers and toes, and expanded and elaborated brains. These trends have continued to develop in the primate order since it first emerged at least 70 to 80 million years ago.

The Anthropoidea, all social and diurnal animals, subsume three distinct superfamilies – Old World monkeys, New World monkeys, and Hominoidea, the apes and humans. Every fragment of fossil evidence so far suggests that human beings evolved among the Hominoidea, primates distributed in the Old World, not the New. For humans to have evolved in the Americas, they would have had to have developed from ancestral roots among the New World monkeys. This group of primates flourishes from southern Mexico deep into South America. All New World monkeys are arboreal and live in small groups. Some have prehensile tails that are adapted for wrapping around branches. They display more variation in both anatomy and behavior than their Old World relatives, and are thought to have evolved from a common higher primate ancestor with the Old World primates, before the Americas split off from Asia some 60 million years ago.

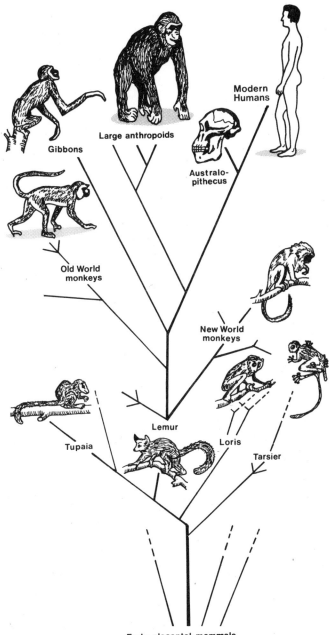

Gibbons

Large anthropoids

Modern
Humans

Australo-
pithecus

Old World
monkeys

New World
monkeys

Lemur

Loris

Tupaia

Tarsier

Early placental mammals

*A generalized family tree showing the evolution of the primates from early
mammals. The New World monkeys branched off quite early and had nothing to
do with the line that led subsequently to modern humans.*

The Old World monkeys are successful animals adapted to both arboreal and terrestrial environments, distributed throughout Africa, India, and southeast Asia. They are all quadrupedal walkers, progressing on all fours. None of them have prehensile tails like New World monkeys. The primitive ancestors of Old World monkeys and the Hominoidea have been found in Egypt, in deposits dating to some 40 million years ago. Perhaps as early as 22 million years ago, the Old World monkeys and the Hominoidea diverged along separate evolutionary lines, lines not replicated in the Americas. Since humans evolved among the Hominoidea, ancestors too of the modern living apes, and no such animals flourish, or ever lived, in the Americas, we can safely assume that humanity evolved in the Old World. Our search for the first Americans must ultimately begin in the cradle of humankind – tropical Africa.

Two million years ago, the population of Hominoidea in East and Southern Africa included not only several species of ancestral apes, but creatures with certain primitive human characteristics. These were the Australopithecines, named after a fossil called *Australopithecus* ("southern ape-man") identified by South African anatomist Raymond Dart in 1924. *Australopithecus* populations varied considerably. Some individuals had larger brain capacities and smaller teeth, features that cause many experts today to consider them early members of the human line (the genus *Homo*). Whatever their correct classification, it is certain that the Australopithecines were different from other higher primates. They walked with an upright posture and enjoyed a larger brain capacity than the apes of the day. The more advanced among them also made tools. This was a crucial innovation, which gave the Australopithecines and their descendants the advantage of what archaeologists refer to as "material culture" in the struggle to survive. (Modern chimpanzees have been found to make tools of a sort, but tool-making can still be thought of as primarily a human attribute.) No longer were biological factors – of the kind for instance that gave polar bears their thick coats and dense layers of fat against the arctic cold – the sole influence on adaptation to the environment. Tools and material culture ultimately enabled humans to act upon and change their surroundings: to cut down trees, to build shelters, to hunt and control other animals.

Ordinarily, when animals die, their experience dies with them. But with the development of material culture, and later speech, humans were able to pass on what they had made and learnt from one generation to the next. They could share ideas, which in turn became behavior patterns that were repeated again and again. These behavior patterns are chronicled by millions of stone tools and other artifacts, by prehistoric dwellings, kill sites, and all the material remains of past human activity that are the "archaeological record" – the archives of world prehistory.

For over a million years, human biological and cultural evolution moved at an infinitesimally slow pace. The earliest primitive humans (called "hominids"), with brain capacities between 600 and 670 cc as opposed to our own average between 1,350 and 1,450 cc, survived with the simplest of toolkits – stone choppers, flake knives and scrapers. They probably used wood and bone artifacts, too, but these have not been preserved. These were tropical and subtropical folk who lived in small bands constantly on the move. As far as anatomists can tell from studying brain casts, their speech organs were rudimentary, so they probably communicated with grunts and signs – warning of danger, expressing pleasure or fear. The savanna they preferred was rich in wild vegetable foods that flourished throughout most of the year. Then as now, abundant mammal herds populated the grasslands and woodlands. But in all probability, our earliest ancestors lacked the means to hunt larger game animals. They were expert scavengers, seizing raw meat from kills made by other predators, perhaps hunting smaller species with stones and simple pointed sticks. They had no fire, no permanent dwellings, no means of protecting themselves from the cold. Humanity was confined to sub-Saharan Africa, and perhaps to parts of the coastal strip of the Near East. As far as we know, no humans were yet capable of adapting to temperate or arctic latitudes. Much of the globe, and certainly the Americas, remained unpopulated by humans.

About 1.5 million years ago, a new form of human being, *Homo erectus*, emerged in East Africa. By 500,000 years ago, *Homo erectus* had adapted to much colder climates than his predecessors. The peopling of the non-tropical world had begun.

Homo erectus had a more rounded skull than earlier hominids, with a few individuals enjoying a brain capacity as large as 1,250 cc. Some anatomists believe that these larger-brained humans were capable of a higher degree of reasoned thought than their predecessors. They also speculate that they may have had excellent vision. Whatever their intellectual capacities, *Homo erectus* populations discovered how to create fire – one of humanity's most revolutionary inventions. No one knows how and when humans first tamed heat. Perhaps they grabbed blazing brands from a lightning-kindled brush fire and kept them fueled day and night until they learned how to make fire for themselves. However it was acquired, fire was a landmark. For the first time, people could warm themselves against winter cold, occupy deep caves and drive away their predator occupants, and cook their food. The hearth may have become a focus for social activity, and allowed human beings to be active during the nocturnal hours.

Even 350,000 years ago the world's human population could be numbered in, at most, the tens of thousands, with people scattered in small bands through Africa, the Near East, in southeast Asia and China, and, perhaps thanks to fire, into the temperate latitudes of west and central Europe and east Asia. The simple stone axes, cleavers, knives, and choppers made by *Homo erectus* appear by the hundred in rockshelters, open sites, and at kill locations.

They were probably multi-purpose artifacts, many of them especially efficient at butchering game carcasses. These distinctive tools were made for hundreds of thousands of years, but are absent over vast areas of the world – in Australia and New Guinea, the arctic latitudes of the Old World . . . and the Americas. There is no evidence that *Homo erectus* ever settled in Mongolia or Siberia, or anywhere within striking distance of the New World.

Archaic *Homo sapiens,* "the wise person," may have begun to replace *Homo erectus* at least 350,000 years ago. Anatomically much more like modern people, with enlarged brain sizes and rounder heads, the new humans were far from dramatic innovators, but they gradually developed a more elaborate toolkit. They were perhaps more skilled hunters, as we shall see. There was greater diversification, too, as hunter-gatherers settled in more extreme tropical environments like rainforests and semi-arid deserts. Humans could also survive fairly cold winters, but they lacked the technological skills and the sewn clothing and specialized toolkit for pursuing game in snow and ice, or extremes of arctic cold. Fire was not enough. On these grounds alone, it seems most unlikely that any human beings crossed into the Americas before 100,000 or 200,000 years ago.

Louis Leakey and Calico Hills

In view of this negative evidence, what are we to make of Louis Leakey's claim that Calico Hills demonstrates human settlement in the New World as early as 100,000 or 200,000 years ago?

Leakey never tired of telling American audiences that human beings had lived in North America very much earlier than many archaeologists believed. In 1963, he gave a series of lectures at Riverside, California, where he met Ruth de Ette Simpson, who worked at the San Bernardino County Museum. She told him about some primitive-looking artifacts that came from Ice Age deposits in arid country east of the Calico Mountains. Leakey and Simpson visited the site, which is situated in the Yermo Fan, an alluvial deposit accumulated long ago by soil and other debris washing out of nearby canyons.

Leakey did not think much of Simpson's "artifacts," but the setting interested him. Out in front of the fan was "a great plain which must have been verdant green, with animals and plants suitable for food. It was ideal." With his customary enthusiastic energy, Leakey walked over the surrounding terrain until he found two chalcedony fragments in a trench wall made by a mechanical digger. This, he said, was the place to excavate. And excavate Ruth Simpson and a group of enthusiasts did – and still do to this day.

The Calico Hills excavations soon yielded promising "artifacts" that were set aside for Leakey to examine on his occasional California visits. Most came from the 6- to 9- foot levels, in a concentration that consisted of some 12,000 specimens. Only three of them did Leakey consider possible artifacts. Even he was doubtful. "Nobody will like them," he said. But the excavations continued, in a second " master pit" 40 feet (12.2 m) from the original one. This time Leakey accepted 43 specimens from the 9-foot (2.7-m) level. There was a circle of cobbles surrounding a shallow basin. When one rock showed signs of heating at one end, the circle was promptly claimed as a hearth. This, and the alleged "tools," were cited as evidence for early human settlement at Calico. Geologist Thomas Clements provisionally dated the site to between 50,000 and 100,000 years ago.

Not for the first time, Louis Leakey found himself the center of controversy. Most of his fellow scientists were very dubious about the site, not only about the artifacts, but also about the possibility of finding human occupation at a location as early as Calico. Some geologists suspected the site was even earlier than Clements argued. Even Leakey's wife Mary – herself a considerable scholar – refused to accept the "artifacts," believing they were formed by natural geological processes.

In 1968 the L.S.B. Leakey Foundation called an international conference of about a hundred archaeologists and geologists at the San Bernardino County Museum to evaluate the site. Leakey's case for early occupation was based on the unusual concentration of flakes in one area, on the fact that his "tools" were only made in chalcedony, as if humans had selected the rock, and, above all, on the hearth. By this time Leakey was a very sick man – he was to die in 1972. So his colleagues were gentle in their public reaction. They pointed out that the Calico "artifacts" were very varied, even more so than 2-million-year-old tools from Koobi Fora in East Africa that were undoubtedly genuine. The concentration of rocks could have been brought together by natural geological forces in a water-transported deposit. Chalcedony was known to be a more fragile rock, and, as such, was much more likely to fracture under natural pressure. As for the hearth, this too could have been formed by natural forces. There were no signs of fire-cracking on the stones, as one would expect on hearth cobbles. Perhaps the heat phenomena on the analyzed rock came from a natural brush fire. The conference ended with profound, if often unspoken, disagreement between Leakey and his Calico excavators, and the wider scientific community.

Research has continued at Calico Hills ever since, mainly in the hands of a small band of devoted people, who believe the site really is an early human camp site. A series of studies under controlled conditions are in progress in attempts to replicate ways in which the Calico "artifacts" were made. Meanwhile, uranium-thorium dating tests on calcium carbonate from the Calico deposits now indicate that the "artifact-bearing" levels are much older than the original estimate, in the order of 200,000 years old.

On the face of it, every form of archaeological logic is against the site. There are no comparable locations in the Americas despite more than a century of intense search. Nor are there settlements of comparable age in even general geographical proximity in northeast Asia. Most archaeologists firmly reject the "artifacts" as being of human manufacture at all. To accept them means accepting pre-Neanderthal occupation in California, something for which there is no evidence whatsoever.

A final determination of the Calico site must await the publication of an exhaustive and definitive report on the stone collections. This we are promised. In the meantime, judging from the evidence published so far and from the "artifacts" themselves, to say nothing of the weight of data now available to us on the peopling of the Old World 200,000 years ago, Louis Leakey's dream of very early human occupation in the Americas remains a dream. Calico Hills is probably an archaeological myth.

Torralba and the Origins of Big-Game Hunting

What is no myth is that by 200,000 years ago archaic *Homo sapiens* populations had colonized most of Africa, Europe, and Asia in tropical and temperate latitudes. Some scholars believe this was the moment when people began systematic big-game hunting, pursuing much larger animals instead of scavenging from predator kills. They cite instances of several large "kill sites," where people camped and butchered game. Among them is Torralba, near Madrid, Spain.

The original Torralba excavation painted a fascinating prehistoric scenario. Several hunting bands living in a deep, swampy valley regularly set brush fires and drove large elephants into bogs. They killed the helpless beasts and butchered the carcasses where they lay, probably exploiting the same location time and again over the years. Clay casts surviving in the archaeological deposits apparently show that the hunters used wooden lances and spears to kill their prey. Unfortunately, this scenario is being modified by more recent research on the distributions of the surviving elephant bones. These suggest that the hunters visited the swamps on a regular basis in order to scavenge the carcasses of elephants already trapped there. So the Torralba peoples' big-game hunting ability is in doubt.

Whatever the final outcome of the Torralba investigations, there can be no question that sometime between a million years ago and the emergence of *Homo sapiens*, human beings slowly became more skilful hunters. Perhaps as early as 300,000 years ago, they took or scavenged not only elephants, but also many other different game species, both large and small. Once primitive hunting skills were established, people seem to have focussed much of their effort on larger herbivores. These offered several advantages: a great deal of meat per carcass, relatively predictable annual grazing movements, and gregarious habits that were easily observed and exploited.

Hunting methods were nevertheless probably still rudimentary, and this may have limited early *Homo sapiens*' ability to colonize areas with extreme climates. Hunters seem to have relied on their stalking abilities and simple game drives to get close to their prey. We know this from one of the earliest kill sites in the world, found at Lehringen in northern Germany. Some time before 130,000 years ago, a group of hunters ambushed a solitary, 45-year-old elephant near a clayey pond. A yew-wood lance wounded the beast in the chest or abdomen. The animal stampeded and became trapped in the water. There it died. The hunters closed in and butchered the carcass with stone flakes, leaving the unused parts in the pond. Millennia later, the excavators found the 6½-foot (1.98-m) yew lance embedded in the elephant. (Interestingly enough yew wood was the favored material of English and French bowmen as late as medieval times.)

Soon after the Lehringen kill, world temperatures began to fall rapidly. By 100,000 years ago, the last major cold snap of the Ice Age was well under way. Great ice sheets centered on the Alps and Scandinavia mantled parts of western and central Europe. Much of North America was buried under ice, too. More southerly latitudes became at times cooler and wetter. World sea levels fell drastically, exposing continental shelves in many parts of the world, joining Alaska to Siberia and many southeast Asian islands to the mainland. The deteriorating climate changed the shape of the world's landmasses, and the distribution of human settlement as well.

The last glaciation witnessed an explosion in human technology and adaptability, as well as the first settlement of arctic environments. The beginnings of this adaptation to much colder climates are associated with one of the best-known prehistoric human forms – the Neanderthals.

The Neanderthals

The first Neanderthal (*Homo sapiens neanderthalensis*) came to light in 1856, when quarrymen found a primitive-looking skull in a cave in the valley of that name in West Germany. Scientists were divided in their opinions. The German anatomist Rudolf Virchow thought the skull with its heavy brow ridges that of a pathological idiot. Others, like the great English biologist Thomas Huxley, realized it was that of an early human. Soon Neanderthal bones turned up in Belgian and French caves, in sufficient quantity for a preliminary description of Neanderthal anatomy. Unfortunately, one of the first studies was based on an elderly individual suffering from arthritis, which distorted images of the Neanderthals' capabilities for generations. For more than a half-century, they were branded as "primitive," shambling humans with pronounced stoops and ape-like features who lived only in caves and used wooden clubs. They became the "cave-men" beloved of cartoonists, the prototype for the "B.C." comic strip run in many newspapers today.

Modern anatomical studies have shown that Neanderthals were very far from brutish and sickly. Their brain capacity was no different from our own.

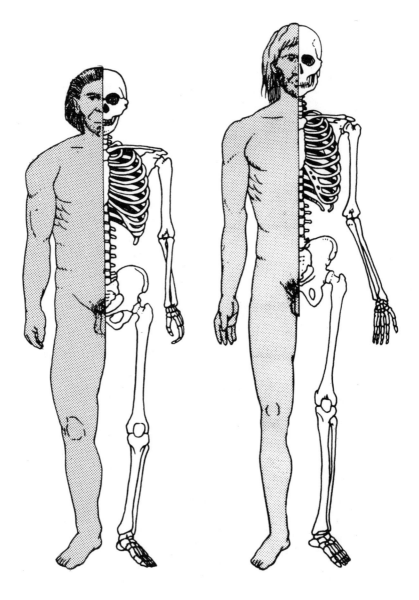

The swarthy European Neanderthal physique (left) compared with that of a fully modern human.

To judge from the enlargement of certain areas of the brain, seen in casts of the insides of Neanderthal skulls, they were capable of at least some form of speech and reasoning. We also know now that the term "Neanderthal" covers a group of prehistoric populations of very diverse physical type, adapted to an extremely wide range of world climates.

We know most about the European Neanderthals. Like their cousins elsewhere, they seem to have been proficient hunters and foragers who utilized fire for warmth and cooking 100,000 years ago. They were squat and robust, well adapted to the arctic environments of western Europe, a climate with long, chillingly cold winters and very short, warm summers. They lived not only in caves and rockshelters, but probably in open camps under skin tents in the warmer months as well.

The Neanderthals still used spears in the hunt, but improved their stone technology. Instead of employing the stone axes and simple flakes of earlier millennia, they struck blanks from carefully prepared flint cores. These they turned into spearpoints trimmed all over their upper and lower surfaces (bifacial points) or on the upper surface alone (a unifacial point). Such points, in a variety of (much more refined) forms, were to become important in many later Asian, Siberian, and American societies. Another Neanderthal innovation was the much more economical use of flint. This was a major consideration wherever big-game hunters ranged over open plains with suitable stone in short supply.

This elaboration of stone technology reflects not only more sophisticated meat processing, but the development of better tools for woodworking, for preparing skins, and for making bone artifacts. The new tool forms may also signal enhanced intellectual abilities, abilities that led the Neanderthals to bury their dead.

Neanderthal burials have come from French and western Asian caves and rockshelters. The skeletons crouch in shallow graves, sometimes accompanied by food offerings. One child skeleton, from Teshik-Tash cave south of Samarkand in the USSR, is associated with five or six pairs of Siberian mountain-goat horns arranged vertically with the tips downward. The horns surround the burial. Almost certainly, the Neanderthals had a belief in life after death.

There are signs of tribal ritual, too. A band living near Rome, Italy, decapitated a man of about 45 and buried his mutilated skull in a shallow trench dug in an inner cave chamber at Monte Circeo. The cave was sealed by a landslide some 60,000 years ago.

Without question, the Neanderthals were intelligent, thinking humans whose rituals and beliefs foreshadowed the immeasurably more elaborate customs of *Homo sapiens sapiens*. But there is good reason to believe they were more "primitive," with simpler cultures than modern humans. Their language system was probably less well developed. They certainly made much less use of bone in their technology, and they never created the sophisticated artistic traditions so characteristic of later Stone Age (Upper Palaeolithic) humans.*

Just over 100,000 years ago, some early Neanderthal hunters probably first encountered the woolly mammoth in central Europe, at places like Weimar-Ehringsdorf in Germany, where elephants could be ambushed and driven into ponds. By 70,000 to 80,000 years ago, perhaps even earlier, Neanderthals were butchering mammoth, reindeer, bison, and wild horse in a cold steppe environment at Salzgitter-Lebenstedt, west of the Harz Mountains in northern Germany, at latitude 52 degrees N. Bone lancepoints made from mammoth rib were used in the chase. Here, and at the 60,000-year-old Königsaue site near Aschersleben Lake in the same general area, Neanderthals camped on lakeshores and in valleys and hunted on the edge of the steppe-tundra. (Steppe is a dry, treeless landscape, typically covered with grass-scrub. Tundra is cold, treeless country mantled with sparse scrub vegetation.)

Sometime between 60,000 and 40,000 years ago, Neanderthal hunters camped temporarily, and probably during the summer, on the continental steppe-tundra at Volgograd, near the Don River in the eastern USSR, at about 49 degrees N. They hunted mammoth, bison, wild horse, and the saiga antelope, an arctic species that flourishes on dry continental steppe even today. Here, as elsewhere, the hunters lived near permanent water, in places sheltered from strong winds, where gallery forests grew, but close to the open plains. These finds show that, at least during summer and early fall, Neanderthal mammoth hunters penetrated temperate, subarctic, and dry, arctic steppe at least as far north as 52 degrees N in central Europe, and 49 degrees N in the eastern Soviet Union.

In the 20,000-odd years before fully modern humans appeared in the Old World about 40,000 years ago, scattered Neanderthal hunting bands were venturing onto the frigid, windswept plains that stretched without interruption from the gates of central Europe right into Siberia. This gradual movement northward into arctic latitudes may have been, at best, a seasonal phenomenon, but a movement repeated at dozens of locations between the Black Sea and northeast Asia. For the first time, human beings were beginning to penetrate arctic frontiers. Why they did so is somewhat of a mystery. One

---

* Old World archaeologists subdivide the Old Stone Age, or "Palaeolithic" (Greek: *Palaeo* = old, *Lithos* = stone), into three very broad technological stages:
Lower Palaeolithic: Stone Age technology based on simple percussion methods, typical of the earliest humans, the Australopithecines, *Homo erectus,* and early *Homo sapiens.*
Middle Palaeolithic: Generally associated with Neanderthal technology. Use of carefully prepared stone blanks and production of large numbers of more-or-less standardized flake tools.
Upper Palaeolithic: Blade technology and blade tools, associated with fully modern humans.
   These terms are little more than convenient labels, which have little or no chronological validity, except in the most general terms.

explanation may be a gradual rise in hunter-gatherer populations in more temperate latitudes that overstressed the carrying capacity of age-old hunting territories, not only in western and central Europe, but in Asia as well.

Only a few sites document Stone Age occupation of all periods in the vast regions of central Asia, Mongolia, and southern Siberia. Such "Lower Palaeolithic" sites as have been reported consist of surface finds of crude choppers and flake tools of doubtful geological association, and even more dubious age. Sites dating to as much as a million years ago, and certainly to 500,000, are well documented in central and northern China, where sporadic later occupation is also recorded, at least as far north as 40 degrees N. In all probability, the situation in central Asia and the Far East was much the same as it was in central Europe – some seasonal hunting on the northern plains, but, at best, only the most scattered of Neanderthal occupation on the fringes of the plains.

Dozens of ancient lake-bed deposits document how after about 40,000 years ago climatic conditions improved slightly, with warmer and longer summers, enabling people to move slightly farther north without highly specialized toolkits. But the warmer summers did not last long. And by 35,000 years ago fully modern humans, *Homo sapiens sapiens*, had taken command, leaving the Neanderthals to die out, or become assimilated.

The Case for Earliest Colonization

Were there, then, human beings in the Americas 200,000 years ago, or did they colonize the New World in Neanderthal times, between some 100,000 and 40,000 years before the present?

Humans were still largely confined to tropical and temperate latitudes 200,000 years ago. To accept Louis Leakey's Calico Hills "artifacts" means that one must search for human ancestors not in the Old World, but in the New. And that, as we have argued, is biologically impossible, for no fossil ancestors or living relatives exist.

Did Neanderthal peoples cross into the New World before 40,000 years ago? Again, the available evidence suggests they did not. The most northerly Neanderthal sites known are at about 52 degrees N, well south of the 60-degrees-plus latitudes of Siberia and extreme northeast Asia, and the Bering Strait. Any claims for indigenous Neanderthal evolution in the Americas would have to explain the complete absence of their fossils (or fossil ancestors) in that continent.

This chapter has chronicled a gradual, 2-million-year peopling of much of the Old World. If one looks at the first settlement of the Americas within the context of this slow-moving scenario, it is almost impossible to support either Calico Hills or the Neanderthal arguments. It seems much more plausible, on a global scale, that the peopling of the New World coincided with the explosion of human settlement that took *Homo sapiens sapiens* to all parts of the world after 35,000 years ago.

Rejecting both of the very early colonization schemes means that fully modern humans were the primeval settlers of the Americas. But how did they first cross into their new homeland? By land or by sea? And when did they arrive? Between 35,000 and 15,000 years ago, or after 15,000 at the close of the last glaciation? These are the controversial questions that have preoccupied archaeologists for generations.

CHAPTER FOUR

Modern Humans Take the Stage

ACT 1, SCENE 2
Europe and Asia 35,000 to 15,000 years ago

Between 40,000 and 35,000 years ago, perhaps the most dramatic development in human history unfolded in many parts of the Old World. *Homo sapiens sapiens*, fully modern humanity, appeared suddenly in Africa and the Near East, and in Asia as well. The new humans evolved from early *Homo sapiens* stock within a few tens of thousands of years, a minuscule timespan in biological terms. They soon occupied every previously inhabited part of the world, replacing or absorbing the Neanderthals who were there before them. The compelling selective force that caused this sudden evolutionary jump remains an enigma. Some physical anthropologists believe that the change resulted from some highly significant, yet inconspicuous development in human life like greater hunting efficiency, a change we cannot identify from the archaeological record. The change may have made the bulky Neanderthal physique an unnecessary and costly burden that consumed too much food. This initiated a rapid reduction in body bulk and perhaps in other special Neanderthal traits such as thick skull bones. The gradual improvement in toolmaking techniques that can be seen in later Neanderthal sites may have played a role, too, giving a selective behavioral advantage to the less robust and more adaptable *Homo sapiens sapiens*.

The moment *Homo sapiens sapiens* appears on the world scene, human cultures become markedly more complex. For instance, after 35,000 years ago the hunter-gatherers of southwest France produced an infinitely more refined and developed artifact inventory. Quite apart from superb new stone tools, they used bone and deer antler to fashion harpoons, spearpoints, even needles for making sewn garments. These were artifacts that could be manufactured in treeless environments and used in pursuit of game of all sizes, exploiting the valuable byproducts from such prey. Within a few thousand years, the new hunters had developed the world's first art tradition, reflected in thousands of rock engravings, cave paintings, and intricately decorated artifacts. Complex symbolism and ceremonial lay behind the artwork, rituals for social behavior that were far more advanced than anything practiced in earlier times.

Wherever *Homo sapiens sapiens* emerged, human populations increased steadily and hunting bands pressed out to the limits of earlier settlement. With their more sophisticated toolkits and greater intellectual capacities, the newcomers were apparently capable of adapting to much more severe climatic regimens. Only a few millennia after the appearance of modern people in Asia and the Near East, hunter-gatherers had crossed open water into Australia, conquered tropical rainforests, and moved far north of previous Neanderthal hunting grounds, perhaps even into Siberia.

Voyagers across the Ocean?

It was modern humans who colonized the two great unpopulated continents – Australia and the Americas. There seems little doubt that the first Australians arrived by sea, but can the same be said of their American counterparts?

All available evidence suggests that Australia was initially reached at least 35,000 years ago, probably a few thousand years earlier, by human migrants from southeast Asia. Even during periods of low sea level, an open-water crossing of about 55 miles (88 km) lay ahead of the first settlers. To cross this wide channel would have required some form of seaworthy craft, even if the crossing was accidental. The archaeologists James O'Connell and Peter White point out that historic Australian aboriginal boats are little more than simple logs or reed rafts. Even the most sophisticated Arnhem Land sewn-bark canoes were only used for open-water journeys of a few miles, perhaps to offlying islands well within sight. Buoyancy problems prevented any longer voyaging. Thus, they argue, the first settlement was an accident, an unwilling journey when offshore winds or unexpected currents carried a family offshore. Not so, speculate other scientists. They believe the journey was a deliberate one, perhaps a crossing toward a great column of smoke from a natural brush fire that acted like a beacon to unknown lands over the horizon. Some also hypothesize that the first Australians were skilled boatbuilders, who lost the art of canoe building once they had the luxury of a vast continent to settle in, an environment quite different from their original homelands. Whichever hypothesis one favors is nothing more than that. In general, however, the simple technology of modern Australian boats makes one suspect that they never had much more elaborate watercraft, and that the original crossing was an accident, one that brought a handful of human beings to a new continent.

Whatever the kind of vessel used, human settlement expanded successfully in Australia. By 20,000 years ago, people were living around the coasts and on the central desert fringes. By 10,000 years ago, the Australians were exploiting every major environmental zone in the continent.

But did the first Americans also arrive by sea? Here we must distinguish between the short potential crossing via the Bering Strait and the vast ocean voyage that would have been necessary to traverse the Pacific (or the Atlantic for that matter). Samuel Haven ushered in the modern era of research when he drew attention to the natural highway from Siberia across the Bering Strait. This icy channel separates Old World from New by some 50-odd miles (80 km), very similar to the distance first crossed by boat to reach Australia. Whether pioneering settlers might in fact have used watercraft to cross the strait, or whether they might have traveled dry-shod over ice floes or on a land bridge at periods of low sea level is an issue that will be discussed in the next chapter. Of more immediate moment is the larger question of an open-ocean crossing.

Both the Atlantic and Pacific Oceans are enormous bodies of water, offering a terrifying variety of weather conditions. The easiest way to cross the Atlantic to the New World from the Old over open water is to follow Columbus from Europe down the northeast trades, from the Canary Islands to the Caribbean. Even this requires seaworthy sailing vessels capable of weathering winds over 35 knots and ocean swells more than 12 feet (3.6 m) high. A north Atlantic crossing is a much more formidable voyage, involving constant headwinds, unpredictable gales, and much larger seas. The earliest authenticated Atlantic crossings were made about AD 1000 by the Vikings, among the most expert sailors ever to have lived. Not even Thor Heyerdahl – whose voyage in recent times in the reed-boat *Ra* caught the public imagination but failed to prove possible ancient Egyptian links with South America – has suggested an Atlantic crossing remotely early enough to have had anything to do with the first peopling of America.

The Pacific dwarfs the Atlantic in the immensity of its open spaces and the length of ocean passages needed to cross from Asia to the Americas, even if you island-hop your way across. The shortest route, from Japan to the outermost Aleutian islands, involves open-water sailing across stormy, icily cold and often fog-shrouded ocean. The tropical routes are thousands of miles longer, and involve unpredictable wind patterns, prolonged calms, and weeks-on-end out of sight of land. Whatever Pacific route might have been followed, prehistoric migrants would have had to possess a technology capable of building strong boats for use on the open sea. And here, crucially, we can consider the evidence of the first colonization of Polynesia, the vast Pacific region that includes New Zealand, Hawaii and Easter Island. Countless excavations have shown that not until about 3,500 years ago, with the advent of the outrigger canoe, did this whole area begin to be colonized. Before then, there were simply no human inhabitants at all. It is scarcely conceivable that migrants thousands of years earlier could have reached the Americas across the Pacific without leaving any trace whatsoever in the intervening islands. As the case of Australia has already implied, primitive boat technology 10,000, 20,000 or 30,000 years ago gave people the ability to negotiate short stretches of water up to 50 or 60 miles wide – but not to navigate thousands of miles of open ocean and survive.

Almost certainly, then, the first Americans crossed from Asia into the New World in the far north, via Siberia and the Bering Strait. But how and when did they get there? For the answer, we need to take a close look at those early *Homo sapiens sapiens* populations that colonized the frontiers beyond the northern limits of Neanderthal settlement.

Mammoth Hunters of the Russian Steppe

The archaeological record of eastern Europe "explodes" with the arrival of *Homo sapiens sapiens* – after about 35,000 years ago. Dozens of sites, as opposed to a handful earlier, document a considerable increase in big-game hunting.

Some 25,000 years ago, mammoth hunters camped at Pavlov and Dolni Vestonice in modern Czechoslovakia, both sites located near much-used mammoth trails. Each year, the mammoth would lumber along predictable migration routes. The hunters would ambush the moving animals at a convenient spot where a nearby slope provided a good butchering surface. The Dolni Vestonice people camped at the edge of a swampy river valley in the late autumn. Judging from modern musk-ox hunting in the Canadian arctic, the hunters were laying in meat as a staple for the long winter months

Reconstruction of the 25,000-year-old hut excavated at Dolni Vestonice in Czechoslovakia. The wooden structure was probably covered by hides weighted down by mammoth bones, branches and earth. The hunter is shown holding a figurine which he has just baked in the fire. One of these so-called Venus figurines was discovered at the site.

that lay ahead. They dried the flesh on the windy, sunny slope nearby. With the ground permanently frozen a few feet below the surface, people could dig through the thaw zone and store the meat in superb natural refrigerators.

Dozens of Upper Palaeolithic camp sites have been uncovered in the three major river systems of the Russian Plain – the Dnestr, Don, and Dnepr, which flow into the Black Sea and the Sea of Azov. The bands tended to cluster in these river valleys, locating their camps on low promontories overlooking large river floodplains. Despite their relatively sheltered locations, the hunters endured a severe climate where winter temperatures may have reached − 40 deg. F (− 40 deg. C), with an average July temperature of + 64 deg. F (+ 17.8 deg. C).

The plains environment, with its dispersed game herds and great distances, made even toolmaking a challenge, for suitable rock outcrops of fine-grained stone were few and far between. The Upper Palaeolithic toolmakers developed a very economic stone technology based on easily portable nodules that could be used and transported for weeks on end. As need arose, they would strike off blades from the precious core, then turn them into light, finished artifacts. They transported and may have traded fine-grained stone over hundreds of miles, and created a great variety of stone artifacts from them – knives, endscrapers, shouldered projectile heads, borers, and "burins" – distinctive graving tools with chisel-like ends. These they used to fashion bone and antler into a fine array of artifacts.

The plains supported a remarkable diversity of large mammals, not just mammoth, but woolly rhinoceros, steppe bison, reindeer, and wild horse – a range of animals so distinctive and so closely linked with Stone Age hunters that Soviet palaeontologists have called it the "Upper Palaeolithic fauna." The hunters supplemented their diet with fish such as salmon, perch, and pike, as well as ducks, geese, and arctic ptarmigan, also wild vegetable foods.

The Russian hunters lived in a variety of dwellings, many of them built around depressions scooped out of the subsoil. Sometimes they used large mammoth bones as foundation walls, perhaps completing the huts with a framework of saplings and hides. Between 18,000 and 14,000 years ago, some groups living at Mezhirich in the Dnepr Valley built elaborate mammoth-bone structures, using neatly arranged skulls and other large bones to form symmetrical wall bases. The builders amassed as much as 46,296 pounds of mammoth bone for each house, acquired from their own kills, and perhaps from scavenged carcasses as well. These were permanent residences, perhaps used for the cold winter months. Other bands lived in oval-shaped dwellings, possibly conical skin tents.

The Ukrainian hunters created images and shared symbols suggesting a complex, imaginative life. They adorned mammoth bones with red ocher designs, carved stylized human figures, and engraved geometric designs on ivory. They wore perforated wolf and fox teeth, necklaces of amber and

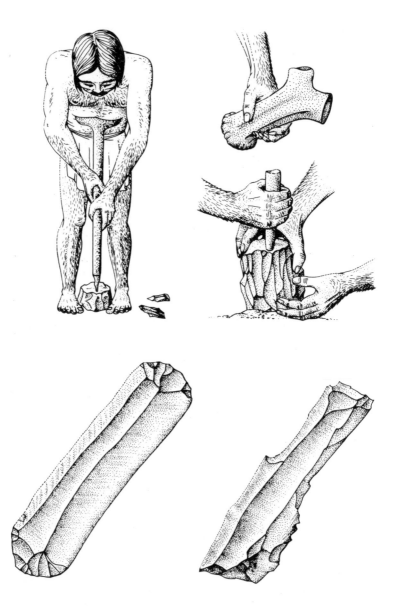

Stone toolmaking reached its apogee in Upper Palaeolithic times. The technology was based on striking blades off a precious core, using a punch supported by the chest (top left) or held in the hand (top right). The resulting blade blanks were then worked into a variety of tools, including endscrapers (above left) and burins (above right). Burins were distinctive tools with chisel-like ends used for grooving wood, bone and antler.

seashell beads. Some of their ornaments came from great distances. Fossil shells found at Mezin came from marine deposits between 372 and 497 miles (600-800 km) distant, amber from a location near Kiev, 93 miles (150 km) away. The exchange networks that brought these exotic objects to the Dnepr extended to the Black Sea in the south and far to the west. These were people with far-flung connections with big-game hunters over thousands of square miles of steppe and river valley.

Cooperation and Coalescence All the evidence from Mezhirich and other sites points to a more elaborate social organization than that enjoyed by the Neanderthals. Olga Soffer of the University of Illinois is one of the few Western scholars to have worked with Soviet scientists in the Ukraine. She believes the fact that the Mezhirich people occupied relatively permanent camps shows they had developed a means of resolving disputes. In a flexible band situation, the disputants would simply move away. Here they apparently lived together for substantial periods of time. They would have had to call on social prescriptions for keeping the peace.

We do not know what sort of institutions these were, but they may have been linked to a form of emerging social status. Soffer notes an uneven distribution of storage pits at some Dnepr sites, as if some households commanded more food supplies than others. Socially prominent families or individuals with surplus food supplies might have been able to direct the labor needed to build the mammoth-bone dwellings. The actual settlements still housed only between 30 and 100 people, but the relationships between different communities may have become formal, and socially binding, just as Ojibwa Indian Medicine Societies in North America are today. Dispersed clans, age grades, secret societies, and other such institutions may now have linked widely scattered groups. Individuals living in camps miles apart may have shared a common clan or age set. For some ritual and ceremonial purposes, a person living in an isolated site might feel closer to people of the same clan living miles away than he or she would to someone living in the same house. Such links would have encouraged closer ties among people than among bands without these social features.

The concentrations of game animals changed constantly throughout the year. Sometimes, the herds gathered in large numbers, at others individual groups were dispersed far over the plains. A tribal type of social organization would ensure links between far-flung groups, who came together at critical periods of the year to prey on great concentrations of game. These were the times of cooperation in the chase, of game drives and communal feasting, of exchanges of gifts and exotic materials, of marriages and tribal ceremonies.

More efficient Upper Palaeolithic hunting and gathering, as well as permanent settlement for many months and sophisticated storage methods, probably promoted slow population growth. As a result, the tribes were in a constant state of flux. Bands would split off as local game herds were decimated, even to extinction. Sometimes sons would take their families into unexploited river valleys several miles away, easing local population pressures. Under such conditions, it was probably inevitable that Upper Palaeolithic hunters expanded far and wide through eastern Russia, and deep into Siberia and northeast Asia. This expansion may have taken a surprisingly short time, for the very nature of the adaptation depended on constant mobility. There was always big game over the next horizon, and, in an environment where everything was spread out, always a chance for bands to work together when the need arose, following behavior patterns that altered little for thousands of years.

The monumental task of tracing this gradual movement of Upper Palaeolithic hunting populations into Siberia has only just begun. The vast landmass that extends north and east from the central Russian plains is almost virgin archaeological territory.

Everything we know about central Asia and Siberia suggests it was a dry environment during the Ice Age, a place of limited glaciation and open tracts of steppe-tundra, and, farther to the south, taiga – northern boreal forest. The taiga was an unattractive habitat for Stone Age hunter-gatherers. Few game animals wandered in the swampy forest. Wild vegetable foods were in short supply, and movement of both animals and humans was much restricted during the summer months, when mosquitoes abounded and the thawed ground was soggy. Taiga is so inhospitable and difficult to move in that it may well have formed a barrier to human settlement. The taiga zones seem to have fluctuated with the climate, expanding during the long millennia of warmer weather between about 40,000 and 35,000 years ago. Extensive taiga, and the relatively limited arctic survival capabilities of the Neanderthals, may have stopped northward and eastward migration during the warm interval. By the time steppe-tundra again stretched northeast, *Homo sapiens sapiens*, not Neanderthals, lived and hunted on the Russian plains.

Siberian Settlements

Two major clusters of Upper Palaeolithic sites provide our best clues to early settlement in Siberia. The first group of settlements occur in the Lake Baikal region, in the Trans-Baikal. The most famous is Mal'ta on the Angara River, near the city of Irkutsk, occupied some time between 25,000 and 13,000 years ago. The settlement covers more than 6,458 square feet (more than 600 sq. m), and includes numerous semi-subterranean houses. Most of them are probably winter dwellings, structures that used large animal bones to support a roof of interlaced reindeer antlers covered with skins or sod. The excavator, M.M. Gerasimov, found many broken bones inside these dwellings, and distinguishes between men's and women's activities inside them on the basis of

27 Human Relatives The chimpanzee is generally regarded as the closest living relative of humans. Like the chimpanzee, we are descended from high primates which evolved in Africa.

28–30 **The Rise of Humanity** The early evolution of humankind is one of the most exciting and rapidly changing fields in modern archaeology. Our ancestors may have split off from apes on the evolutionary tree before 4 or 5 million years ago. By about 2 million years ago a variety of hominids, including *Australopithecus africanus* (*left*), lived in tropical Africa. *Homo erectus* (*right*) evolved in Africa over 1.5 million years ago and eventually colonized large areas of Asia and temperate Europe as well as the tropics. This hominid used slightly more elaborate tools than its predecessors, and sometimes hunted large

mammals. *Homo neanderthalensis* was an early form of *Homo sapiens* with much greater intellectual and technological capacity than earlier humans. The Neanderthals flourished after 100,000 years ago and adapted to considerable extremes of arctic climate and cold winters (as in the scene *below*). Although there is some evidence of Neanderthal burial customs and, perhaps, of ceremonial life, these people had relatively limited communicative abilities and, apparently, were no match for fully modern humans, *Homo sapiens sapiens*, who emerged about 40,000 to 35,000 years ago.

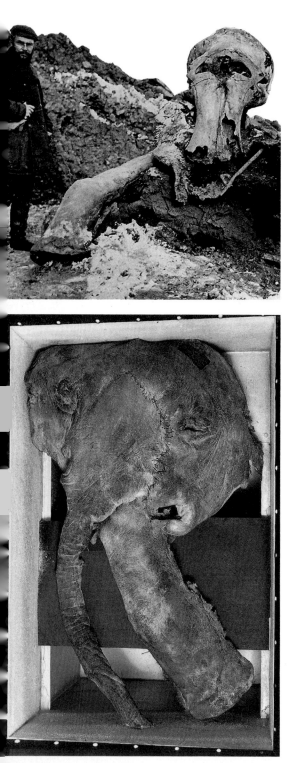

31–34 **Monarch of the Ice Age Plains** The arctic mammoth was the largest Ice Age mammal to roam the vast steppe-tundra of northern Europe, Siberia, and Beringia. Fortunately, the permafrost conditions of the far north have preserved some remarkably complete carcasses for modern scientists to study. A British Museum reconstruction (*below right*) is based on these finds and on Palaeolithic cave paintings, as well as fossil bones. With its heavily insulated hide and long hair, soft, pad-like feet, and compact body mass, the gregarious mammoth was well adapted to extremes of arctic cold. Perhaps the most famous frozen mammoth carcass came from Beresovka in Siberia in 1901 (*left*). More than 39,000 years ago, the mammoth had slipped and fallen, becoming enmired in swampy ground. Unable to free itself, it lay

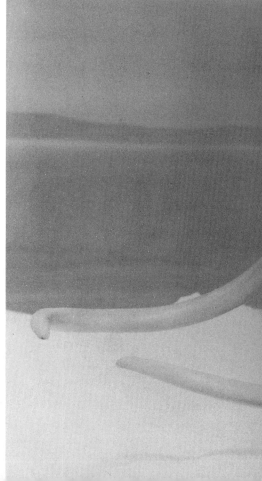

in a sitting position. Wolves had eaten most of the head and back by the time scientists arrived. Their dogs ate some of the meat without apparent harm. Another Siberian mammoth, this time 12,000 years old from the Berelekh area (*right*), was so well preserved that the long hair on the legs could still be stroked. Mammoth carcasses are much rarer on the Alaskan side, in what was once eastern Beringia (*below left*). Here the head, trunk, and leg of a young mammoth are preserved.

35–37 **Voyagers across the Oceans** Did humans make long-distance voyages and colonize the Americas thousands of years ago? The issue has been debated since the days of the conquistadors. Thanks to excavations in Labrador and Newfoundland, and researches in Viking sagas, we now know that Vikings landed in North America about AD 1,000 (*below*, view of the famous Oseberg ship). They came via Greenland. But did other long-distance voyagers like the Polynesians (*left, above*) reach the New World? Although they colonized Easter Island and the Hawaiian Islands, prevailing trade winds and the huge distances involved make it highly unlikely that Polynesian outrigger canoes reached the Pacific coasts of the Americas. Even if they did, the first Americans had arrived many thousands of years earlier.

Although some scientists claim that Japanese mariners landed in Ecuador, their hypotheses are based on the flimsiest parallels with Asian artifacts. There are also claims that ancient Egyptians, Phoenicians, and other Mediterranean peoples colonized the Americas. Norwegian adventurer Thor Heyerdahl made two attempts to cross the Atlantic in the *Ra* (*left, below*), a replica of an Egyptian papyrus boat. The first attempt failed, but the second succeeded. Heyerdahl claims this shows the Egyptians were ocean voyagers. In fact, all it proves is that a moderately seaworthy downwind vessel can navigate the tradewinds to the New World. The first Americans had crossed by another route at least 10,000 years earlier.

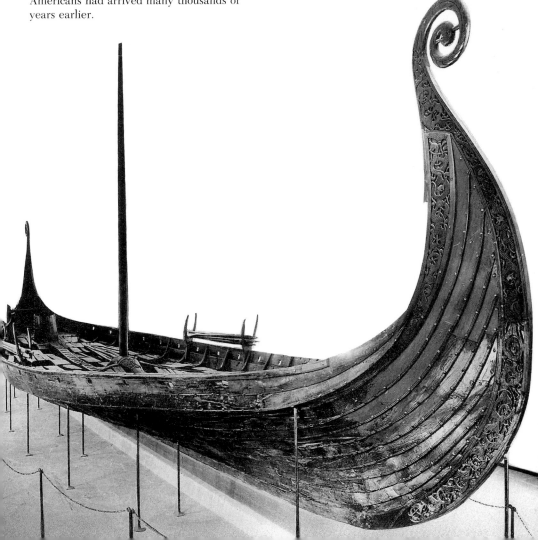

38 **The First Americans** A reconstruction painting of a small band of primeval Beringians. The band members wear sewn clothing and carry simple weapons.

artifact distributions. The women stayed close to the settlements, while the men ranged widely in search of mammoth, woolly rhinoceros, and reindeer on the surrounding steppe.

Mal'ta is famous for its ivory carvings that include depictions not only of mammoth, but of women and wild fowl as well. The Mal'ta people also deliberately buried arctic foxes after skinning them, and a child burial came from the site, one of the few examples of a Russian Upper Palaeolithic individual yet discovered. More recent, and as yet largely unreported, excavations have confirmed the impression of a society whose way of life strongly recalls that of the west Russian big-game hunters.

The Angara flows into the Yenesei River, where further distinctive Upper Palaeolithic sites are to be found. The rich Afontova Gora II site was excavated in the 1920s, and is thought to date to as early as 21,000 years ago, on the basis of a single radiocarbon sample. Dwellings and diet were similar to

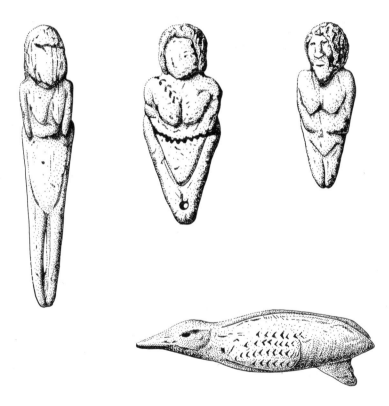

The famous ivory carvings from Mal'ta on the Angara River in Siberia include these three female figurines and an arctic waterbird.

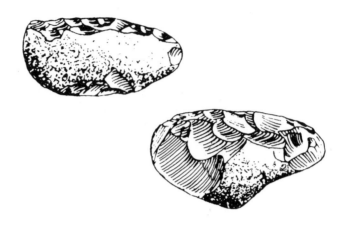

Two "skreblos," the steep-sided choppers made on pebbles and found in the area of the Yenesei River in Siberia.

Mal'ta, but the artifacts are quite distinct. They include large tools known as *skreblos* – steep-sided choppers with jagged edges usually made on pebbles. Unlike west Russian sites, burins are rare; these were bone engraving tools, so perhaps it is no coincidence that engraved art objects are likewise scarce. Some of the Yenesei stone artifacts may resemble the pebble choppers, tiny blade tools ("microblades") and wedge-shaped scrapers made in northeast Asia perhaps as early as 20,000 years ago.

A second group of Upper Palaeolithic settlements lies in the Middle Aldan Valley, far to the east of the Yenesei. In 1967, the Soviet archaeologist Yuri Mochanov from the Scientific Research Institute in Yakutsk in northeast Siberia excavated the important site of Dyukhtai (or Diuktai) cave, close to the river floodplain. He found mammoth and musk-ox remains associated with spear and arrow points flaked on both surfaces ("bifaces"), burins, blades, wedge- and disc-shaped cores, as well as large stone choppers that may have served as butchery tools. The cave deposits were undisturbed by thawing, freezing, and other local climatic phenomena, so Mochanov was able to obtain some reliable radiocarbon dates that ranged between about 14,000 and 12,000 years ago.

Mochanov made a clear distinction between the Mal'ta-Afontova tradition of the west that had no bifacial artifacts, and his Dyukhtai people who made fine bifaces. In the 1970s, he argued that Dyukhtai hunters had followed mammoth and other big game into the New World about 11,000 years ago. Their culture had first flourished, he believed, some 18,000 years ago in the Aldan Valley, with an ultimate origin in Inner Asia.

But Mochanov had second thoughts about the dating of his Dyukhtai people. He found new sites on the banks of the Aldan, one at Ezhantsy with a radiocarbon date from a sand-and-pebble terrace of about 35,000 years, another with somewhat later dates. These finds led Mochanov to develop a different hypothesis about the Dyukhtai culture. Between 40,000 and 35,000 years ago, he believes, a local form of *Homo sapiens sapiens* evolved in northern China from primeval Neanderthal stock, a form with physical traits akin to those of modern American Indians. These entirely hypothetical people began to move north towards the Middle Lena about 35,000 years ago. During the following 10,000 years, they settled in the Middle Aldan and extreme northeast Asia. They then colonized North America sometime after 25,000 years ago, much earlier than he had originally argued.

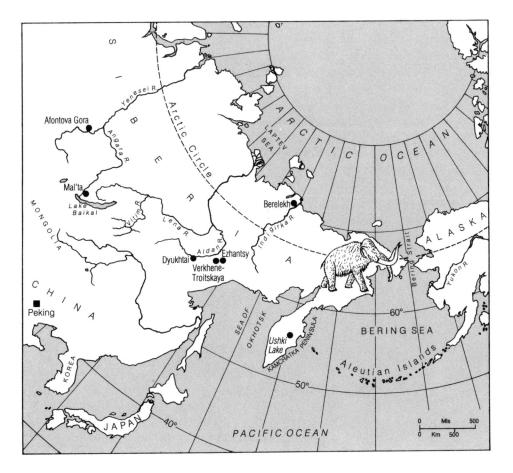

Northeast Asia and western Alaska, together with place-names mentioned in the text.

Unfortunately, Mochanov's new sites from the Middle Aldan have serious chronological problems. In the first place they are terrace deposits that contain vertically concentrated accumulations of artifacts and animal bones in alluvial sediments that have been subjected to violent seasonal perturbations such as are commonplace in subarctic regions. Furthermore, the radiocarbon samples were taken from wood fragments, which, Alaskan experience has shown, are often much older than the deposits in which they are found, having survived for centuries, if not millennia, in the ice-cold, sometimes perennially frozen deposits. The new Mochanov sites are open locations where his dates and vertical bone artifact associations cannot be taken at face value.

Most American, and some Soviet, scholars believe that the Dyukhtai culture is no older than about 18,000 years ago, on the basis of locations like Verkhene-Troitskaya, with a radiocarbon date of that age. At that site, well-made bifacial tools, asymmetrical knives, points and scrapers were found, as well as wedge-shaped cores and microblades. Certainly the Dyukhtai tradition was widespread over northeast Asia after 14,000 years ago. The Berelekh site at 71 degrees N, near the mouth of the Indigirka River, is the northernmost known. It lies just upstream of a "mammoth cemetery" where at least 140 animals perished in spring floods. Only two mammoths were actually found at the humanly-occupied site, together with numerous bones of the arctic hare. These particular Dyukhtai people used not only microblades and bifacial artifacts, but bone and ivory artifacts as well. Broadly contemporary Dyukhtai sites, dating to the closing millennia of the Ice Age, are found as far west as the Angara River, to the south in the Amur Valley, on the coastal plain of the Sea of Okhotsk, even in the Kamchatka Peninsula and perhaps in Japan. Some of the same artifact forms also occur in Alaska, but somewhat later than in Siberia.

Is Mochanov correct in arguing that the Dyukhtai tradition originated somewhere in northern China and Inner Asia? We can evaluate this hypothesis from two angles, one biological, the other archaeological.

An Argument with Teeth in it

Many physical anthropologists, the redoubtable Aleš Hrdlička among them, have pointed to biological similarities between Siberians and North American Indians, but few of them with the thoroughness of Christy Turner. His dental laboratory at Arizona State University is littered not with artifacts, but with human teeth and jaws. Turner is an expert on the study of changing physical characteristics in human teeth. He pores over tooth crowns and roots, for the differences and similarities between them give clues to the degrees of relationship between prehistoric populations. These tooth features are more stable than most evolutionary traits, with a high genetic component that minimizes the effects of environmental differences, sexual dimorphism, and

UPPER JAW

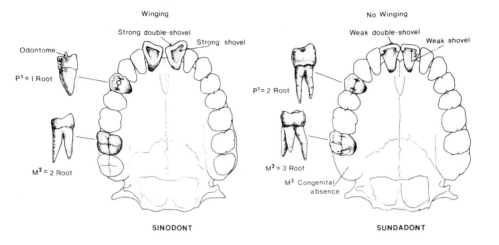

SINODONT

SUNDADONT

LOWER JAW

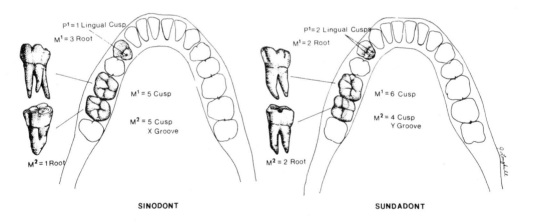

SINODONT

SUNDADONT

Some of Christy Turner's theories about the peopling of America are based on differences between the teeth of so-called Sinodonts (northern Asians and all native Americans) and Sundadonts (eastern Asians). Sinodonts display among other features strong incisor shoveling (scooping out on one or both surfaces of the tooth), single-rooted upper first premolars, and triple-rooted lower first molars.

age variations. Aleš Hrdlička and other early physical anthropologists examined teeth characteristics, too, but Turner is working in an era when much more is known of the evolutionary characteristics of teeth, and many more early specimens are available for examination.

After examining the teeth of more than 4,000 individuals, ancient and modern, from the Old World and New, specimens going back as far as Upper Palaeolithic and Paleo-Indian times, Turner has developed a set of hypotheses about the first settlement of the Americas which he relates to archaeological evidence from China and Siberia.

Turner points out that prehistoric Americans display many fewer variations in their dental morphology than do eastern Asians. Their crown- and root-trait frequencies are similar to those of *northern* Asians. He calls these characteristics "Sinodonty," a pattern of tooth features that includes incisor shoveling (the scooped-out shape on the inside of the tooth), double-shoveling (scooping out on both sides), single-rooted upper first premolars, and triple-rooted lower first molars, among other features. Sinodonty only occurs in northern Asia and the Americas. So far, Turner has been able to examine but a small sample of Asian teeth. His earliest evidence for Sinodonty comes from northern China about 20,000 years ago, but he believes it emerged very much earlier, perhaps as early as 40,000. Turner assumes a common origin for all *Homo sapiens sapiens* populations. He argues that the Sinodont north Chinese may have evolved from a more generalized southeast-Asian population, people they resemble more closely than the eastern Siberians and native Americans who evolved from them.

The few Upper Palaeolithic skeletons from the Lake Baikal area do not display Sinodonty. A child found buried at Mal'ta shows Caucasoid (European) rather than Mongoloid (Asian) features, and no Sinodonty. The simpler teeth of prehistoric Europeans from Kostienki, Mal'ta, and other Russian locations display none of the traits that add mass to the tooth crown. This adaptation, so characteristic of Sinodonts, is thought by Turner to be an adjustment to the dentally-demanding conditions of arctic northeast Asia. The morphological differences are so striking that Turner believes Europeans and eastern Asians (whom Turner calls "Sundadonts") had nothing to do with the peopling of the Americas. Thus, he argues, the New World was populated by Sinodonts from east Asia.

Christy Turner's research is based on dental morphology, not archaeological sites. Such anatomical data is really a study of evolutionary divergence, using statistical calculations that allow one to date the approximate moments at which Sinodont populations split off from the ancestral Chinese groups. The first of these divergences led, Turner believes, to the Paleo-Indian migration. He hypothesizes that the settlement of the New World took place through eastern Mongolia and the Upper Lena Basin, across eastern Siberia, and from there along the now submerged continental shelf to Alaska. At present, we lack critical assessments of Turner's researches, for he has yet to publish complete information and statistics on his teeth samples. However, his argument that there is a dental connection between the Americas and north China must be taken seriously, and provides an interesting framework for the archaeological finds.

Some support for Turner's dental work comes from distributions of genetic markers in modern American Indian populations. A team of physical anthropologists from all over the United States has collaborated on a study of the variants (called Gm allotypes) of one particular protein found in the fluid portion of the blood, the serum. All proteins "drift," or produce variants, over the generations, and it has been discovered that members of an interbreeding human population will share a set of such variants. Thus by comparing the Gm allotypes of two different populations one can work out their genetic "distance," which itself can be calibrated to give an indication of the length of time since these populations last interbred.

The research team sampled thousands of Indians from four cultural groups in western North America, and found their Gm types divided into two groups, with the Aleuts and Eskimos of the far north forming a third one. One group is thought to relate to the Paleo-Indians. More than 14,000 Central and South American Indians shared the same grouping as well. The scientists believe this result demonstrates that there was a single, early migration of hunter-gatherers, who evolved later by cultural differentiation. Two further migrations, giving rise to the present-day Athabaskan and Eskimo-Aleut populations respectively, took place at a later time into North America.

Precious little Gm data comes from northeast Asia, but enough for the research team to write that "North-eastern Siberia appears to be a good candidate for the ancestral home of contemporary North Americans. It has the genetic variation, geographic proximity, and geological history required of such a homeland."

Microblades, Reindeer, and Migration Routes

If the biologists are right in thinking that there were three distinct migrations into the Americas, and Turner's data points to northern China as a major dispersal point, are there archaeological sites in this general area that support their hypothesis, or, for that matter, Mochanov's general theory of Dyukhtai origins?

There are certainly numerous late Stone Age sites that date to later than 20,000 years ago, and some that may be even earlier. According to Chinese archaeologists Tang Chung and Gai Pei, there were late Stone Age hunter-gatherers in northern China at least as early as 30,000 years ago. Sometime between 30,000 and 15,000 years ago, microblade technology came into use, reaching a high degree of sophistication between 15,000 and 10,000 years ago.

The tool inventory includes not only microblades, but characteristic wedge-shaped cores. The two Chinese scholars claim that the same complex blade technology was widely distributed over much of northeast Asia and northwest America.

Locations with microblades and other small artifacts are undoubtedly abundant in the Japanese archipelago after 20,000 years ago. There are also claims of human occupation in Japan before 30,000 years ago, but these are controversial. The Korean peninsula has likewise yielded microblade sites dating back perhaps as far as 20,000 years ago. Undated surface sites with basically similar artifact inventories have been reported from Inner and Outer Mongolia, Manchuria, and south and west China, but they may well date to the very end of the Ice Age and early post-glacial times.

At present, however – as we have seen – there is no solid evidence for Siberian sites dating to earlier than about 18,000 years ago, and microblades there seem to be much later than that. Nor can definite links between Chinese and northeast Asian sites be documented, even if they are suspected. The only possible link may be a very general one, an adaptive one. American palaeontologist Dale Guthrie believes the Dyukhtai microblades were inset into antler shafts as slotted points, and links the distribution of microblade production to that of reindeer. Could it be that this inset-weapons system emerged in China, other parts of eastern Asia, in Siberia, and northwest America, as a widespread adaptation to tundra conditions, where migratory reindeer herds roamed? Perhaps the widespread microblade techno-logy reflects a widely shared and successful material culture that emerged at the very end of the last glaciation and flourished well into post-glacial times.

While some scholars are beginning to think along these lines, Christy Turner argues in terms of actual population movements. He believes that his Sinodonts could only move north and east, for the way west and south was blocked by other, Sundadont, *Homo sapiens sapiens* populations. Any movement northward would have been shaped by the course of major river valleys and other topographic features. Turner moves his Sinodonts into eastern Mongolia about 20,000 years ago, via the north-flowing Vitim River. From the Upper Lena Basin they could reach the "thickly-iced Arctic coast near the much reduced Laptev Sea." Here they turned east along the exposed (today submerged) continental shelf on the north coast of Siberia. This route led the ancestors of the first Americans to their new homeland.

A different route via the southern coast of Siberia is proposed by the Soviet archaeologist Nicholai Dikov, working on the Kamchatka Peninsula. Dikov argues that the earliest period when one can speak of cultural relations between Asia and America corresponds to a period of early human settlement at Ushki Lake on Kamchatka. A series of large prehistoric settlements on the shores of the lake are said to be separated by sterile bands of volcanic ash. The lowest and oldest layer, "cultural layer VII," has been radiocarbon-dated to around 14,000 years ago. The people lived in large, tent-like houses buried partially in the ground and apparently occupied for long periods of time. They lived off both hunting and fishing, using stone-tipped spears, and perhaps bows and arrows. Many artifacts were bifacially flaked, including stemmed points and leaf-shaped knives. Dikov believes the stemmed points "influenced the development of stem types" in North America, and also finds similarities with Japanese specimens, but his comparisons do not hold up under close scrutiny. Dikov theorizes that contemporaries of the early Ushki people could have moved along the southern edge of the Bering land bridge and along the northwestern coast of North America before sea levels rose at the end of the Ice Age.

Few Westerners have first-hand experience of the Ushki site, so it is difficult to assess Dikov's interpretation, or to establish its connections, if any, with the Dyukhtai tradition. Turner finds it hard to accept Dikov's arguments about the southern Siberian migration route on climatic and geographical grounds, for the topography is rugged and of low productivity. One interesting find from later Ushki levels is extremely significant. A burial of a domesticated dog dated to about 11,000 years ago is the earliest record of this vital animal in the far north. Perhaps this was the point at which dog-sled travel became a viable means of getting around on arctic ice, a technology that was to have momentous consequences in later millennia.

The Stage is Set

We are now at the outer frontiers of northeast Asia, on the shores of the Bering Strait. We have followed *Homo sapiens sapiens* across open water to Australia, and deep into arctic latitudes for the first time. Truly modern humanity was capable of conquering almost any environmental extreme, and of making short passages over open water – provided there was land in sight at the other end. Offshore navigation by the stars and true deep-water vessels were probably a much later cultural development.

The initial settlement of the northern steppe-tundra may have been relatively rapid, simply because the natural carrying capacity of the plains was so low and people were constantly on the move, covering enormous distances within a short time. (Some Australian aborigine groups exploit territories over thousands of square miles.) The move north and east may have begun very soon after the emergence of *Homo sapiens sapiens* some 35,000 years ago and never stopped. The process of constant, gradual expansion was to continue right into recent times, as people developed ever more effective ways of exploiting subarctic and arctic plains, valleys, and coasts, and hunter-gatherer populations rose. The exact dating of this process remains, in its earliest stages, unknown. But Stone Age peoples were at the threshold of the

Americas, in northeastern Siberia, almost certainly by 18,000 years ago, just possibly much earlier than that.

We have now identified the most likely ancestors for the first Americans – Sinodont late Palaeolithic hunters and foragers with a dental and genetic morphology remarkably similar to that of the American Indians, who subsisted off big game, smaller animals, perhaps fish, and some wild vegetable foods. At some point, a few of these people, with a culture developed over thousands of years, walked or paddled eastward, across the Bering Strait, the only logical route into the Americas. We must now examine the manner of their crossing, and evaluate two competing hypotheses as to the date when it first occurred – between 35,000 and 15,000 years ago, or later, after 15,000.

PART THREE

THE CROSSING

---

*"Theirs are shapes only dimly seen,
a shadowy people who came on stage
on tiptoe when the lights were low."*

Thomas Canby, 1979

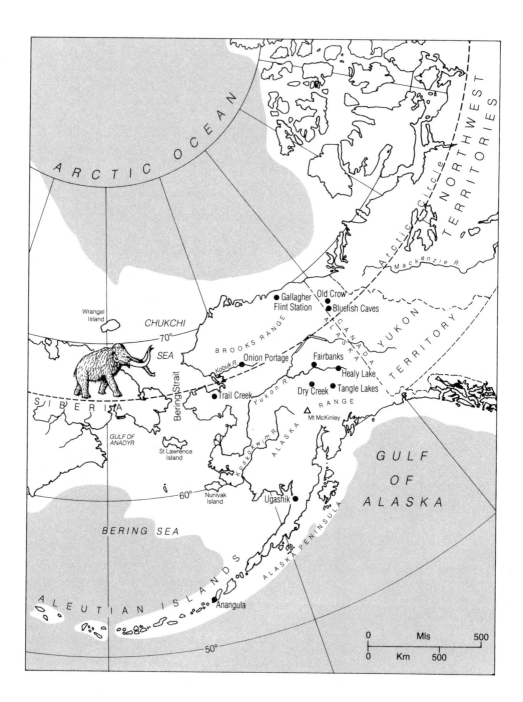

Beringia (untinted area) as it would have been at its maximum extent some 20,000 years ago.

The following labels appear on the map:

ARCTIC OCEAN

NORTHWEST TERRITORIES

Arctic Circle

Mackenzie R.

CHUKCHI SEA

Wrangel Island

70°

BROOKS RANGE

● Gallagher Flint Station

● Old Crow

● Bluefish Caves

YUKON TERRITORY

CANADA / ALASKA

SIBERIA

Bering Strait

Kobuk R.

● Onion Portage

● Fairbanks

● Healy Lake

Yukon R.

● Dry Creek

● Tangle Lakes

● Trail Creek

GULF OF ANADYR

St Lawrence Island

Kuskokwim R.

ALASKA RANGE

△ Mt McKinley

GULF OF ALASKA

60°

Nunivak Island

● Ugashik

BERING SEA

ALASKA PENINSULA

ALEUTIAN ISLANDS

● Anangula

50°

0   Mls   500

0   Km   500

CHAPTER FIVE

Beringia

The ship sailed slowly northward. Anxiously, the Russian explorer Vitus Bering peered to port and starboard, hoping for a glimpse of land through the impenetrable fog. Even on this August day in 1728, the air was chilly and uninviting. Nervous about ice and apparently out of sight of land, Bering gave the order to head south. That very day, he glimpsed the Diomede Islands in the middle of the strait. Had the weather been clear, he would have sighted Alaska a few miles away to port. It was not until four years later that two other Russian seamen discovered the North American side of the strait.

Bering Strait is a desolate, windy place. Even in summer the winds can howl through smoky mists, cutting visibility to a few yards. Savage winters last for nine months in these latitudes. For eight months a year the strait is ice-covered as far south as 60 degrees N. It is a somewhat unspectacular place, bounded on the Alaskan side by lowlying coastal plains, numerous lakes, and some low, rolling hills. The Siberian coastline is more rugged and steeper. But, for all its unremarkable scenery, the strait is the only sea route from the north Pacific to the Arctic and north Atlantic oceans. Modern Americans tend to think of the Bering Strait as an impenetrable barrier that separates them from an alien, Communist world. The political boundary is, of course, meaningless. In prehistoric times, an Eskimo could readily cross from the Old World to the New in a skin boat. Common linguistic and cultural traditions survive to this day on both sides of the strait. For much of the time from as early as 30,000 until some 12,000 years ago, the Bering Strait was dry land, part of a vast northern lowland known to scientists as Beringia.

This bleak landscape is the highway by which Upper Palaeolithic people crossed into the New World. We must now search this chilly region for signs of very early settlement, and try and reconstruct the environmental setting for both our chronological scenarios: between 35,000 and 15,000 years ago, and for a later crossing.

The Discovery of Beringia

When archaeologist Samuel Haven wrote of the Bering Strait in 1856, he had no idea that it had once been dry land. Like José de Acosta, he assumed that "short stretches of navigation" had stood in the way of any overland journey from Asia. However, in 1887, a geologist named Angelo Heilprin pointed out that, while the tropical animals of the Old and New Worlds had little in common, those of more temperate latitudes displayed fewer differences. Furthermore, the fauna and flora on both sides of the Bering Strait were almost identical. Thus, he argued, the two hemispheres had once been connected in northern latitudes and, if humans walked across, in quite recent times.

Seven years later, another geologist, George Dawson, took soundings in the strait, found shallow depths, and was convinced a "wide terrestrial plain" had once connected Asia and Alaska. When mammoth bones came to light on the Unalaska and Pribilof Islands, doubt turned to certainty. The strait had been dry land during part of the Ice Age.

The early geologists based their arguments on comparisons between fossil animals found on both sides of the strait as well as on soundings and land-based geomorphological data. They argued that earth movements or continental uplift had separated the two continents.

There matters stood until 1934, when a well-known geologist, R.A. Daly, popularized the idea that the world's sea levels had fluctuated markedly during the Pleistocene. These sea-level changes were the result of major fluctuations in the amount of water locked up in the great ice sheets that had covered the earth's surface during the glaciations. These are called *eustatic* changes to differentiate them from *isostatic* alterations caused by adjustments in the earth's crust, as the land reacted to the massive weight of continental ice sheets. These theories of glacial eustasy and isostasy provided just the theoretical framework that Bering Strait geologists needed. Three years later, Swedish scientist Eric Hulten used the Soviet term "Beringia" to describe a great arctic lowland, an isolated land where many arctic and boreal plants took refuge during the bitterly cold glacial phases of the Ice Age. Beringia, he argued, had been the route by which early hunter-gatherers had reached the New World.

In the late 1930s, the technology of underwater exploration was so rudimentary that the experts had little more to work with than a handful of crude deep-sea cores and land-based geological observations. Today American and Soviet ships have probed the waters of the strait with grabs and core borers. They use sophisticated acoustical reflection techniques to penetrate soft, sea-bottom sediments and the bedrock beneath them. These new surveys revealed a very flat plain of soft sediment generally less than 9.8 feet (3 m) thick. The entire floor of the Chukchi Sea and the northeastern Bering Sea was until some 14,000 years ago an exposed coastal plain that was in the process of being dissected and denuded by many streams.

The underwater probes of recent years have yielded a complicated, and often conflicting, jigsaw puzzle of data about Beringia, but they have shown that Eric Hulten was right. About 18,000 years ago, Beringia was a large and impressive landmass extending from Siberia across the Bering Strait, and deep into Alaska and northwest Canada. During the most intensely cold millennia of the last glaciation, the great North American ice sheets effectively isolated Beringia from southern latitudes. There was less glaciation in Siberia and relatively easy communication between Asia and Alaska. So, for many millennia, Alaska was biogeographically part of Siberia.

An Ever-Changing Landscape

It is one thing to establish the topography of a sunken landmass, quite another to reconstruct its convoluted history. As Ice Age sea levels rose and fell, the Bering Strait alternated between ocean and dry land in a complicated series of geological events that can only be studied from surviving high-sea-level beach lines on present-day coasts and from deep-sea cores.

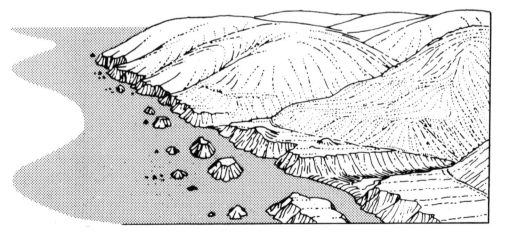

During the Ice Age there were many alternating periods of high and low sea level, and one way geologists study such variations is by looking at so-called raised beaches, higher shorelines left by seas well above those of the present day. The illustration shows a late Ice Age raised beach on the Pacific Coast of California north of San Francisco.

Some clues as to the fluctuations of Ice Age sea levels come from the tropical waters of the Caribbean. In 1970, the geologists W.S. Broecker and J. van Donk described some Caribbean deep-sea cores, in which they traced major changes in water temperature during the Ice Age, using inorganic particles and cold-water foraminifera. Broecker and van Donk noticed a remarkably cyclical temperature-change pattern over hundreds of thousands of years. Every time the world climate became cooler, it did so at a very slow rate, taking as much as 90,000 years to change from temperate to extreme cold conditions. The cooling process was irregular, too, with prolonged intervals of equilibrium, or even temperate climate, that lasted as long as 20,000 years. In dramatic contrast, the process of deglaciation took but a tenth of the time. The great ice sheets of Europe and North America retreated rapidly. Sea levels adjusted fast as water poured back into the oceans. The land crust compensated for the reduced weight of continental and mountain ice by rising considerably. All this adjustment took place within periods as short as 10,000 years.

Twice, some 125,000 years ago, and again approximately 14,000 years before the present, the world climate warmed up rapidly. Broecker and van Donk called these moments of rapid warming "terminations," and argued they would have occurred all over the globe. These, then, would be periods when central Beringia – the land bridge – was flooded.

To gain some idea of the magnitude of climatic change, one has only to compare the appearance of northeast Asia and Alaska today with that of 20,000 years ago. Then, the earth's northern latitudes were locked in bitter arctic conditions, conditions so extreme they were quite unlike any found on earth today. At the height of this last glaciation, three gigantic continental glaciers mantled northwest Europe, Greenland, and the northern latitudes of North America. So severe was the glaciation that sea levels were at least 280 feet (85 m) lower than they are today all over the world. Beringia was not two landmasses separated by a watery strait, but a diverse, lowlying continuum, part of an enormous, arctic continent. Huge, interconnected and unglaciated plains and lowlands extended all the way from southeast Europe, to southern Siberia, through the Lena River Valley, along the exposed ranges of the continental shelf, then onto the dry plains adjoining the Chukchi and Bering Seas and into Alaska.

These dramatic changes in sea level and climate are of vital archaeological importance, for they form the backdrop to the first human settlement of the Americas. When the land bridge was exposed, it would be possible for people to walk across to Alaska dry-shod. When it was submerged, they would have had to paddle over open water – or risk their lives walking on ice floes – to the land dimly visible on the other side. When, therefore, was the land bridge in existence? Recently, a group of experts on Beringia collaborated on a study of the land bridge, based on research in many disciplines. One of these experts,

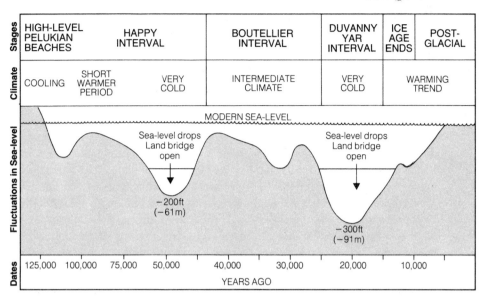

Stages	HIGH-LEVEL PELUKIAN BEACHES	HAPPY INTERVAL		BOUTELLIER INTERVAL	DUVANNY YAR INTERVAL	ICE AGE ENDS	POST-GLACIAL
Climate	COOLING	SHORT WARMER PERIOD	VERY COLD	INTERMEDIATE CLIMATE	VERY COLD	WARMING TREND	

MODERN SEA-LEVEL

Fluctuations in Sea-level

Sea-level drops Land bridge open

−200ft (−61m)

Sea-level drops Land bridge open

−300ft (−91m)

| Dates | 125,000 | 100,000 | 75,000 | 50,000 | 40,000 | 30,000 | 20,000 | 10,000 |

YEARS AGO

Chart giving an approximate indication of climate and sea-level fluctuations over the last 125,000 years in the Bering Strait area.

David Hopkins of the University of Alaska, has spent much of his career working in the far north. He has developed a tentative sequence of land-bridge fluctuations over the last 125,000 years:

Pelukian Beaches Hopkins begins by identifying a well-defined high-sea-level "terrace" that lies on either side of the strait, between 50 and 100 feet (15 and 30.5 m) above modern sea level. These "Pelukian" beaches (named after exposures at Peluk Creek, near Nome, Alaska) are at varying heights and contain both warmer mollusks and others similar in temperature range to those in the area today. Hopkins believes that the higher Pelukian terraces coincide with Broecker and van Donk's 125,000-year "termination," a period when the climate was at least as warm as today.

Happy Interval Then the cooling process began, and continued for tens of thousands of years. The term "Happy Interval," coined by Hopkins, is perhaps a misnomer, for the climate became increasingly cold. Alaskan glaciers reached their maximum extent during these millennia. Around 100,000 years ago, the climate warmed up briefly and sea levels returned to near-modern levels to form the lowermost of the Pelukian beach terraces. But the cooling resumed. Sea levels fell to at least − 200 feet (− 61 m) about 50,000 years ago.

Boutellier Interval A lengthy period of intermediate climate and less extensive glaciation then ensued. Hopkins names this after a stratified location in southwestern Yukon Territory, where organic soils were sandwiched between two ice sheets. The Boutellier Interval may have lasted from about 44,000 to 30,000 or 25,000 years ago. Some 400 centuries ago, the sea level was not far below its present position. The land bridge was probably no more than a narrow isthmus that was flooded periodically. The climate was still severe, with snowy winters and short, dry summers.

Duvanny Yar Interval Some 25,000 years ago, temperatures again declined, ushering in a period of extremely dry continental climate in Beringia documented by an exposure at Duvanny Yar on Siberia's Kolyma River. The Pacific was between -295 and -330 feet (-90 and -100.5 m) below modern levels. The land bridge now stretched from Asia to Alaska and covered much of the Chukchi Sea. Its southern coastline extended from the Gulf of Anadyr in Siberia to the Alaskan Peninsula in the New World. The winters were long, cold, and extremely dry. Strong winds swept across the land bridge, lowering air temperatures by wind-chill factors to depths unimaginable by modern standards.

Duvanny Yar ends in what Broecker and van Donk called "Termination 1," that moment when the recovery from the low-sea-level point began. This warming trend began about 15,000 to 14,000 years ago. Hopkins and his colleagues have traced the rapid flooding of the Bering Strait from submerged shorelines. As sea levels rose, so the geography of the flat land bridge changed dramatically. The Bering Strait and Gulf of Anadyr were submerged when the sea level rose to -157 feet (-48 m). Around 13,000 years ago, St Lawrence Island was still a peninsula of the Alaskan mainland, when the sea level stood at -124 feet (-38 m). While much of the Siberian coastline assumed its present configuration about 10,000 years ago, freshwater peat was still accumulating off the Alaskan coast in what is now 65 feet (19.8 m) of sea water. The American coastline was still up to 63 miles (100 km) offshore at the very threshold of modern times.

A Crossing by Sea or Land?

Geologists are still arguing about many of the minor details of this sequence. However, they agree that for two long periods, sometime between 75,000 and 45,000 years ago, and again from about 25,000 to 14,000, the Bering land bridge was exposed.

If Upper Palaeolithic people settled in extreme northeast Asia as early as 35,000 years ago, they would have gazed eastward over open water. To cross the strait, they would have needed some form of boat. Assuming that such settlement existed – and for discussion purposes we should assume it did – were Upper Palaeolithic people capable of navigating the Bering Strait? Had they done so, they would almost certainly have relied not on wooden boats, for the environment was probably largely treeless, but on skin canoes.

About the only evidence for early Upper Palaeolithic navigation comes from Australasia. As we saw in the previous chapter, the first Australian settlers had to cross a channel some 55 miles (88 km) wide, and they probably did so on simple log or reed rafts. At its narrowest, the Bering Strait may be a similar distance across (50 miles or 80 km), but sea conditions are much severer in the far north. Raft crossings on usually placid, warm tropical seas are one thing, venturing offshore in arctic waters quite another matter. Even in the slightly warmer conditions of 35,000 years ago, the Bering Strait would have been a jumble of grinding ice floes for much of the summer. In winter, darkness and pressure ridges, snow drifts and harsh winds would have rendered the frozen sea impassable to even the boldest traveler. And to judge from modern arctic hunters, anyone who hunted in these latitudes was very cautious indeed. Offshore navigation in the most seaworthy of skin canoes would have been, at best, a seasonal activity, confined to the few warm weeks of summer, when the threat of crushing ice leads receded. Even then, only the most experienced and well-trained watermen would survive sudden storms or a ducking in waters where people fall victim to hypothermia in a few short minutes.

Did the Upper Palaeolithic Siberians have boats 35,000, or even 15,000 years ago? We simply do not know. They were probably well aware that animal skins sewn round a framework of bone or wood might form a primitive boat capable of supporting one person, or more. They may even have used such craft to hunt sea mammals close to shore. But, like their very distant Upper Palaeolithic relatives far to the south, it seems unlikely that they went far from land, even if lowlying shores were visible on the horizon. There might, of course, have been accidental crossings, but even these seem a remoter possibility in the far north. When the anthropologist Richard Nelson lived and worked among Alaskan Eskimos in the 1970s, he observed that they were the most cautious of hunters, who invariably minimized risks on land, ice, or water. We can safely assume that a similar caution ruled in Upper Palaeolithic times. Arctic hunters cannot survive any other way. With a diversity of large and small land mammals ashore, they may have depended far less heavily on sea mammals and fishing than the Eskimo peoples of more recent prehistory. Their seamanship and navigational skills were probably correspondingly less well developed.

The theoretical arguments, and they are theoretical, seem strongly against a sea crossing. Most likely, Upper Palaeolithic bands crossed into the New World over the flat, lowlying land bridge, either during the height of the last glaciation between 25,000 and 15,000 years ago, or soon after, as the land bridge began to be submerged once again.

If we reject a boat crossing, a crossing that is so far undocumented on either side of the Bering Strait, we must then ask another question. Was the Bering land bridge capable of supporting human life?

Life on the Land Bridge

Make no mistake about it, the Beringian climate was extremely inhospitable, and the land-bridge environment probably quite unlike anything now found on earth. Monotonous expanses of dry arctic taiga and tundra cover much of northeast Asia and the northern latitudes of the New World today. These are some of the coldest places in the world. At the height of Ice Age glaciations they were even colder. Siberia and Alaska are dry today. They were even drier 18,000 years ago. On the face of it, Beringia would seem to have been completely unsuitable for human settlement. However, many palaeoecologists believe it was a refuge for both animals and humans during the cold intervals of the last glaciation. Therein may lie clues to the first colonization of the Americas.

Most of what we know about this submerged land comes from locations on both shores of the Bering Strait. (Some fossil mammoth bones have, however, been brought up by seabottom grabs.) The modern climate is so cold that ancient plant remains sometimes survive in a near-perfect state, refrigerated in prehistoric muds and peats. They also turn up in such esoteric places as late-glacial animal burrows, and tend to be isolated finds, although they have shown that cottonwood trees, and possibly aspens, grew on the land bridge. Fortunately, the science of palynology – pollen analysis – provides a much more comprehensive, if tantalizing, view of ancient Beringia.

Back in 1916, the Swedish botanist Lennart von Post discovered that tiny fossil pollen grains found in Scandinavian bogs could be used to reconstruct Ice Age vegetation over thousands of years of prehistoric time. As any sufferer from hay fever knows, our own air carries a myriad of tiny pollen spores, many of them from trees and grasses dozens of miles away. A constant pollen "rain" descends on the earth, a rain that reflects the natural vegetation around us. Von Post argued that samples of fossil pollen from stratified prehistoric swamps would chronicle changes in vegetational cover at the end of the Ice Age and even earlier. He found dramatic vegetational changes in Scandinavia. At the end of the Ice Age, arctic tundra covered northern Europe. As the ice sheets retreated, this gave way to birch cover, then to mixed oak forest as the climate warmed up. In places, von Post and his successors found Stone Age artifacts in polliniferous layers. So they were able to tell the archaeologists what the vegetation, and to some extent the climate, had been like at the time.

Palynology has illuminated the Bering land bridge like a searchlight. Dozens of core-borings from lake beds, swamps, muds, and other Ice Age deposits have revealed a unique association of arctic plants that flourished on the lowlying plains between 18,000 and 13,000 years ago. The botanists have combined the pollen data with studies of the modern vegetational cover of what remains of Beringia today. The result is a fascinating, and controversial, picture of a unique Ice Age landscape.

Pollen expert Steven Young, a palaeoecologist from Vermont, says that the present vegetational scenario reflects a state of knowledge "still fragmentary and often equivocal enough to allow a variety of interpretations." In 1937, Eric Hulten pointed out that Beringia was a distinctive subcontinent, not just a corridor between the Old World and the New. He also dismissed notions that the land bridge had been a plain of gently waving grass, where half-naked hunters had pursued big game from Asia into a new continent. Beringia was a treeless land, Hulten said. There had been no exchange of Alaskan and Siberian forests throughout the Ice Age. Somewhat later, in 1964, botanist Paul Colinvaux of Ohio State University wondered if, perhaps, the southern shore of the land bridge had been warmed by the Japanese current and had offered a less bleak homeland for both animals and humans. However, his pollen samples from the Pribilof Islands showed that this coast was just as harsh and forbidding as the tundra-covered interior.

Paul Colinvaux heads a school of thought that argues that the land bridge was "an unproductive place, invaded by small migrating populations of herbivores, largely confined to river systems." The food resources for human beings, he says, would have been scarce and unpredictable at best. Colinvaux argues from pollen data that central Beringia was covered with sparse tundra during the height of the last glaciation, until at least 14,000 years ago. He conjures up a "vision in the mind's eye of a dusty plain, stretching to the horizon, vegetated between the bare patches with a low mat of sedges and grasses looking like a drier version of modern arctic plain." An arctic tundra fauna lived on the plains, a fauna somewhat similar to the rodents of the modern tundra. Such large mammals as existed were outliers of much bigger populations that lived in more forested terrain on the neighboring landmasses. Colinvaux believes the land bridge was inhospitable and barren until about 14,000 years ago, when rising sea levels and retreating ice sheets caused radical changes, perhaps even bringing moist tundra and scattered patches of forests to the land bridge.

Palaeoecologists like Young, and the palaeontologist Dale Guthrie of the University of Alaska, take a less pessimistic view: a hypothesis that Colinvaux calls "the assumption of a land bridge fit for big-game animals and human heroes to live in." They talk and write of a long-vanished ecosystem where many different animal species lived in productive harmony, just as they do on the African savanna today. Young and others interpret Alaskan and Yukon pollen diagrams somewhat differently from their colleagues. They argue for steppe rather than tundra. They point to the dominance of grasses and sedges in the pollen diagrams of the time, and to the high percentage of *Artemisia*, the wormwood. These percentages imply better drainage, some summer thawing and dryness, and a more steppe-like grass cover. They believe the land bridge would have been covered by a patchwork of very different types of vegetation.

The Young-Guthrie interpretation argues that south-central Beringia was home to many marshes and shallow ponds. Perhaps these conditions favored grass-dominated wetlands, where large herbivores would find summer fodder. In land-bridge times, several large rivers, among them the Anadyr and the Yukon, must have crossed the coastal plain. They carried great volumes of water when summer glacial ice melted, much more than today, creating floodplains of considerable size. Small, local drainages and tributaries may have supported stands of tall willow brush, again an ideal food for large herbivores. Nearer the southern coast, deltas and coastal flats might have supported freshwater marshes, ponds, and slow-moving streams with their own sedge-meadow flora. There were probably extensive dune fields covered with coarse grass, like the enormous fossil dune field south of the Brooks Range that is the size of the state of Indiana.

Steven Young's reconstruction of the land bridge appears to be based on a broader spectrum of palaeoecological data than Colinvaux's. His vegetational map is based not just on ancient pollen samples alone, but on modern botanical data collected from Alaska and Siberia. He notes that present-day Beringian flora is distributed in isolated patches, as if previously continuous ranges of vegetation types had been disrupted by a catastrophic change – in this case the submergence of the land bridge where many now-rare species once flourished in profusion. He is quite prepared to find cottonwood and other tree and brush species in this harsh environment.

This unique vegetational pattern is found only in scattered relic associations today, but we know considerably more about it from Siberia than we do from Alaska. As long ago as 1929, the Russian botanist Alexei Tugarinov described this form of arctic steppe as "open landscape, noticeably xeric [dry], rather cold, with little winter precipitation." Its grasses and cottonwood scrub supported a mammal fauna that included mammoth and saiga antelope, something that a mere southward extension of the present-day tundra would never have done. At this time, he added, dry, windy conditions blew clouds of glacial dust (loess) over the plains and formed large dune fields in many places.

Was this the vegetational cover of the land bridge, a cover capable of supporting large herbivores? Paul Colinvaux believes that the land bridge pollen diagrams reflect a pollen "rain" from tundra rather than steppe. He feels that the closest analogies for Siberian steppe-tundra come from the modern tundra landscape of Wrangel (Vrangelya) Island in the Arctic Ocean, at 72 degrees N. He argues that those who call the central Beringian landscape steppe-tundra are misunderstanding how the Russians use the term. The land-bridge environment was, he says, "a broad expanse of frozen silt." Here the continental summers spawned great dust clouds that blew over a thin, thawed land surface. There were few places where herbivores could graze and people could hunt them. Today, the plant complexes of Siberia and Alaska are quite different. Many botanists believe the similarities that exist probably resulted from connections much earlier than the last glaciation. Thus, the Siberian steppe-tundra may not have extended into North America. Colinvaux's hypothesis suffers from one major defect. Late Ice Age mammals *did* cross the strait. There must have been something for them to eat on the way.

Geologist J.V. Matthews of the Geological Survey of Canada has attempted to navigate the morass of controversy and look at the Beringian landscape through more multidisciplinary eyes. He believes the high percentages of wormwood portray a tundra vegetation that was better drained than today. This vegetation was not a monolithic, unchanging tundra or steppe, but a mosaic that included both extensive tracts of steppe and tundra, low uplands, and lowland areas that differed considerably from modern tundra. This environment was somewhat drier and more steppe-like than modern-day Alaska. Matthews looks farther afield than pollen diagrams and plant remains. He points out that the fossil insects found in Alaskan deposits include occasional finds of a grassland beetle, *Harpalus amputatus*, which does not occur in modern tundra. On the other hand, weevils and other beetles suggest scanty vegetation and dry conditions. Even more important, he observes that the dung beetle *Aphodius* can represent between three and ten percent of insect samples, an insect typically associated with hoofed mammals. In contrast, post-glacial deposits contain an abundance and diversity of ants, conifer-loving beetles, and insects that live in or near the water.

The participants in the steppe-tundra controversy agree only on a few basics. They agree that Beringia was largely treeless, the vegetation dominated by herbaceous plants, with alder, dwarf birch, and heath shrubs found in rare, more sheltered localities. This was sparse vegetation, but, judging from the mammalian population, it may have been more productive than the thin flora of modern tundra or the montane and polar desert areas of today.

Mammoths and the Late Ice Age Bestiary

Everyone, whether optimist or pessimist, agrees that Beringia was linked to a panorama of interconnected landscapes that spilled over from central Asia into eastern Siberia, across the land bridge into Alaska. These diverse landscapes supported what Soviet palaeontologists call the "mammoth" or "Upper Palaeolithic" fauna.

In the year 1901, reports reached Moscow of a remarkable "devil creature" half buried in arctic mud at Beresovka, deep in northern Siberia. It turned out to be a refrigerated woolly mammoth that had become mired one summer tens of thousands of years ago, then deep frozen in near-perfect condition. The hair and coat were well preserved, the remains of the mammoth's last meal were still in its stomach. The carcass was so fresh that the scientists were tempted to try the meat. They settled for feeding it to their dogs, with no apparent ill effects. Dozens of Ice Age mammoths have come to light in Siberia since then, most of them dating to between 45,000 and 11,000 years ago. All had died of natural causes, some in landslides, others in deep mud. Others fell into deep pits in the permafrost. Every spring flood washed mammoth carcasses into quiet rivers like the Berelekh on the East Siberian Sea, where they were macerated. More than 140 animals have come from the Berelekh mammoth "cemetery" alone. All these discoveries have given Soviet scientists a remarkably complete knowledge of these magnificent herbivores.

Contrary to popular belief, *Mammuthus primigenius* was not a gigantic beast – not that it was small, either, for at shoulder height it stood up to 11 feet (3.4 m) tall (compared with up to 13 feet (4 m) for an African elephant). The mammoth differed considerably from modern tropical elephants. It had relatively shorter limbs and longer body, probably an adaptation to its plains grazing habitat. African elephants are browsers that use their longer limbs to feed on branches and shrubs. The mammoth had broader feet, adapted to support its heavy body in marshy, poorly drained terrain. A combination of elastic fibers, fatty tissues, and laterally extending toes provided a cushion like an automobile tire to support the mammoth's weight. They were probably difficult animals to enmire.

Beringian mammoths were imposing beasts, with high, massive heads and great, curved tusks. Thick hair covered every part of the body except the soles of the feet, even the ears and trunk. The underwool was up to 6 in. (15.2 cm) deep. Siberian carcasses show that mammoths fed on cottongrass, sedges, mosses, and small trees. Their winter sustenance probably included dry grasses, willow, birch, and perhaps larch twigs.

The mammoth may have been the giant of the Upper Palaeolithic fauna, but steppe bison were large animals, too. They were heavily built, with a large head, massive horns, and a coat as much as 30 in. (76 cm) deep to protect them against arctic winds. The musk ox was another gregarious animal, which survives today in Canada's Northwest Territories, and has been reintroduced to Nunivak Island in Alaska. This is a thickset animal with a sluggish blood circulation in the legs to protect it against the cold. These remarkable beasts can easily survive temperatures of up to -50 deg. F (-45.5 deg. C). Not only that, they can secure food from beneath snow up to 8 in. (20 cm) deep without any trouble.

The saiga antelope (*Saiga tatarica*) migrates seasonally in enormous herds. It is a fast runner, capable of speeds up to 40 miles an hour, a plains animal with large hooves for digging under snow and running over it, and a nose adapted to filter flying dust. The saiga still inhabits Siberia, as does the caribou (the North American reindeer), another gregarious beast with a regular migration pattern based on open, tundra-type landscape. Then there were the

Ice Age deposits all the way from western Europe to Siberia and Alaska yield remains of woolly mammoth (top left), steppe bison (top right), wild horse (above left), and reindeer/caribou (above right) – shown here as depicted by Upper Palaeolithic artists in southwest France.

small animals. Ground squirrels fed on grasses, berries, and insects, hibernating in winter. Lemmings and voles lived both on steppe-tundra and in marshes, as did the white-furred arctic foxes that lived off them.

Woolly mammoth, steppe bison, wild horse, and reindeer/caribou are found in Ice Age deposits all the way east from western Europe right into Siberia, Alaska, and the Yukon. In Asia, this glacial fauna included both extreme arctic and more temperate forms from southern latitudes, which could venture north in open country. The mix included arctic fox, saiga antelope, musk ox, and the yak. North-south exchanges were impeded by rough terrain in Alaska and the Yukon. The Upper Palaeolithic fauna was remarkable for its diversity, and for its dominance by grazers and hoofed mammals. It also included some formidable predators, including arctic panthers, the short-nose bear, and a variety of foxes.

Soviet biologists N.K. Vereshchagin and G.F. Baryshnikov have not only examined Ice Age carcasses and bones, but also compared the ecology of the Upper Palaeolithic fauna with that of the modern arctic community. Their scenario for Beringian mammalian ecology reads like this: the thick woolly coats of mammoth, bison, horse, and musk ox protected them against a climate colder and drier than today. Why drier? All the animals had pelts with skirtlike fringes that hung near the ground. Had the climate been wetter and more maritime, the skirts would have frozen, then thawed, with lethal effects on their owners. Furthermore, the ears and tails of all Beringian mammals were small compared with those of living species, reducing the amount of body-heat loss by exposure of body surfaces to the cold air.

The steppe bison, horse, and saiga are fast-moving animals that flourish on firm, dry soils. Many of the smaller animals were burrowers, preferring firm soils for the purpose. Beringia was so dry that snow cover was probably thin and often blown away, exposing dried vegetation for mammoth and other ungulates to consume during the winter.

Whether or not all the animals in the Upper Palaeolithic fauna existed together in Beringia at one time is highly uncertain. Some experts even doubt whether the fossil mammals from ice-rich Siberian silts and similar fetid "mucks" on the American side represent full-time inhabitants, as opposed to seasonal migrants. Most fossil bones are discovered at the base of geological exposures having eroded from stratified levels, so there is no way of establishing their exact geological age. About the only way to prove the association of different animals is to date the bone collagen from recently thawed bones.* J.V. Matthews did just that and assembled a list of a minimum

---

* A typical modern bone, degreased and air dried, consists of inorganic matter (mainly calcium phosphate and carbonate) and 15-20 percent collagen, an insoluble protein. Well-preserved bone from cold and dry environments still contains sufficient collagen for dating after as much as 40,000 years of burial. Radiocarbon dating from bone collagen is hard because it is difficult to remove contaminants like humic acid. Bone-collagen-based dates tend to be regarded as somewhat less reliable than readings taken from more conventional organic samples like wood charcoal.

of eight species that date to between 25,000 and 18,000 years ago. His samples come from a wide geographical area, and the dates have large statistical errors. But Matthews argues that bison, caribou, mammoth, and horse, as well as two forms of musk ox, a wild sheep, and arctic predators, made up a mammalian community with twice as many species as that of the modern tundra.

Repeated associations of the same basic members of the Upper Palaeolithic fauna at Siberian sites must be more than coincidence, Matthews points out. He claims Beringia supported a diverse mammalian fauna 18,000 years ago. If it did, then the vegetational cover was considerably more productive than modern tundra.

The Productivity Paradox

If there were large herbivores on the Bering land bridge, how did the harsh environment support them? The problem comes down to a basic question: how does one keep a mammoth alive and well on an arctic land bridge?

The land bridge could have supported a diversity of herbivores, *provided* it had sufficient variety, *and* quantity, of plant communities to do so. (For some species, like the mammoth, which feed more or less continuously and process large quantities of low-quality browse, quantity was especially important.) Had such communities been present, wild horses and other small hoofed mammals could have lived on dry upland sedges, grasses, and low shrubs. The plains gave way to areas of much higher productivity in lowlands and river valleys, areas covered with about 5 percent tall shrubs and 10 percent wet sedge moss. These were the places where grazers, browsers, and perhaps, people flourished. Valley-bottom meadows and willow-shrub vegetation would have been intensively grazed, as they are today by musk oxen. In the process, animals manured the meadows with their droppings and decaying carcasses. These processes again improved production and nutrient values. The grazing animals would have pruned and trampled the natural vegetation, preventing organic accumulation and helping the soil to retain warmth during the grazing season.

Under these conditions, the grazing animals would have helped one another, too, with some species digging holes in the snow used later by smaller, more selective, feeders. The mammoth and horse ingest large quantities of low-quality fodder, especially tall and medium-height grasses. Their feeding activities helped create patches of higher-quality short grass for more selective grazers like steppe bison. The result was a grazing succession in which each ungulate species created and maintained a level of environmental diversity to serve the needs of other animals in the same area.

Everyone agrees Beringia was a dry place, with strong winter winds and relatively thin snow cover. In spring, the snow cover would be blown off much earlier than it is today. The spring rains would fall on bare soil warmed by the longer, sunny days of the new season. Perhaps even more important than spring rains were the large snowdrifts accumulated in many places by winter winds. They often lay nearest the warmest spots in the landscape during the spring and early summer solar radiation peak. Thus, constant moisture sources lay next to areas with the most favorable radiation. As this patchwork of snowbanks melted, so the neighboring areas enjoyed a period of "protein spurt." Perhaps the Beringian ungulates moved from one favored location to another as the snow thawed throughout the annual growth season of four or five months. Thus, fresh fodder was available from spring until the first late fall snows. It is interesting to observe that the Beringian fauna included animals like the horse that were intolerant of heavy winter snow, grazers with large bodies that clearly enjoyed a long season of abundant food.

Botanists Lawrence Bliss and James Richards have used the present arctic vegetation and ecosystems to produce a model of possible environmental usage by Beringian herbivores 25,000 years ago. Their model assumes that the densities of individual herbivore species were similar to those of modern arctic environments. However, the herbivore biomass of Beringia may have been up to three-and-a-half times that of modern arctic ecosystems with their lower species diversity. Bliss and Richards point out just how critical vegetational diversity would have been. For example, a 5 percent willow-shrub coverage was vital, for mammoth and moose are estimated to have received between 40 and 70 percent of their diet from this source. With less willow, both mammal, and perhaps human, population densities would have been lower.

Not even the most ardent proponents of the steppe-tundra hypothesis envisage Beringia as a land teeming with vast herds of herbivores. More likely, these animals were scattered through the landscape, concentrated at dozens of special sites, in lowland meadows and near rivers. Not all the mammal species would have been in the same place at once. They would have succeeded one another, utilizing patches of the bare, treeless environment in an endless succession of grazing patterns that persisted as long as the continental ecosystem remained intact.

All of this seems like a plausible, even captivating, hypothesis, but where did humans fit into the picture? So far, no artifacts, worked bones, or traces of human settlements have come from the submerged parts of Beringia. So we must fall back on intelligent speculation. We know that Stone Age peoples lived off the land in eastern Siberia, even during the coldest millennia of the last glaciation. Theoretically, at any rate, they could have survived comfortably on the arid plains of the land bridge only a few miles away.

If humans lived on the land bridge, what were population densities like? Bliss and Richards have developed the steppe-tundra scenario to accommodate this variable. They used modern herbivore densities and calculations of possible harvestable rates for different animals in their computations. A mammoth harvestable biomass, for example, is about 4 percent of the total population a year, that for bison and horse about 9-10 percent. Using these data, they estimated a potential human carrying capacity of between 15 and 25 people per 1,000 square kilometers, a figure roughly equivalent to that for modern Eskimos living off land and sea resources alone. The Bliss and Richards figures hint that a steppe-tundra Beringia was capable of supporting reasonable numbers of people, perhaps even more than modern tundra because their calculations did not allow for a larger ancient biomass. These hunter-gatherers would have been capable of greatly influencing the density and diversity of herbivore populations.

A Shadowy Scenario

The Bering land bridge stands revealed as an arid, even desolate, land, but one that supported a surprising diversity of mammals, large and small. The human players are still absent, but their presence on the now-submerged plains seems a haunting possibility. If Upper Palaeolithic people were present in Siberia, there is absolutely no reason why they should not have ventured onto the land bridge.

At what moment, then, did human settlers first cross into the Americas? Unfortunately, the high sea levels of modern times have flooded most places where one might search for coastal settlements, villages where early fisherfolk and sea-mammal hunters may have lived as they ranged slowly north and eastwards in Alaska. But even if such coastlines were accessible to archaeologists, we might not find the kinds of specialized sea-mammal hunting cultures that were to flourish in the far north much later in prehistory. Without effective canoe technology, the Stone Age peoples who lived on Beringia's coasts may have been severely limited in their ability to exploit maritime resources. Almost certainly, such people would have relied heavily on terrestrial hunting, just as the Dyukhtai people did. And, as land-based hunters, such settlers would have crossed into Alaska dry-shod, when the land bridge was in existence.

A Stone Age hunter arriving at the borders of the Bering land bridge would have had no idea he was gazing at a natural highway into a new continent. The flat, gently undulating landscape receded to the far horizon, apparently a continuation of his homeland. It was unpromising terrain, but one where the expert big-game hunter could find sustenance to tide his family through even the coldest months. Schooled over the millennia to arctic environments, to months of plenty followed by seasons of near starvation, late Stone Age hunter-gatherers gradually trekked into Beringia, where they subsisted for thousands of years. At some point, perhaps as early as 25,000 years ago, or much later, as the land bridge began to submerge, they hunted their way across to higher ground in the east that took them away from the chilly Pacific and ultimately into the Americas.

We must now examine the question of first settlement on the basis of archaeological evidence from the New World itself.

CHAPTER SIX

Alaska and the Yukon Territory

ACT 2, SCENE 2

The Northwestern Reaches of the New World

The lowlying, varied landscape of the eastern shores of the Bering Strait is sparsely populated even today. The best way to see what remains of Ice Age eastern Beringia is to fly over the coastline across the North Slope, then south to the modern city of Anchorage and on to the Aleutian island chain. On a clear day, you look down on a land of considerable environmental contrasts. In the extreme north, treeless tundra plains lead down to the Arctic Ocean and stretch all the way across Alaska and northern Canada. Poorly drained and swampy in summer, savagely cold, dry, and windy in winter, the plains are bounded on their southern border by the treeless Brooks Range. The Alaskan portions of these highlands were once glaciated. They become the British Mountains in Canada, and lie just north of a great tract of flat lowlands and low, rugged woodlands traversed by two rivers. The Yukon rises in Canada and the Kuskokwim in Alaska. Both flow into the Bering Sea and witness huge annual Pacific salmon runs that have provided valuable food supplies for local peoples for thousands of years. The Alaska Range rises at the southern edge of the state. Massive and glaciated, it merges with the Aleutian Range that forms both the Alaska Peninsula and the Aleutian Islands that extend more than 1,000 miles (1609 km) into the north Pacific. To the east rise the Richardson and Mackenzie Mountains of the Yukon and Northwest Territories.

"The Traditional Gateway to America . . .?"

About 18,000 years ago, during the Wisconsin glaciation,* glaciers covered the Alaska Range and the Alaska Peninsula, as well as the Brooks Range, but much of eastern Beringia was ice-free, drier than today. The exposure of the

---

*In the New World, the last major phase of the Ice Age (Würm in Europe) is known as the Wisconsin, the term we will use from this point onward.

Bering land bridge shifted rainfall moisture sources further south. Cooler sea temperatures and southward shifts in storm tracks reduced evaporation in the northern Pacific. Palaeontologist Dale Guthrie of the University of Alaska has cataloged dozens of finds of bison, wild horse, and mammoth fossils from late Ice Age deposits in central Alaska. These, he believes, show that this portion of eastern Beringia carried substantial tracts of grassland that was more productive than the tundra and forest of post-glacial times. It was not until sea levels rose after 14,000 years ago and average temperatures and humidity increased dramatically that birch, willow, and other shrubs spread widely over Alaska. By 9,000 years ago the last remnants of steppe-tundra had vanished. The rich mammalian community of full glacial times was succeeded by caribou – the dominant species since then. About 6,000 to 5,600 years ago, spruce forest expanded westward into parts of Alaska from northwest Canada.

Some archaeologists believe that the ice-free areas of Alaska were uninhabitable during the last glaciation. Others have called it "the traditional gateway to America." Most modern archaeologists would agree with the late J. Louis Giddings, who wrote in 1960 that "a very sparse Arctic population spread over the belt of northern climate, neither pursuing nor evading pursuit, but simply existing and adjusting at random to the environment, the sons sometimes hunting beyond the range of their fathers but never really leaving home." The problem is to find archaeological sites that document this – or any other – hypothesis.

Louis Giddings spent his career studying the archaeology of Alaska and the Bering Strait. He complained that many scholars thought of Beringia as a mere passageway on the human route south into the Americas. For thousands of years, he argued, Eskimos and Aleuts had flourished on the shores of the strait, developing their own distinctive adaptations to its diverse environments. Had not much earlier peoples likewise settled there for long periods of time? Many scholars have a hunch he is right. The problem again is to prove it.

What Kind of Hunters Are We Looking For?

Is there any archaeological evidence for human settlement in eastern Beringia during land-bridge times? One of the problems is to decide what one is looking for, what the technological capabilities of the first Americans might have been. Everyone agrees that anyone wanting to live in the far north would have had to have crossed the necessary technological "threshold" to live there. This threshold must have included not only adequate, tailored clothing and shelter, but means of traveling over snow and ice. In later times, this meant dog sleds, snow shoes, even shoe attachments for walking securely on ice floes. Not only did arctic hunters have to be expert in the chase, and at fishing and gathering, but they had to develop storage technologies for food surpluses to tide them over scarce winter months. An arctic lifeway meant a high degree of seasonal mobility, and an ability to cope with constant scarcity, as well as cycles of plenty. The debate surrounds not so much the way of life, but the toolkits one would expect to find in the archaeological record that reflect it.

The experts disagree profoundly. Richard MacNeish, an archaeologist with more than forty field seasons behind him, several of them in Alaska, has argued that the first settlers were "technologically unsophisticated," and "unskilled as hunters." Alan Bryan, a Harvard-trained advocate of early human settlement, has gone even further and suggested that the "basic Paleo-Indian tool kit contained few, if any standardized stone or bone tool types." In contrast, University of Alaska archaeologist William Workman says that "only specialized big game hunters with sophisticated lithic [stone tool] technologies could have survived in Beringia . . . lithic industries so crude as to raise legitimate doubts about their human authorship do not have to be taken seriously in the New World."

Anyone who thinks of eastern Beringia as merely a corridor – and a simple one to cross at that – should pause and look at modern traveling conditions in these northern latitudes. Judging from today's environment, it was easier to move around during the winter. A hunting band traveling on the arctic coastal plain of the far north in summer in modern times could not move far: thousands of lakes and swamps hinder movement. Conditions may have been drier and colder in Ice Age times, but may still have been adverse in summer. However, disregarding weather and restraints on movement imposed by the particular nature of their hunting, Stone Age people could walk almost anywhere over the frozen plain between October and June, perhaps as much as 20 or 30 miles (32 to 48 km) a day if they wanted.

Some modern travel information places mobility in perspective. To travel from the summit of the Anaktuvuk Pass in the Brooks Range via the John River southward to the Koyokuk River in central Alaska today involves a distance of about 150 miles (241 km). In summer, you have to battle swampy, pond-filled thickets and forest. The journey will take at least ten days, perhaps as much as three weeks, depending on what you can find to eat on the way. In the winter you can walk on the river ice and cover the same distance in about five days, and in even less time with a dog sled. Add the variable of the long months of winter darkness and you have a very restricted travel season indeed, perhaps late fall and spring, the very periods when game like caribou moves to new feeding grounds.

Even without these travel restrictions, eastern Beringia was an isolated land during the height of the last glaciation, 18,000 to 25,000 years ago. This was partly because of vast ice sheets to the east and south – which we will look at in some detail in Part Four – but also on account of rugged topography. Geography offered powerful incentives for people to stay in Beringia. If Stone Age people lived there, it was their homeland, not merely a corridor.

It is hardly surprising that the level of speculation vastly exceeds the amount of archaeological data from Alaska and the Yukon. Archaeology in the far north is a highly seasonal activity. Fieldwork is crammed into a short, two-to-three-month period when the surface layers of the earth melt. Even then, evidence of early human occupation is hard to find, and even harder to discover *in situ*. The unglaciated parts of Alaska and the Yukon territory cover an enormous area that has barely been scratched archaeologically. Nevertheless, progress is being made. For example, a generation ago, the Yukon was almost virgin archaeological country. Today, about a thousand sites are known, but not many are more than a few millennia old.

The Enigma of Old Crow

Despite years of patient endeavor, no one has yet found an archaeological site in Alaska and the Yukon that can be securely dated to earlier than about 15,000 years ago. The most intensive research concentrates in the Yukon, where ancient glacial lake basins offer a happy hunting ground for palaeontologists. Between about 25,000 and 14,000 years ago, the vast Laurentide ice sheet covered much of Canada and extended as far west as the Richardson Mountains and covered Bonnet Plume Basin in the Yukon. The ice diverted local rivers north and west, where they drained into three large glacial lakes now represented by Bell, Bluefish, and Old Crow Basins.

Old Crow Basin, close to the Alaskan border, contains the sediments of lake deposits laid down during the last glaciation, downstream of the Laurentide ice sheet. The palaeontologist C.R. Harington of Canada's National Museum of Natural Sciences has been collecting Ice Age mammal bones from Old Crow since 1966, bones eroding from the streams that dissect the ancient lake basin. The very first year's investigations yielded a caribou tibia that had been fashioned into a butchery (fleshing) tool. The working end displayed a fine saw edge for removing flesh from hides. The bone could only have been worked when it was fresh. Original radiocarbon tests on the inorganic fraction of the caribou bone produced a reading of about 27,000 years. Two mammoth long-bone fragments showing possible, but dubious, human workmanship from the same collection gave similar dates.

On the face of it, the caribou bone artifact was a revolutionary step forward in the study of the first Americans, but in fact the Old Crow tools were controversial from the day they were discovered. All Harington's finds came from *redeposited* sands and gravels of the Old Crow River valley. They had been carried some distance from their original burial place, probably by flood waters. Following up Harington's work, Richard Morlan of the Archaeological Survey of Canada and other archaeologists and palaeontologists have spent years interpreting the jigsaw puzzle of old stream beds, lake deposits, and other layers that criss-cross the Old Crow Basin. The clays and silts of the

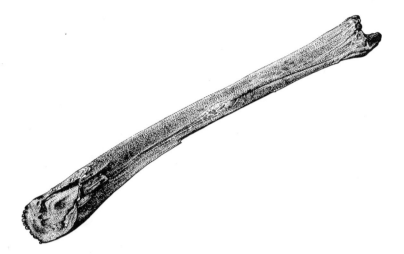

The famous bone "flesher," or device for removing flesh from hides, found at Old Crow. Originally the bone gave a radiocarbon reading of 27,000 years, but recent tests suggest it may be only 1,300 years old. Length about 10 in. (25.4 cm).

late Wisconsin lake are as much as 15 feet (4.5 m) thick. Below them lie alluvial deposits and some lake sediments, radiocarbon-dated to between 31,000 and more than 54,000 years ago.

The river and lake bed sediments between the two lake episodes represent a long period of time during which countless streams and rivers deposited and eroded the layers of the basin. One prolonged floodplain land surface was weathered during a period of intensely cold climate. Morlan calls this "Disconformity A," a break in the sedimentary record underlain by an easily identified layer of volcanic tephra (ash). The Old Crow tephra is a vitally important chronological marker. University of Toronto scientists fission-track-dated the tephra to less than 120,000 years ago; it may in fact be as young as 87,000 years. The erosion event that produced Disconformity A has been dated by bone-collagen dates on bones resting on the contact zone to less than 40,000 years ago. The silts and sands that lie above Disconformity A contain bone and ivory "artifacts," "worked" specimens from caribou, mammoth, bison and other mammals. Radiocarbon dates obtained from wood fragments in these levels range from "infinite" on redeposited samples to about 31,000 years ago for wood found 13 to 15 feet (4 to 4.6 m) above Disconformity A. No indisputable "artifacts" have been found in the deposits under Disconformity A, where mammalian fossils occur in abundance.

The Old Crow stratigraphy seems to form a definite pattern, the first traces of "human occupation" appearing on and above a land surface that was exposed during a period of intense cold, perhaps the early Wisconsin glaciation. It implies in fact that Stone Age peoples were living in eastern Beringia before 30,000 years ago, perhaps even before 50,000 years ago. This is a surprising conclusion, in view of the evidence already discussed for 25,000 years as the very oldest likely date. How reliable, then, is the Old Crow material?

Quite apart from the patchy geological evidence, the artifacts themselves and the circumstances under which they were found have fueled controversy. None of the Old Crow specimens are made of stone, all are fashioned from animal bones, apparently modified when they were fresh, or "green," to use the technical term. And all of them were transported from their original resting place by flood waters and other agencies.

Richard Morlan and his colleagues have studied the "worked" mammoth and other mammal bones from Old Crow in exhaustive detail. Since these are not associated with stone tools and other traces of human occupation, Morlan has somehow to demonstrate that the flake scars and fractures on the bones were made by human hands, not by geological processes or predator teeth. Superficially, the Old Crow "artifacts" look like simple tools. A generation ago, they would probably have been accepted as humanly manufactured without a murmur. Then, simple observations of flaking, polish, or abrasion on a bone were sufficient to classify a specimen as humanly made. Today, archaeologists rely on biomechanical and technological arguments. This type of research was pioneered by the biologist C.K. Brain on Australopithecine bone accumulations in South Africa. Anatomist Raymond Dart had claimed that Australopithecines had used an "osteodontokeratic" material culture of bone, teeth and horn long before they had made stone tools. His studies were based on little more than the bones alone, and on the assumption that the caves were habitations rather than refuges. Brain went beyond examining the form of the bones, making long-term observations of bone fractures made by non-human primates. He showed that Dart's bone fractures were in fact the remains of cheetah kills, and that the bone fractures were not the result of human toolmaking.

The Old Crow bones raise much the same types of questions. Did the first inhabitants of eastern Beringia rely on fresh bone at the expense of stone, using basically the same methods to fashion mammoth bone tools that they would have used on stone cores? Robson Bonnichsen of the University of Maine experimented with bones from animal cages at the Alberta Game Farm. He also observed the fractures left by Cree Indians breaking bones open for marrow, as well as bones worked over by a Siberian tiger. He claims that the spiral types of fracture found on many of the Old Crow bones are identical to those produced by the marrow-extracting Cree – bones also chewed by their dogs. Thus, he writes, "spirally fractured bones are indicative of man's presence and reflect patterned human behavior." In fact, as the well-known archaeologist Lewis Binford of the University of New Mexico has shown in both Africa and Alaska, modern animals regularly produce spiral fractures when they break up limb bones – and one would imagine that large Ice Age predators were even more adept at this.

Richard Morlan also studied polished, cut, and flaked bones from Old Crow. A few bone fragments exhibit cuts that appear identical to those made experimentally on fresh bone and antler with stone flakes. At first he believed these were butchery marks, resulting from the human dismemberment of big-game carcasses. Others were claimed to be ground, polished, and scratched. But Morlan has shifted his ground, for he realizes that we know little of how large carnivores break bones. We know a great deal about the fracturing properties of fresh, as opposed to dry, bone, which breaks much more easily. The trouble is that small bone pieces so often found at places like Old Crow frequently lack the diagnostic attributes. For example, some of the "green-fractured" mammoth bones that are claimed as humanly fractured fragments may in fact have been broken by some natural agency after they dried out. There are other phenomena in the arctic environment that have the ability to modify bone. Ice exerts great force during the annual spring thaw, as do subsurface soil movements, when thawed deposits move over permanently frozen ones below. Such soil creep and fast-moving flood waters transport angular grains of silica that may produce incisions on bones that could be confused with human butchery marks.

Morlan did reject many of the claims that these, and the spirally fractured bones, were humanly worked. But he commented on a pattern of mammoth-bone flaking and fracturing that defied explanation as the work of predators. Mammoth bones, he argues, are too large for carnivores to flake and fracture. Nor can he identify any natural phenomena that could account for the fracture patterns. Thus, by argument of elimination, humans worked the mammoth bones. This is a dangerous line of reasoning, for we know relatively little of the processes that can modify and break mammal bones once they are buried. Until we can eliminate the possibility that the bones were modified by natural agencies, we cannot claim that they are of human manufacture, however convincing the "flakes" and "cores" look.

The famous caribou flesher found at Old Crow is undoubtedly a humanly manufactured artifact. Since it was found in soil that had slipped away from its original layer, no one has any idea where it originally came from. Morlan has recently obtained a new linear-accelerated radiocarbon date for the flesher, a reading of about 1300 years. This seems more plausible, since the artifact is very similar to caribou fleshers made by the eastern Kutchin Indians of Alaska and the Yukon to this day. The revised dating for this artifact leaves just Morlan's bone cores and flakes as evidence for human activity at Old Crow, and these are still a question mark.

We have dwelt on Old Crow at some length because it is an excellent illustration of the difficulties of interpreting very early American sites. When the caribou flesher first came to light, the discoverers placed a great deal of faith in such an obvious artifact. The original date of 27,000 years was based on carbon obtained from what was assumed to be apatite, a substance that is known to undergo diagenetic exchange of carbon. Collagen, the material used for the revised date, does not. This may account for the 26,000-year discrepancy between the two readings. What is refreshing about the Old Crow research is that the investigators have not been afraid to take a long, sober look at their initial conclusions. After years of patient research, their original enthusiasm has eroded to the point where the existence of early human occupation at the site is now considered a real question mark. Meanwhile, research on the mammoth-bone flakes and cores continues in an attempt to establish beyond all reasonable doubt whether or not there is a late Ice Age technology at the site.

The scientists associated with the site have always been careful to reassess and evaluate their finds, but others have been less restrained in their enthusiasm. Old Crow kindled great excitement among advocates of very early settlement in the Americas. Although the new dates for the caribou flesher may have led him to change his mind, some years ago, Alan Bryan – an archaeologist who believes passionately in very early Americans – described the Old Crow finds as "a remarkably sophisticated and specialized bone and antler industry." Few archaeologists would go so far today.

Bluefish Caves

In the late 1970s Jacques Cinq-Mars of the Archaeological Survey of Canada excavated the important site at Bluefish Caves in the Keele Range about 40 miles (64.4 km) southwest of Old Crow. Some 15,000 years ago, the caves lay within sight of windswept glacial lakes. Cinq-Mars found a layer of glacial, wind-blown dust known as loess in the caves. This layer is very lightly packed and varies in thickness from 1 foot (30 cm) to 6 feet 6 in. (3 m), and is overlain by a humus-rich rubble and modern soil. Pollens from the silt layers confirm that the stratigraphy has not been disturbed and document a rise in birch forest between about 14,000 and 12,000 years ago. They also show a vegetational shift from herbaceous tundra to a shrub tundra during the period of loess deposits. Outside Cave I lay a large pile of bones of late Ice Age mammals. A butchered mammoth bone from Cave II gave a bone-collagen reading of 15,550 ± 130 years ago, while a horse femur from Cave I gave a date of 12,950 ± 100 years ago. Animals found in the loess include mammoth, horse, bison, elk, and caribou.

Cave I yielded some unquestionable stone artifacts, including a graving tool with a characteristic chisel-shaped edge made on a chert flake, some biface trimming flakes, microblades, a wedge-shaped core, and a variety of chert flakes, all of them made on rocks brought to the site from elsewhere. The tools were found scattered in the wind-blown silt layers with the animal bones. Some of the animal bones from the loess show scraping, cutting, and piercing marks that were similar to those from Old Crow.

Cinq-Mars has correlated the radiocarbon-dated bones with the loess layers. He believes that Bluefish Caves contain evidence of human occupation dating to between 15,000 and 12,000 years ago, with the most likely date being closer to the more recent end of the timescale. He also wonders whether the broken bones hint at even earlier human occupation, perhaps as early as 23,000 to 24,000 years ago. However, the specimens suffer from the same interpretative problems as the Old Crow specimens, and must remain controversial.

Despite several seasons of excavation, the stone artifacts from the loose wind-blown silts of Bluefish Caves are still dated in only the most general terms. But if the dates are correct, then people making microblades that would not be out of place in the Dyukhtai tradition of Siberia were living in eastern Beringia by 12,000 years ago, perhaps some millennia earlier. The fractured bones from the lower levels of the same site and Old Crow *may* be evidence for even earlier human occupation, but few archaeologists are prepared to accept them as indisputable tools.

The Land Bridge is Submerged

Beringian pollen diagrams paint a dramatic picture of rapid vegetational and sea-level changes at the end of the Wisconsin glaciation about 14,000 years ago. Major vegetational changes were underway within 2,000 years. The land bridge was fully flooded by 10,000 years ago. Central Beringia was dry land for a very short time, geologically speaking. The herbaceous tundra landscape lasted a mere 8,000 years or so, from about 23,000 to 15,000 years ago. As the sea encroached, the mammal population must either have dwindled and eventually crashed, or moved inland to east or west.

During these 2,000 years of major climatic change, any human populations would have been under stress, especially in the most favored areas where band densities were greatest. Many groups may have starved to death, or moved away, adjusting to new environmental conditions. Animal migrations away from the submerging land bridge into eastern Beringia may have led to a greater variety of mammals in Alaska and the Yukon than at the height of the Wisconsin glaciation. Humans would presumably have followed the mammals.

Paleo-Arctic Hunters

Frederick Hadleigh West of the Peabody Museum in Salem, Massachusetts, is among those who believe that the rapid changes at the end of the Wisconsin glaciation caused human populations not only to move off the land bridge, but out of Beringia southward into warmer latitudes as well.

West's hypothesis gains support from fairly well-documented finds of post-glacial occupation dating to as early as 11,000 or 12,000 years ago. Most are scatters of stone artifacts found in caves and on small open sites the length and breadth of interior Alaska and into the Yukon. Many of the artifacts, simple tools used for hunting and processing food, have been linked by their finders to possible Dyukhtai equivalents in Siberia.

The first finds came in the 1930s. Archaeologist Nils Nelson made his reputation in the American Southwest in the 1920s. In 1937, he was in Alaska and published a description of a Stone Age site discovered four years earlier on the campus of the University of Alaska in Fairbanks. The Campus site was an unspectacular find, a confused scatter of stone tools including fine cores and blades. Nelson was working in a complete archaeological vacuum. Prehistoric Alaska was still unknown territory, so he looked to the Old World for typological parallels. Nelson had visited the Gobi Desert in Mongolia, and he compared the Campus artifacts to Stone Age tools from that distant locality. This was the first serious attempt to link early American artifacts with Old World prototypes.

The Campus site was almost unique until the 1950s. Then Helge Larsen excavated two caves at Trail Creek in western Alaska in 1949-50. One yielded not only small blade cores, but, from its lowermost level, some bone projectile points slotted with narrow grooves as if to receive small, microblade insets. These hunting weapons were highly effective at penetrating tough hide. A radiocarbon date on some nearby caribou bone dated the spear- or lance-heads to about 9,000 years ago. Further dates on bison and horse bones (probably not killed by humans) gave dates of about 13,000 and 15,800 years ago respectively. Above all, the Trail Creek cave occupations were associated with the broken bones of caribou, a seasonal migrant that was very much the dominant prey for post-glacial northern hunters.

The Trail Creek caves and other scattered finds of wedge-shaped cores and small blades caused much theorizing in the 1950s about a "Northwest Microblade" tradition in Alaska and the Yukon Territory, a tradition that probably had its origins in Siberia. Then, in the mid-1960s, a number of discoveries defined this shadowy cultural tradition more closely. Frederick West discovered the Donnelly Ridge site in southwest Alaska. This contained similar artifacts to those from the Campus site – snapped flakes, and in particular small cores with elliptical striking platforms created by removing a transverse flake. The blades removed rarely exceeded 2.5 in. (5 cm) in length.

West compared Donnelly Ridge with sites near Mt McKinley in central Alaska and the Campus artifacts. He subsequently grouped all these sites, including Trail Creek cave, into a microblade-and-core tradition he named the "Denali Complex," after the site of that name. West claimed that Denali sites display a high degree of similarity, "such as would be expected of the components of a larger entity having common historical roots, occupying the same region, and, in all likelihood, occupying a restricted span of time."

West was so impressed by the widespread distribution of his new complex that he looked for cultural parallels in Upper Palaeolithic Siberia. At first he had no radiocarbon dates to work with, but later readings gave a chronological range for Denali sites between about 11,000 and 8,000 years ago. Despite their later date, West has argued that they were contemporary with the somewhat similar tools near Lake Baikal in Siberia (presumably Dyukhtai, although West does not specifically say so).

As West defined the Denali Complex, Douglas Anderson was excavating the Onion Portage site on the Kobuk River, some 124 miles (199.5 km) from the Chukchi Sea. Louis Giddings had originally found the site, but he died in an accident before he could excavate there. Anderson, one of his graduate students, was involved in the original discovery. He took over the project and excavated several locations near the river. Onion Portage itself is a 2-mile (3.2-km) long old meander of the Kobuk River that served as an Eskimo portage route before the days of motorboats. The site lies at the upriver end of the portage, close to the modern river. Excavating the deeply stratified hillsides and gullies in 1965 and 1966, Anderson uncovered three prehistoric occupations, the earliest of which yielded artifacts that were quite different from more recent tools. They lay between 11 and 20 in. (30 to 50 cm) below the present ground level on part of an ancient land surface, much of which had been eroded away later by spring meltwater from upslope. All that survived of what may have been a permanent settlement were stone artifacts.

Anderson named this artifact assemblage "Akmak," after the location at Onion Portage. It consisted of more than 500 artifacts and tool fragments, which could be divided into eight different classes. Anderson at once recognized Campus-site-like cores and blades in the collection. He pointed out that similar artifacts had come from other sites in the Brooks Range and on the North Slope. Thus, he argued, Akmak must pre-date 8,000 years ago in this part of Alaska. The Akmak occupation was partially sealed by a later, quite different occupation (named the Kobuk Complex), which has been radiocarbon-dated to about 8,400 years ago.

Meanwhile, West surveyed the Tangle Lakes region on the south slope of the Alaska Range, where he discovered sixteen more "Denali Complex" sites. The lakes lie at about 2,800 feet (853 m) above sea level in birch and scrub tundra country. West found his Denali sites just above an ancient shoreline of the lakes, roughly 100 feet (30.5 m) above the modern water level. The sites were occupied by hunters some 10,000 years ago, maybe earlier. They probably pursued caribou and other herbivores that flourished on the grassland and dry vegetation along the lake shores. About 8,000 years ago they abandoned the Tangle Lakes area.

What exactly is West's Denali Complex? Does Akmak belong within it? Denali is still ill-defined, apparently dating to later than 11,000 years, perhaps as much as a millennium earlier. Many archaeologists prefer to use other terms, such as "Beringian Tradition" and "Paleo-Arctic" to classify the earliest archaeological sites in eastern Beringia. The Denali Complex itself has been redefined on at least one occasion. The result is mild terminological confusion that puzzles experts, let alone the casual observer. The term "Beringian Tradition" subsumes both Dyukhtai and Alaskan microblade sites, and reinforces the idea that Siberia and extreme northern North America were one cultural province during early settlement. However, the term "Paleo-Arctic" is perhaps the most widely used, because it is the sort of general label that reflects a great variety of different human adaptations during a period of increasing environmental diversity and change. The Paleo-Arctic toolkit is highly varied, at present an archaeological entity that defies precise classification, partly because we lack the dated sites to do so, and also because the bone and wood artifacts that were such a vital part of it are missing.

Paleo-Arctic sites are remarkable for their small cores and microblades, the tiny bladelets that are far smaller than the normal Upper Palaeolithic blade. There are marked, even striking, similarities between Paleo-Arctic and later Dyukhtai artifact collections. Most striking of all is the diminutive size of much of the stonework. The same relative scaling down in size is found throughout the Old World. It coincides with the closing millennia of the Ice Age. No Alaskan Paleo-Arctic sites are at present known that date to earlier than about 11,000 or 12,000 years ago. Almost certainly, the Alaskan Paleo-Arctic is a terminal Palaeolithic phenomenon, a scatter of sites that reflect human adjustment in both northeast Asia and across the Bering Strait to the radically changed climatic conditions of the late Wisconsin and early post-glacial times.

We do not know for certain whether earlier technology was used in the Americas *before* microblades and other small tools came into fashion. A very few sites offer tantalizing clues. One is Dry Creek, on the Nenana River valley in the northern foothills of the Alaska Range. The lowest levels, "Dry Creek 1," radiocarbon-dated to about 11,100 years ago, contain some cobble and flake tools, as well as broken blades, thin bifacial knives, and points. Roger Powers of the University of Alaska compares the Dry Creek toolkit to a collection of "Upper Palaeolithic" stone tools from Kukhtyi III in eastern Siberia, a site that the Soviet scholar Mochanov considers to belong within his Dyukhtai tradition. Neither the lower level of Dry Creek nor Kukhtyi contain any microblades. A later Dry Creek level, "Dry Creek 2," dating to about 10,700 years ago, includes clusters of microblades and other artifacts.

Dry Creek 1 is still almost unique. The shores of Healy Lake on the middle Tenana River valley yielded the Village site, whose lower levels contain bifaces, concave-based points with thinned bases, and subtriangular knives

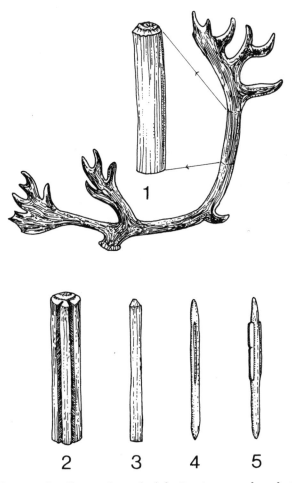

A marked feature of toolkits at the end of the Ice Age was the relative scaling down in the size of much of the stonework. Tiny bladelets known as microblades were used to make projectile heads, as shown here. A length of antler is cut off (1) and given two parallel grooves (2) to remove a triangular segment (3) which is then pointed, rounded and itself grooved on one or both sides (4). The microblades are mounted in the grooves (5) to produce a razor-sharp weapon head.

that remind one of Dry Creek 1. This occupation level, which is dated to between 12,000 and 11,000 years ago, also contains microblades, but these may have been introduced into the earlier levels by later wind disturbance of the sandy deposits. The Healy Lake bifaces have such pronounced thinning at the base that they look almost like the fluted points so characteristic of very early settlement further south in the New World.

There are a number of other early Alaskan sites that cannot be described as representative of Denali or other microblade sites. These include the Gallagher Flint Station in the north-central Brooks Range, the Groundhog Bay site from southeastern Alaska, and the Kagati and Ugashiik Narrows locations in the southwest. Most of these sites contain large core and flake tools, a wide range of bifaces, including simple projectile points and occasional large blades. Clearly there was considerable cultural diversity in eastern Beringia by 11,000 years ago, diversity that reflected a great variety of adaptations to different maritime, tundra, and river-valley or mountain environments.

A key element in this diversity was the sea coasts. Unfortunately the post-glacial shorelines are buried under later high sea levels. Only two or three sites contain tantalizing glimpses of an early maritime adaptation at a late stage in Beringia's history. The Anangula site lies about a third of the way along the Aleutian chain, atop a 65-foot (19.8-m) cliff. The many radiocarbon dates range as early as about 8,800 years ago, but most of the occupation is probably later. These people made blade tools of various sizes, but few microblades in the Denali sense. But microblade sites are found in the Alexander archipelago area of southeast Alaska, dating to between about 8,800 and 4,000 years ago. Not that the absence of such artifacts at Anangula or even inland means much: the people may well have relied heavily on bone artifacts, as prehistoric Eskimo and Aleuts did in later millennia.

We cannot yet identify specific cultures within this scattered distribution of archaeological sites in the 12,000-to-10,000-year range. Some contain bifaces, others microblades. Sometimes both are found together. This diversity of sites and artifacts poses some interesting questions. Do the sites without microblades and those with represent two distinct cultural traditions in eastern Beringia, one of which was earlier than the other and the direct ancestor of the first Americans? Or do they indicate different, but contempo-raneous adaptations to varied environments that supported different game populations? Do, for instance, sites with high percentages of microblades reflect an emphasis on caribou (reindeer) hunting using bone or wood arrows inset with small stone barbs? Did the first bands to venture further south into the Americas take only tools appropriate for hunting game like mammoth with them, much heavier tools than fine microblade-inset arrows? There are as yet no straightforward answers.

"Existing and Adjusting at Random"

We are left with a patchwork of short scenarios and hypothetical reconstruc-tions. This jigsaw puzzle of clues can be arranged in a series of tentative, and highly conservative, propositions.

The first is entirely impressionistic. Despite the evidence from Australia, one has the distinct sense that the Upper Palaeolithic peoples of between 35,000 and 25,000 years ago are most unlikely to have crossed the 50-odd miles of the Bering Strait by boat. They were above all land-based hunters, without the canoe technology or the incentive to make the dangerous crossing. Most probably, first settlement of eastern Beringia took place in land-bridge times, at some point after 25,000 years ago.

Second, there is, *at present*, absolutely no *unimpeachable* evidence for the human occupation of eastern Beringia before 15,000 years ago – if we insist, as we should, that data for any form of prehistoric human occupation, however ancient or modern, *must* be found in a dated, primary association. Holmes and Hrdlička made this point more than a half-century ago, and it is just as valid today. This raises the possibility that eastern Beringia was settled only when Stone Age people retreated to higher ground as the land bridge submerged after 14,000 years ago.

Third, the earliest relatively well-attested archaeological site in eastern Beringia is Bluefish Caves, which may date to between 15,000 and 12,000 years ago. The artifact collections from these excavations are too small to allow detailed comparisons with Siberian equivalents.

Fourth, after 12,000 years ago, a variety of Paleo-Arctic occupations developed in Alaska and the Yukon. They display a wide range of different toolkits, some with microblades, others with small bifaces, projectile points, and snapped flakes. These occupations include Frederick West's Denali Complex, Dry Creek, Akmak, and other sites. We do not know whether there was an ancestral Upper Palaeolithic culture in eastern Beringia, a culture that perhaps used larger artifacts. If such a population existed, then it was certainly a very scattered one.

Fifth and last, any late Stone Age occupation of eastern Beringia was an easterly extension of long-flourishing Siberian hunting traditions, perhaps the little-known Dyukhtai tradition. This *may* just possibly date to as early as 30,000 years ago in the Middle Aldan region, but is probably considerably later, around 18,000 years and after. Dyukhtai survived into post-glacial times, by which time hunters were using smaller stone artifacts, many of them microblade tools mounted in bone and wooden shafts in an "inset-weapons" technology. This same diminution can be witnessed on the Alaskan side as well, but we do not know whether this originated in Alaska and the Yukon, or was introduced from the west. One tends to forget that even less is known about Siberian prehistory than eastern Beringian.

Whatever the precise date of first settlement, and whatever the way in which it happened, we are now at a historic moment in the human story. To those who crossed the Bering Strait for the first time, the trek into eastern Beringia would have seemed like nothing more than the opening up of another hunting territory. We know now it was a watershed in human development, a moment to pause and wonder at humanity's startling ability to adapt to the extremes of life on planet earth. Human beings first evolved in the relatively undemanding tropical environments of Africa, then progressively mastered ever more harsh climates, in Europe, the Near East, and Asia in the hundreds of millennia that followed. A mere 35,000 years ago, *Homo sapiens sapiens* expanded rapidly into even more severe arctic landscapes and open steppe-tundra, where winters lasted three-quarters of the year, and where people were huddled in smoke-filled dwellings for months of total midwinter darkness. Eventually they came to the frontiers of a vast continent. Soon they were to wander into the heart of the Americas and explode into a new chapter of human history.

PART FOUR

THE FIRST AMERICANS

"*Believers, agnostics, and sceptics can be found in all fields, where the evidence is difficult to obtain, often difficult to interpret, and subject to valid differences of opinion. We need only think of theories of biological evolution, or of continental drift, to find parallel situations in disciplines other than archaeology. So in archaeology it is not useful to tally up votes, invoke authority figures, or descend to name calling.*"

Clement Meighan, 1983

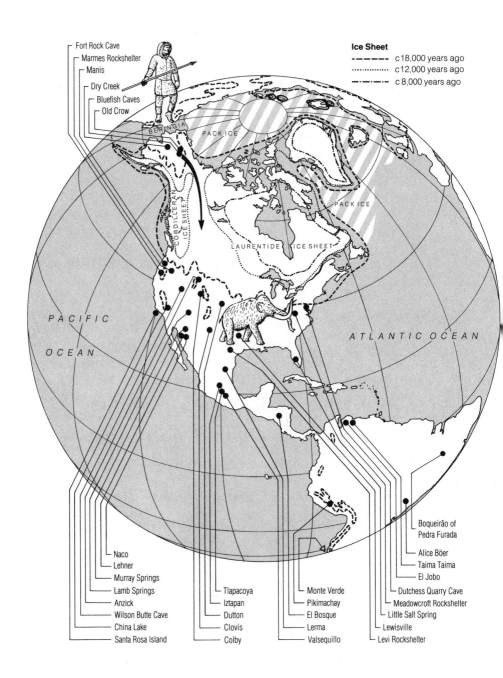

Fort Rock Cave
Marmes Rockshelter
Manis
Dry Creek
Bluefish Caves
Old Crow

Ice Sheet
------ c 18,000 years ago
··········· c 12,000 years ago
-·-·-·- c 8,000 years ago

PACK ICE

BERINGIA

CORDILLERAN ICE SHEET

PACK ICE

LAURENTIDE ICE SHEET

PACIFIC
OCEAN

ATLANTIC OCEAN

Naco
Lehner
Murray Springs
Lamb Springs
Anzick
Wilson Butte Cave
China Lake
Santa Rosa Island

Tlapacoya
Iztapan
Dutton
Clovis
Colby

Monte Verde
Pikimachay
El Bosque
Lerma
Valsequillo

Boqueirão of
Pedra Furada
Alice Böer
Taima Taima
El Jobo
Dutchess Quarry Cave
Meadowcroft Rockshelter
Little Salt Spring
Lewisville
Levi Rockshelter

The Americas during the last stages of the Ice Age, when human colonization took place, perhaps via the corridor between the Cordilleran and Laurentide ice sheets.

CHAPTER SEVEN

The Ice-Free Corridor?

INTERLUDE

Before examining the evidence for more southerly first settlement, we should take a look at the virgin continent that lay to the south of Beringia during the Wisconsin glaciation. For tens of thousands of years, North America, like the rest of the world, suffered through the fluctuations of the last Ice Age glaciation. During much of that time, great continental ice sheets waxed and waned over the north, mantling much of Canada and the northern United States in deep and impassable glacial ice that affected the entire landscape.

Wisconsin, the Last Great Glaciation

We know from deep-sea core studies that the Wisconsin glaciation began more than 100,000 years ago, with an inexorable cooling of world temperatures and major advances of huge ice sheets in northern latitudes. The earlier stages of the Wisconsin are still imperfectly documented, but, in any case, at that time the New World was uninhabited. The geological chronicle is much more complete for the later stages.

In the so-called *Mid-Wisconsin* phase, from about 60,000 to 25,000 years ago, there was a prolonged period of glacial retreat. As the climate ameliorated somewhat, sea levels rose, perhaps as high as their present levels in places. With the possible exception of a much-reduced ice sheet around Hudson Bay, most of northern North America was freed of glacial barriers. For those 35,000 years, any (hypothetical) human settlers would have encountered environments not very different from modern tundra and boreal forest, the latter a harsh landscape, even for present-day Athabaskan Indians in Alaska. "I hope that you will return again, and that we will be here to see you," call out the Koyukon Indians to migrating flocks of birds in the fall. Their call is like a prayer for survival through the lean months.

But the fact is, there is so far absolutely no evidence for human settlement in North America in the Mid-Wisconsin.

The *Late Wisconsin* began about 25,000 years ago, when the so-called "Laurentide" glaciers centered on Labrador and the Keewatin areas of Canada expanded south, west, and east, eventually coalescing in a huge ice sheet. For years, geologists thought in terms of a great, domed ice mass centered on Hudson Bay, up to 2.6 miles (4.2 km) thick, and about the area of the present Antarctic ice sheet. Today the Laurentide ice sheet is painted in less spectacular terms, as a complex and much thinner glacial mass made up of many independent glaciers fused into a single, frozen wilderness. Its end moraines* extended from the Atlantic seaboard, across the southern shores of the Great Lakes, into southeastern Alberta. These are cumulative bound-aries, representing an average rather than a fixed front, for the ice sheet was in constant flux. The glacial margins advanced and retreated with great rapidity, at times as much as 3,250 feet (990 m) a year.

The Laurentide ice sheet reached its maximum extent between 22,000 and 17,000 years ago, at a time when the mountain ranges of southern Alaska and British Columbia were heavily glaciated. As the Laurentide expanded, so did a "Cordilleran" glacier complex in the west. This mountain glaciation mantled the northern Strait of Georgia after 25,000 years ago, developed around Vancouver after 17,500, and expanded vigorously to about 30 miles (48 km) south of Seattle by about 14,500 years ago. The ice extended down the Pacific coast, leaving only occasional ice-free pockets. The Cordilleran ice seems to have reached its maximum extent later than the Laurentide.

The Ice-Free Corridor: Myth or Reality?

For at least 10,000 years after 25,000 years ago, great icy barriers would have inhibited travel between Beringia and the southern latitudes of the New World, but did they stop it altogether? In the 1950s, when Canadian geologists reported that Cordilleran ice flowed down the eastern flanks of the Rockies, but apparently did not abut the Laurentide ice sheet, archaeologists were mesmerized by the idea of an "ice-free corridor." In the 1960s, the corridor soon became a prehistoric superhighway that beckoned the Paleo-Indians south from Beringia into warmer climes. It passed into the popular imagination. "Doubtless it was a formidable place," wrote Thomas Canby of the National Geographic Society in 1979, "an ice-walled valley of frigid winds, fierce snows, and clinging fogs . . . yet grazing animals would have entered, and behind them would have come a rivulet of human hunters." The picture is appealing – but was it reality?

When the idea of a corridor first surfaced in the 1950s, the remote belt of land that stretched north from the US-Canadian border to the Arctic Ocean

---

* Ice Age geologists identify the distribution of the Laurentide and other ice sheets from glacial "tills," and "moraines," the rock rubble caught up in the body of a glacier as it moves, and the jumbled deposits left at the sides and ends of glaciers when they advance and retreat.

was geologically almost unknown. Now, a quarter-century later, the jigsaw puzzle of glacial boundaries in this inhospitable region is partially assembled. Nat Rutter of the University of Alberta divides the corridor route into three parts. The corridor begins on the eastern slopes of the Mackenzie and Richardson mountains and in the Mackenzie valley. Here the Laurentide ice penetrated to the mountains, but much of the range was unglaciated. The Laurentide and Cordilleran ice sheets did not coalesce there. Even at the height of the Late Wisconsin, there were ice-free areas in the mountains where people could have traveled, but the terrain was very rough.

Between the British Columbia and Alberta borders and southward to the Edmonton-Jasper area, the two ice sheets did coalesce. Continuous sheets of glacial rubble linked ice flowing down the Rockies to the Laurentide sheet. There are signs that the linked sheets diverted ice flow southward. This area of the corridor is closest to the massive Cordilleran ice sheet west of the Rocky Mountain Trench. The ice spilled over the Rockies during part of the Late Wisconsin, blocking the ice-free corridor, presumably during the glacial maximum, but the date is uncertain.

Between Edmonton and the US-Canadian border, extensive Cordilleran and Laurentide glacial deposits never approach one another. Throughout the Late Wisconsin, an ice-free passage extended in places from the western edge of the Laurentide ice-sheet to the mouths of the major river valleys coming from the Rockies.

Geologically, then, the ice-free corridor was at least a partial reality. The crux of the geological argument centers on the strength of the Late Wisconsin glacial advance. Andrew Stalker of the Geological Survey of Canada has likened the corridor to a giant zipper, with the zipper parting from the south to the north as successive glaciations waned. He thinks the Late Wisconsin glacial advance was much weaker than many of his colleagues believe. Stalker also places the Laurentide ice front farther east than does Nat Rutter. Working near Medicine Hat, Alberta, Stalker discovered two Late Wisconsin tills (the glacial rubble deposits) separated by a thick alluvial soil containing an abundance of fossil animals. These tills overlie silts and clays radiocarbon-dated to between 28,600 and 25,000 years ago. The fossils included mammoth, saber-toothed cats, western camel, and other species. Stalker believes this is evidence for a retreat of some magnitude of the Laurentide ice, perhaps about 20,000 to 19,000 years ago. Thus, in his opinion, the best time for humans to move through the corridor was either around 19,000 years ago, at a time of minor glacial retreat, or after 14,500 years ago, post-glacial times. However, the Medicine Hat section of the corridor is very controversial. There is a possibility that some of the layers are redeposited, that is, not in their original sequence due to subsequent disturbances.

Stalker's arguments are based on the most fragmentary of geological evidence, and, in any case, are by no means the only issue. The ultimate question is not whether the corridor itself existed, but whether it was capable of supporting human life.

Anyone who has clambered over loose boulders and through frigid meltwater stream beds to reach a modern glacier knows just how rugged the terrain can be. The corridor was fronted to the east by the Laurentide ice margin, undoubtedly a harsh, raw, and ever-changing landscape. The Cordilleran front was less well defined by valley glaciers and mountains. So the corridor twisted and turned, changing from century to century as ice sheets waxed and waned. The climate must have been brutal. If the Laurentide ice sheet was high domed, then arctic winds may have been funneled down the narrow defile with a wind-tunnel effect. If, as now seems likely, the Laurentide ice sheet was thinner, the corridor may have been less funnel-like. Even so, local winds and climatic effects could have made the ice sheet margins a very frigid environment indeed, a place with immature soils and minimal vegetation.

Movement through the corridor might have been restricted by large meltwater lakes that formed at the margins of the ice sheets. These were cold, iceberg laden, and biologically sterile, with unstable shorelines – difficult country even at the most favorable times of year. Only south-facing slopes in the corridor and occasional sheltered uplands may have supported enough plant growth for a few musk oxen. Farther to the south, the environment may have been tundra-like near the ice sheets. The boreal forests and forest-tundra so prevalent in the north today only flourished well south of the Laurentide ice sheet during the Late Wisconsin.

At the height of the Late Wisconsin, the ice-free corridor was, at best, one of the most barren and impoverished landscapes that human beings could possibly exploit. Even in the slightly more favorable millennia that preceded and followed the glacial maximum, the environment in the corridor would have been a major challenge. The meager vegetation would support few animals, large or small, and where animals would not go, humans would not either. The topography would have caused severe problems too. The human traveler would have had to traverse miles of rugged glacier surfaces. Even today, mountaineers avoid glaciers whenever possible. They are mazes of crevasses, meltwater, and crumbling rock. Only those with the most compelling reasons to do so would cross such terrain. *Limited* glacial travel was always a feasible option, especially for people who knew how to minimize the risks and costs of such journeys. We can assume that Beringian hunters would have had such skills, but it is a very different matter to claim that just because they had such skills, they used them to settle southern latitudes. In all probability, much better food resources lay in the far north, in Beringia. There was probably little, if any, incentive to traverse this chilly and inhospitable highway between 25,000 and 15,000 years ago – always assuming human settlers had reached the starting point in eastern Beringia this early.

Skin Boats and Shoreline Routes

If the ice-free corridor was a barrier to human settlement, what about other routes? Even though the Laurentide ice sheet covered most of northern and northeastern Canada, there were ice-free areas in a chain across the top of the arctic archipelago and down the Baffin Island-Labrador coastline. There may have been ice-free landmasses, but they were almost certainly incapable of supporting human life. It is only at the latitude of Nova Scotia that the Late Wisconsin Atlantic coast was sufficiently hospitable to serve as a human habitat.

The Canadian archaeologist Knut Fladmark is a versatile scholar who has worked at a wide range of different archaeological sites – everything from Paleo-Indian settlements to historical locales. He has discovered evidence of comparatively early human settlement on the Queen Charlotte Islands of British Columbia. Research here is in its infancy, but preliminary work suggests colonization of this region at least as early as 12,000-10,000 years ago. Fladmark points out that the Pacific coast of North America was relatively warmer and potentially more productive than other shores. The Cordilleran ice sheet extended to the ocean in many places during the Late Wisconsin, but, again, patches of unglaciated coastline were probably exposed as sea levels sank to new lows. Were these areas accessible from mainland Beringia? We do not know. If they were, then the chances are that these ice-free areas were more productive than the arctic ones. The Pacific coast might have sustained human life, especially societies that used skin boats and other technological innovations adapted to the pursuit of marine mammals. Unfortunately, there is no evidence that such societies existed in Beringia during Late Wisconsin times.

Did the first Americans arrive in southern latitudes along Ice Age coasts, then move inland? If they did, then their sites are buried under modern sea levels, and we would need a lot of luck and difficult and costly underwater archaeology to find them – until, that is, another glacial episode obligingly lowers world sea levels again. Such settlement on a large scale seems unlikely, however, for everything we know about the earliest settlers hints that they were terrestrial hunters and gatherers, with a lifeway adapted in part to the pursuit of large Ice Age mammals.

What is "Proof" of Early Settlement?

In 1966, Gordon Willey of Harvard University, the doyen of American archaeologists, wrote that "Man's radiocarbon-dated presence in the Americas can be placed no earlier than about 10,000 BC [12,000 years ago]." He was working on a magisterial compilation of archaeological data from the entire New World, a compilation based on extensive traveling and his encyclopaedic knowledge of American archaeology. Willey is a conservative observer, with an unrivaled sense of archaeological data and of the criteria needed to date an archaeological find securely. After examining thousands of artifacts and hundreds of sites, he added that "as things stand now, [earlier settlement] will not be demonstrated beyond reasonable doubt until a complex or assemblage of materials attributable to it are found stratigraphically beneath artifacts of the well-known, 10,000- to 12,000-year-old bifacially flaked lanceolate or leaf-shaped point class. . . . No amount of forceful argument, on the basis of present data, will change this situation."

Two years before, in 1964, another archaeologist, Alex Kreiger, had proposed what he called "a pre-projectile point horizon" to account for the scattered sites that seemed to document occupation before the well-known Clovis sites of the period after 11,500 years ago. Willey allowed that he believed, although not beyond reasonable doubt, in this horizon and earlier settlement. What was needed was definitive proof. He summarized the great difficulties of finding earlier archaeological sites, the same problems faced by Charles Abbott a century before: the difficulties of identifying crude early tools, the lack of stratified sites with secure dating, and the damage wrought by millennia of erosion and deposition, to say nothing of modern industrial development. Willey's statement about "forceful argument" can be put another way: the whole subject of first settlement generates emotional reactions, even among the most placid of scholars.

Every year, sometimes at the American Anthropological Association convention, and invariably at the Society for American Archaeology meetings, earnest panelists rise to discuss and evaluate their latest discoveries, from North America, Central America, and the far south. Those who believe that human beings lived in the Americas before 15,000 or 20,000 years ago present their latest finds – an early cave site in Brazil, a possible mammoth kill in Mexico, an isolated hearth in the Midwest. Slides of excavations and artifacts document stratigraphic sequences, associations of artifacts, and radiocarbon dates. Year after year, proponents claim that this is "accumulating" evidence for the presence of early humans. Year after year, their conservative opponents politely disagree, pointing to unsatisfactory stratigraphic conditions, to "hearths" that are probably of natural origin, or, more commonly, to stone artifacts that simply do not seem to be humanly manufactured at all. In the end, everyone goes home convinced they are correct.

On first acquaintance with the enigma of the first Americans, the newcomer is likely to throw up his hands in horror and emerge from library, museum, or conference confused by a plethora of claims and confusing data. The confusion is compounded by talking to scholars actively involved. Those who believe in a high antiquity for the first Americans sweep you along with their enthusiasm, sometimes insisting that very early sites must be judged by less rigorous criteria than later settlements. "Remember these sites are very old," one eminent proponent of very early settlement told me. "The artifacts have lain in the ground for a very long time. How can you apply the same rules as you do to much later Paleo-Indian or Maya sites?" I resisted the temptation to draw the speaker's attention to the rich cave and open sites of Africa and Europe that date to far earlier than 17,000 years ago, and yet enjoy magnificent preservation.

All too often, those who insist on stricter stratigraphic and chronological criteria are accused of being legalistic. "It is a matter of arbitrary definitions," writes Mexican archaeologist José Luis Lorenzo. He accuses many archaeologists of inflexibility, of holding archaeology to a 14,000-year limit. The issue, he says, is obscured under a layer of "pettifogging legal phraseology." He wonders whether, one day, the archaeologist studying the first Americans will need not only a team of lawyers at the excavations, but a notary public to verify the discoveries!

Alas, it is not a matter of being legalistic, it is a matter of satisfying basic scientific guidelines. Many of the claimed early sites do not even remotely satisfy the strict archaeological and geological criteria established for such discoveries by William Holmes and Aleš Hrdlička in the early years of this century. Except for the development of dating methods like radiocarbon, these have not changed one iota since Folsom was excavated in 1926. Allowing for new dating methods, and for more sophisticated recovery methods, they may be simply restated:

Clearly defined stratigraphy, and a clear understanding of the stratigraphic context of the finds, and the formation of the layers in which they were found.

Reliable and consistent radiocarbon dates, or dating established by some other widely accepted chronological method.

If possible, field and laboratory evidence from other disciplines to support the chronological and geological context. A good example of such evidence would be concordant pollen samples.

The presence of humanly made artifacts in a primary stratigraphic context, artifacts that are established as being of human manufacture according to strict scientific criteria.

These guidelines have been applied successfully to very early sites indeed in many other parts of the world. The Leakeys and other palaeoanthropologists have wrestled with these criteria when digging 2-million-year-old sites in East Africa. Soviet scholars use them in Siberia, British prehistorians apply them when studying early farming in southern Britain. Why, then, should any different criteria be applied to early American sites? Emotional instinct and impassioned argument are no substitute for sound archaeological reasoning based on carefully excavated data.

When visiting sites and looking at very early artifacts, I have sometimes felt a sense of historical *déja-vu*. It is like being transported back to the 1910s, when claim after claim for early settlement was surfacing, and each in turn was undermined by closer scrutiny. As the curtain rises on the final act of our play, we must apply level-headed scientific criteria to a scatter of archaeological sites as widely separated as Idaho and Chile. And in doing so, we should remember that the accumulated evidence from the Old World and the arctic northwest points to Stone Age people having finally conquered the frigid plains of Beringia no earlier than about a theoretical date of 25,000 years ago – with the oldest well-documented sites in Alaska and the Yukon Territory falling in the period after 15,000 years ago.

CHAPTER EIGHT

On the Track of the Earliest Settlers

ACT 3, SCENE 1
The Americas before 11,500 years ago

Our quest for the first settlers now takes us on a journey through the temperate and tropical latitudes of the Americas. We visit rockshelters and possible big-game kill sites from the Great Plains to Midwestern river valleys, the islands and deserts of the far west, central Mexico, the Peruvian Andes, and the wet and cold landscape of south-central Chile. Everywhere we go there are tantalizing hints of pioneer Americans in the epoch before 11,500 years ago. But how substantial are these traces of settlement preceding the period when the Clovis hunters burgeoned across the continent?

Projectile Heads and Mammoths: the Western United States

We saw in the previous chapter how Knut Fladmark's preliminary work along Canada's Pacific coast gave a suggestion of human settlement there as early as perhaps 12,000-10,000 years ago. It is therefore striking to discover that so far the most coherent western US evidence for pre-Clovis hunters lies only a little to the south, in the modern states of Washington, Oregon and Idaho, at sites dating back to 12,000, possibly 14,000 years ago.

During the early 1970s, on Washington's Olympic Peninsula, a rancher uncovered the bones of a mastodon (an archaic form of elephant) with the broken tip of a bone fragment in one of its ribs. The bone had grown around the wound, for the beast had survived the attack and later perished in a bog, where hunters had butchered part of the carcass. Called the Manis site, it was visited several times by human predators. The mastodon lay alongside three bison, a caribou, a duck, and a muskrat. Radiocarbon dates from seeds, wood, and other vegetable remains from the mastodon-bone level suggest that the carcass was butchered at least 12,000 years ago, but the precise date of the kill is uncertain. Unfortunately, none of the artifacts from this well-documented association are sufficiently finished for us to be able to compare them with those from other sites. They are mostly sharp flakes, like those used by hunters everywhere.

Elsewhere in Washington State, stone stemmed projectile heads are found at a variety of sites, among them the Marmes Rockshelter on the lower Snake River. Ten radiocarbon dates from the earlier levels of the rockshelter date this early occupation to between at least 10,800 and 8,700 years ago.

There are isolated reports of early occupation levels in caves and rockshelters in Oregon and Idaho. Fort Rock Cave in south-central Oregon contains a gravel layer sealed under an occupation level radiocarbon-dated to about 9,000 years ago. Two poorly worked obsidian projectile points and some flakes came from the gravel. The earliest radiocarbon date for the layer is $13,250 \pm 720$ years ago.

The Wilson Butte Cave in south-central Idaho provided a home for prehistoric peoples for thousands of years. The lower levels date, on geomorphological and sedimentary grounds, to a period that is transitional between the Wisconsin and post-glacial times. Two radiocarbon dates of $14,500 \pm 500$ and $13,000 \pm 800$ years ago came from a representative bone sample from the lowest levels. Three humanly made stone fragments, including a broken biface, were discovered near the bottom of the cave. Although there may have been some disturbance of the lower strata by burrowing animals, the early bone dates do seem to tie in with the Fort Rock evidence. They suggest that what we may be looking at is fragmentary colonization of the US Pacific coastal and inland regions in the very early post-glacial period after 14,000 or 13,000 years ago.

But there are those who would argue strongly for much earlier, Wisconsin-period dates. Phil Orr, an archaeologist at the Santa Barbara Museum of Natural History, was an enthusiastic excavator of early settlements and more recent Chumash Indian sites on Santa Rosa Island, in the Santa Barbara Channel, and on the nearby California mainland. Digging on the island, he was delighted to come across some depressions filled with fire-reddened earth mixed with small amounts of charcoal, depressions very occasionally associated with burnt, fragmentary bones of dwarf mammoth – small elephants that stood no more than 6 or 7 feet (1.8–2.1 m) tall. The charcoal gave a wide range of radiocarbon readings, as late as 11,000 years but also as early as 37,000. Orr was convinced by colleagues that the mammoth had been cut up and cooked by very early hunters indeed.

However, the geological context of the finds leaves many questions unanswered. Geologists have argued that mammoth bones could have been washed into natural depressions in the soil by floods or heavy rains, then been burnt by natural forest fires tens of thousands of years ago, forming what might look like "hearths." Many of the weathered bedrock sediments have been oxidized to the same color as the burnt "hearths," so it is difficult to distinguish them. All the alluvial deposits on the island contain dwarf mammoth bones and charcoal, and none of them are associated with stone tools. The earliest genuine human occupation on Santa Rosa Island is thought to date to much more recent times, to about 7,500 years ago. Almost certainly, 37,000-year-old human occupation of the island is a myth.

China Lake Valley overlaps the extreme northwest part of the hot and inhospitable Mojave Desert in east-central California. During the Wisconsin, and during the wetter post-glacial millennia, a constantly fluctuating lake filled the valley. The marshes and grasslands on its shores provided excellent forage for large mammals such as mammoth, camels, bison, and wild horses. For thousands of years, later prehistoric peoples camped on well-drained knolls along the boundaries between the marshes and grasslands. These were temporary encampments, where hunter-gatherers settled for a few days during their seasonal rounds.

For more than fifteen years, Emma Lou Davis of the Great Basin Foundation in San Diego has spent her weekends searching for very early prehistoric sites by the shores of the lake. She has excavated a number of locations where stone artifacts are associated with large mammal carcasses. The "Mammoth I" site yielded a bone scatter, a weathered chert chopper, and flakes associated with an ancient soil surface. This could be linked to another mammoth bone scatter, where ivory was radiocarbon-dated to $18,000 \pm 4,500$ years ago. The date is unreliable, however, because the sample has been heavily mineralized by the local soil geology. Davis uses this unreliable date and a correlation with a soil from another lake that formed between 16,000 and 14,000 years ago to estimate the age of "Mammoth I" as somewhere around 14,000 years ago. Despite this highly speculative dating, she claims the artifacts are prototypes for later Clovis forms. Davis has plotted scatters of artifacts on surface sites elsewhere near the lake. She says these were butchery sites or camps but admits there are no stratigraphic associations or radiocarbon dates to support her claims.

Unfortunately, Davis has little more to go on than careful speculation. The China Lake sites are an intricate distribution not of stratified sites, but of surface occurrences, sometimes linked to lakeshore levels or ancient soil horizons. There is well-documented later occupation in the China Lake region, but any earlier sites must remain questionable until the stratigraphic matrix of such discoveries is established. This may prove impossible in China Lake's harsh environment, with its thin soils and continual lakeside fluctuations. The prehistoric peoples who visited the lake were transients, moving from one temporary encampment to another. They left behind few tools, and most of those were food-processing artifacts, tools used for skinning and butchery. Many of them were convenient flakes with the sharp edges needed to slice through fresh meat for a few minutes before being discarded – the sort of artifacts every Stone Age hunter used when the need arose. As such, they have no chronological or classificatory significance whatsoever.

Sites of greater substance, though equally controversial early dates, have been found to the east, on the Great Plains.

Dennis Stanford is an archaeologist at the Smithsonian Institution, a strong-minded scientist who believes firmly in strict adherence to basic stratigraphic and dating principles when interpreting early sites. In the mid- to late 1970s, he excavated two sites, one near Selby (the Dutton site), and the other at Lamb Spring, both on the High Plains of Colorado. The Dutton and Lamb Spring finds were large mammal bone accumulations in lake beds that formed between 20,000 and 17,000 years ago. Some of the bone collagen from Lamb Spring was dated to about 13,000 years ago. Stanford noticed at once that many of the bones appeared to have been broken open and butchered. There were flake scars, too, as well as bones with localized areas of high-gloss polish. Similar phenomena could be seen on modern humanly worked bone and on known prehistoric artifacts. But were the bones worked by prehistoric big-game hunters? If they were, then the hunters made no use of stone artifacts at either of the two sites – a most unusual practice.

The Lamb Spring site was certainly a prehistoric kill site that had been visited by later hunters, from at least 10,000 years ago, right up to the historic period. But had human beings preyed on game drinking at the spring in even earlier times? Stanford carried out excavations between 1979 and 1981. He found the remains of more than thirteen mammoths, as well as extinct camels, wild horse, and bison. Some of the bones lay in piles, but no stone artifacts or other definite traces of human occupation came from the pre-10,000-year levels.

Like his colleagues at Old Crow in the Yukon, Stanford enlisted the help of biologists, who had studied modern carnivore habits and recently-deposited bison and moose bones in the wild. They observed, amongst other things, that natural edge flaking, abrasion marks, and polish effects could be seen on these moose and bison bones. Thus the scientists concluded that at the Colorado sites, just as at Old Crow, there was no way of disproving the hypothesis that the ancient bone accumulations were the result of non-human agents. In the end, bone expert Gary Haynes (no relation to C. Vance Haynes) argued that many of the edge marks were caused by a combination of natural agencies: gnawing by large carnivores, trampling by elephants and other big animals, and soil pressure within the deposits.

Stanford, Robson Bonnichsen, and others even enlisted a recently deceased twenty-two-year-old elephant named Ginsberg from the Boston Zoo as a guinea pig. With difficulty, Stanford fractured some of Ginsberg's limbs with a 12-pound (5.4-kg) boulder. He made cores and flaked thin bone pieces off them to use as cutting tools. Then he butchered Ginsberg with his "artifacts." The waste products and edge polish were very similar to those of some of the Colorado specimens, but he found that there was what he called a "grey area" between his obvious, humanly made tools and those produced by natural agencies. "At present," he wrote, "a clear and simple resolution is not possible."

In their earliest phases, Dutton and Lamb Spring are probably natural bone accumulations.

Further south, in Texas, there are other sites claimed to show very early settlement. Levi Rockshelter near Austin, Texas, has an extremely complicated stratigraphy, for both erosion and constant roof falls have convoluted the occupation deposits. A Clovis occupation, complete with characteristic projectile heads, overlies two indistinct "pre-Clovis" levels. Unfortunately, both suffer from poor definition. The earliest occupation level is hard and cemented to the back of the cave, the second found in unconsolidated rock fall and roof debris. Neither is securely dated.

The Lewisville site in Denton County, Texas, was found during a river-basin survey in the 1950s. Excavations in 1956 yielded the remains of twenty-one areas, interpreted as hearths. The excavators recovered a Clovis-type point, a stone chopper, and several flake tools. Several radiocarbon dates of over 37,000 years were obtained from the hearths. Three schools of thought subsequently developed concerning the site. One argued that the artifacts were intrusive, the hearths natural, and the site not a site at all. A second held that the Clovis point was intrusive, but the other artifacts were *in situ* and part of an earlier cultural tradition. Still a third group of scholars flatly rejected the dates and said Lewisville was a Clovis camp. Since the site had been flooded by a reservoir, no one could confirm their hypotheses.

A timely drought in 1978 brought the reservoir water level down to a point where the site could be reexamined. Army Corps of Engineers archaeologists moved in at once. They cross-sectioned a burnt area and confirmed that it was indeed a human hearth. However, they also found that the owners of the hearth had burned lignite from lower levels as fuel, so the carbon elements in the radiocarbon samples were much earlier than the occupation they dated. Almost certainly, Lewisville was a Clovis camp site, a place where hunters dug hearth pits into earlier fossil-bearing levels.

The very earliest dates in the west and far west do not, then, stand up to detailed examination. Fort Rock and Wilson Butte Caves may indicate first colonization this far south after 14,000 or 13,000 years ago, but no archaeological site west of the Mississippi River has yielded proof of anything earlier than that.

Rockshelters and Sink Holes: the Eastern United States

When Canadian archaeologist George MacDonald summarized the evidence for pre-Clovis occupation east of the Mississippi, he remarked that for some scholars penetrating the 12,000-year-boundary for human settlement had become an ardent quest, "almost a search for the Holy Grail. Like most quests, however, it occasionally requires the suspension of logic and the acceptance of arguments on faith alone."

There are many sites where claims of pre-Clovis occupation have been made, some of them quite promising. Among them is the Kimswick site just west of the Mississippi in Missouri. Here a fluted point was found in direct association with mastodon bones. The excavators claim there is a possibility that the kill is pre-Clovis rather than later.

The site that has generated most discussion in the east is Meadowcroft Rockshelter in southwestern Pennsylvania, an excavation that merits extended discussion.

Meadowcroft Rockshelter James Adovasio is an experienced archaeologist with a reputation for careful, thorough excavation. When he announced the discovery of Meadowcroft Rockshelter, a deep prehistoric site on Cross Creek, a small tributary of the Ohio River, and 30 miles (48.2 km) southwest of Pittsburgh, his colleagues took notice. Between 1973 and 1977, Adovasio excavated Meadowcroft with a multidisciplinary team of geologists, soil scientists, and botanists.

Meadowcroft is a large south-facing rockshelter with a sheltered area of 914 square feet (85 sq. m). A prevailing west wind carries smoke and insects away from the shelter during the hot summer months. Perennial springs and the creek are close by. The latter flowed some 15 to 20 feet (4.6 to 9.1 m) higher when the site was occupied. The creekside shelter is close to uplands that once abounded in big game.

Adovasio excavated the intricate stratigraphic layers of the rockshelter three-dimensionally, in small grid squares, passing most of the occupation deposits through fine wire mesh. The excavations revealed no less than eleven strata, the lowest, Stratum I, containing no evidence of human occupation. The Meadowcroft levels have been dated by more than seventy radiocarbon samples, one of the most thorough dating programs ever carried out on an archaeological site in North America. They show the rockshelter was occupied from at least 12,000 years ago (possibly, and controversially, much earlier) to nearly 700 years ago.

The deepest level containing traces of human occupation is known as Stratum IIa. Adovasio and his colleagues divide this into three subunits. The uppermost of these three is dated to between about 10,950 and 7,950 years ago. It is separated from Middle Stratum IIa by a layer of rock spalls from the roof and walls of the shelter. This middle zone accumulated between about 12,950 to 10,950 years ago, while the lowermost subunit, again sealed by rock spalls, has yielded seven radiocarbon dates ranging from 19,600 to 13,240 years ago. The 19,600-year date is the deepest date from the rockshelter that is associated with materials of *indisputable* human manufacture. Adovasio claims it marks the onset of human use of Meadowcroft.

While everyone agrees that Meadowcroft was occupied *after* 12,000 years ago, controversy surrounds the dates from the middle and lowest units of Stratum IIa. The geologist and archaeologist Vance Haynes considers the early dates anomalous. He argues that Stratum IIa charcoal samples contain large percentages of soluble humic acids, or "dead" carbon in the form of coal particles, that are older than the residue in which they were found. This residue should be insoluble if it is true charcoal. The reason the humates are older, argues Haynes, is because old acids in groundwater are permeating, or have in the past permeated, Stratum IIa. Thus, the dates are older than they should be. However, in all but one of the samples from Lower and Middle Stratum IIa, the humates are younger than the solid fraction in the samples. The one exception had humates that were only 1,000 years older. Adovasio points out that low-order reversals such as this within large series of dates do occur. But the vast majority of the Stratum IIa samples have younger humate fractions, effectively ruling out any fears of non-particulate contamination. After exhaustive testing, Adovasio is certain that no older humates exist at the site. Even if they did, they would have to have been transported in solution by moving groundwater. Since calcium carbonate is preserved intact in the sediments within the rockshelter and none of the sand grains in the Meadowcroft sediments show any rounding from groundwater movement, arguments for humate percolation may be invalid.

Adovasio also submitted a check sample to the Oxford Radiocarbon Laboratory for accelerator dating, a sample from the lower layers of the cave that were not associated with human occupation. Charcoal residue was dated to $31,400 \pm 1,200$ years ago, the humic acids from the charcoal to $30,900 \pm 1,100$. These samples agree closely with another sample also from an unoccupied level of $30,710 \pm 1,140$. The new dates appear to support Adovasio's view that the dates for the lower levels are not contaminated.

The radiocarbon dates from 11,000 to about 16,000 years ago are associated with small humanly struck blades, delicately flaked unifaces, and bifaces, including an unfluted, lance-shaped projectile point, as well as abundant stone flaking debris. The $19,600 \pm 2,400$-year-old date comes from an apparent basket fragment and was associated with only stone working debris. Thus, the dating evidence suggests human occupation at the very end of the Wisconsin glaciation, with just a possibility of earlier visits.

Is there palaeoenvironmental evidence that can provide clues? Meadowcroft's rich flora and fauna provide a fascinating chronicle of the changing prehistoric environment. No less than 45 species of mammals and 68 of birds are represented in the 11 strata, as well as 30,000 plant fragments, also terrestrial and freshwater molluscs. The gastropods show that the local environment stayed essentially stable for at least 11,000 years, a woodland of oak and hickory flourishing in a temperate climate much like that of today. Turtles, snakes, and turkeys attest to these climatic conditions as early as

11,300 years ago. The floral remains go back even further, and document a "mixed coniferous-hardwood" vegetation throughout the "entire 16,000 years represented by the floral remains." The presence of oak, hickory, and walnut in Stratum IIa argues against boreal forest or tundra conditions occurring anywhere near the site when the earliest strata were forming. All the plant species found in the excavations are found in the area today.

Does this impressive palaeoenvironmental archive contradict the early dates, which would place the middle and lower subunits of Stratum IIa in the later part of the Late Wisconsin and early post-glacial times? Haynes and others argue that both the fauna and flora from Stratum IIa are of a type that flourished in the area *after* the Wisconsin ice sheet had retreated. The closest the Laurentide ice sheet came to Meadowcroft was about 31 miles (50 km) north of Cross Creek – and somewhat further away during the later part of the Late Wisconsin. They imply that tundra or boreal forest conditions would have likely dominated the Meadowcroft area at the time. Thus the palaeoenvironmental data and the radiocarbon dates do not "fit." Adovasio counters by pointing out, correctly, that only eleven identifiable animal bone fragments come from the controversial levels. He agrees that the botanical evidence from the same levels hints at temperate conditions at Meadowcroft. However, he points out that the shelter faces south, and lies in a sheltered area of east-west drainage that might foster a more temperate ecology. Meadowcroft lies at a lower altitude than the surrounding uplands, and enjoys a greater number of frost-free days. Perhaps the floral evidence reflects a locally more temperate setting, one that made the site attractive to human occupants during the height of the Late Wisconsin.

Meadowcroft is still a tantalizing question mark, its earliest occupation levels a matter of continued academic debate. Meanwhile, the search goes on for comparable sites nearby, especially locations where radiocarbon dating and palaeoenvironmental conditions are such that the anomalies in the present site can be addressed. No one denies that Meadowcroft was occupied at least 12,000 years ago, making it one of the earliest sites in North America. At present, however, the evidence for even earlier occupation must remain in suspense account.

Sink Holes in Southern Florida Dozens of isolated projectile points have been found throughout eastern North America. They testify to widespread, but scattered, Paleo-Indian occupation from Clovis times about 11,500 years ago, if not earlier. Unfortunately, few of these discoveries come from stratified or well-dated sites, so locations that approach even the most conservative dates for the early Meadowcroft levels are rare.

Some idea of the potential for spectacular archaeological discoveries from this early time can be gained from recent finds in southern Florida, where underwater archaeologists have recovered human remains, artifacts, and the

39, 40 **Creatures of the Far North** Musk ox
(*above*) can now survive north of 80 deg. N.
In Upper Palaeolithic times, they roamed as
far south as 30 deg. N. Caribou are
gregarious animals which migrate in herds.
Northern hunters would live off the same
caribou herd for generations.

41–43 **A Frozen Landscape** With nine-month winters and short, warm summers, the far north (*left*, view of the Alaska Range) was, and still is, a harsh environment. Permafrost conditions mean that early archaeological sites like Bluefish Cave I (*bottom*, detailed view of "bone pit") in the Yukon can only be excavated for a few weeks a year. Small wonder that early sites are so rare. But the refrigerated soil provides excellent preservation for Ice Age carcasses, like this 31,000-year-old bison from near Fairbanks, Alaska (*below*).

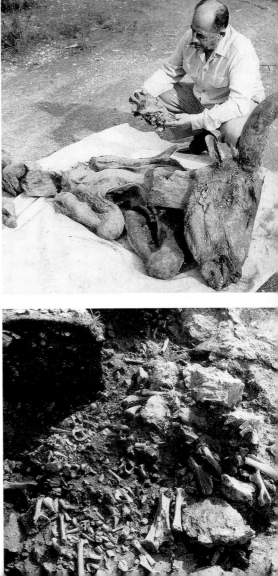

44, 45 Pennsylvania Controversy The Meadowcroft Rockshelter in Pennsylvania is a tantalizing archaeological puzzle. The excavations are seen (*right*) in 1973, near the beginning of the seven-year project. A site grid has been laid out, and the upper levels of the rockshelter are being probed. Towards the end of the excavations in 1978 (*below*), the excavators had reached bedrock. The large white tags on the walls of the trench indicate the major strata identified by the excavators. Smaller labels locate features and places where various other samples were taken. Despite meticulous excavation, questions are still raised about the reliability of radiocarbon dates from the lower levels of the shelter. Meadowcroft lay a relatively short distance from the Wisconsin ice sheets. Some scientists believe it would have been uninhabitable before post-glacial times.

46–48 **A Brazilian Enigma** French excavators have made claims for very early human settlement at the Boqueirão of Pedra Furada rockshelter in northeastern Brazil (*above*). Many shelters in this area are painted with animal and geometrical art, which dates to post-glacial times, although the excavators claim paintings as early as 17,000 years old (*below*). The Pedra Furada excavations (*left*) have dug 9 feet (3 m) into the shelter, yielding what are claimed to be humanly made artifacts dating to as early as 32,000 years ago. Many scientists are doubtful about the French claims and await further details of the finds.

49, 50 **Peru and Venezuela** Only a few claimed early South American locations merit close scrutiny. Pikimachay Cave, "cave of the fleas," high in the Peruvian Andes (*left*) provides well-documented post-glacial occupation. Richard MacNeish believes humans visited the cave as early as 20,000 years ago. Taima-Taima in Venezuela (*below*) yielded a mastodon kill that may be up to 13,400 years old. However, the projectile point found with the bones is of a type used after about 11,000 years ago, so Taima-Taima could be somewhat later.

bones of extinct animals from natural sink holes. Until the early 1970s, most Paleo-Indian projectile head finds came from the beds of north Florida rivers. Everyone believed that the first settlers had wandered south at the end of the Ice Age and hunted game along the rivers, ambushing animals at shallow crossings. Then scuba divers started finding artifacts and animal bones in water-filled natural sink holes in the limestone country of southeast Florida. These revolutionized perceptions of Paleo-Indian life in the southeast.

Experts believe that the sink holes were used during a time of low sea level at the end of the Ice Age. The freshwater hydrostatic head in the area is directly related to ocean sea levels. At a time of lowered sea level, present-day surface rivers would leave large sink holes that could be used by human beings. Carl Clausen, Wilburn Cockrell, and other archaeologists have recovered a wealth of palaeoenvironmental information from the sink holes. This reveals that Florida was cooler and drier, not the lush environment that it is today. Many Paleo-Indian settlements are submerged under modern high sea levels. The interior populations were probably sparse, and concentrated in river and sink-hole areas, where game would also feed.

At Warm Mineral Springs in Sarasota County, Cockrell and his colleagues found a human burial on a ledge 42.6 feet (13 m) below the modern water level. The dead man had been deposited in an earthen grave that had subsequently been submerged. A shell spearthrower hook lay with the skeleton. This burial was radiocarbon-dated to about 10,300 years ago. Some further human remains have come to light below a 9.8-feet (3-m) ledge at the Springs, in the same clay layer as the bones of a ground sloth and a saber-toothed tiger and other extinct species. The site reveals that the Paleo-Indians were exploiting not only large game but animals as small as the raccoon and the frog, as well as plants. Some of the Warm Mineral Springs occupation is thought to be more than 11,000 years old.

An even more spectacular find came from Little Salt Spring not far away. The collapsed shell of an extinct giant land tortoise that had been killed with a wooden stake thrust between shell and plastron lay broken and carbonized 85.3 feet (26 m) below the sink-hole lip. The stake has been radiocarbon-dated to about 12,000 years ago. The excavators surmise that the tortoise was impaled with the stake, then turned over and cooked in its own shell. Portions of an immature mammoth, an extinct sloth and bison, and another turtle, as well as several smaller mammals and birds lay nearby. By 10,000 years ago, the water level had risen to 36 feet (11 m) below the lip, and white-tailed deer had become common prey. Little Salt Spring yielded the head of a boomerang-like artifact made from oak, which looks remarkably similar to those made by Australian aborigines.

Most likely, the Paleo-Indians who visited the sink holes hunted most of the animals that flourished in the vicinity, as well as collecting wild vegetable foods. They appear to have camped for short periods around major water

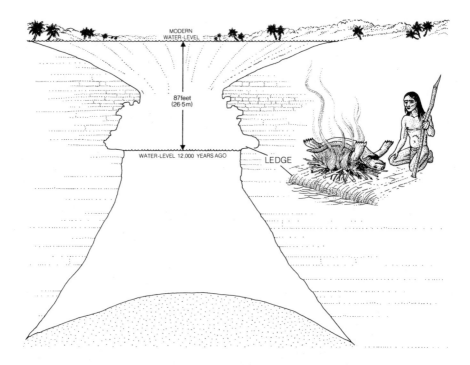

Little Salt Spring in southern Florida preserves ancient deposits dating back some 12,000 years. A remarkable find of that age was of a Paleo-Indian who had apparently fallen into the spring. He must have swum to a dry ledge just above the contemporary water level, because his remains were found there together with those of a turtle he probably cooked for food. When the meat ran out, he simply starved to death.

sources, lingering to consume their prey after making a kill. Since water supplies were irregular and widely dispersed, the hunter-gatherer population may have exploited huge territories to support a very low density of people per square mile.

There are hundreds of Florida sink holes that still await archaeological exploration, many of them known to contain artifacts and animal bones. Such sites offer some of the best opportunities we may ever have for recovering evidence of pre-Clovis occupation in North America at the very end of the Ice Age. New discoveries are reported almost yearly, and recent excavations in the Vero Beach area of southern Florida may well reveal occupation as early, if not earlier, than that already discovered at Little Salt Spring.

The perishable artifacts, well-preserved human remains that sometimes even yield brain tissue, and wide range of animal bones make the Florida sink hole sites unique in the New World. Elsewhere in the east, there have been numerous claims for pre-Clovis occupation, but none of them have stood up to close scrutiny. Many sites may be later than their radiocarbon dates allow, because of as yet undetected contaminants in the acidic soils of the northeast. For example, a fluted point from the Dutchess Quarry Cave in New York State has been dated to about 12,500 years ago. It comes from a layer containing caribou bones, but the date is regarded as being much too early for the artifacts associated with it.

Most Paleo-Indian sites in the east date to later than 10,000 years ago. But we appear to have solidly documented evidence for human occupation in the southeast by 12,000 years ago. Perhaps new discoveries in the Florida sink holes will help resolve the thorny problem of Meadowcroft's early occupation levels.

Enigmatic Flakes and Choppers: Central America

The search for pre-Clovis peoples has gained fresh impetus in recent years from new fieldwork in Central and South America, which has yielded results which would seem at first glance to contradict the fairly convincing pattern emerging from North America.

Richard MacNeish of Boston University made his archaeological name by chronicling the domestication of maize in prehistoric Mexico in the 1950s and 1960s. He has also worked on many early caves and open sites where very early human artifacts might be found. MacNeish is no archaeological conservative. In 1983, using but a scatter of poorly documented finds, he elaborated Alex Kreiger's "pre-projectile point horizon" into an entire sequence of early prehistoric occupation for Central America. This dated back, at least hypothetically, to as early as 30,000 to 40,000 years ago.

MacNeish's earliest stage is "characterized by chopping/chopper tools," dating to more than 30,000 years ago. There are few artifacts to place in this stage: some undated surface finds from San Isidro, in the Nueva Leon area of Mexico; a "few artifacts in high terrace gravels indicative of high antiquity" from Tamaulipas, which MacNeish believes are later; and some doubtful tools from the Tlapacoya area near Mexico City. These vaguely defined finds are joined by a Nicaraguan site named El Bosque.

The archaeologists Alan Bryan, Richard Morlan, Ruth Gruhn, and William Irving spent three weeks at El Bosque in 1975. They excavated a scatter of giant sloth bones – the animal had become trapped in the original swamp or bog – and uncovered a blackened area with heavily pulverized bone and extensive thin beds of pebbles. Dates from the bones ranged from 22,600 to greater than 32,000 years ago. Bryan and his colleagues believed the blackened area consisted of humanly made hearths or ash pits. Some small, flat chert fragments came from the trenches, but these did not seem to be convincing artifacts. Many observers at a field conference on the site considered the pebble concentrations and "hearths" were the result of large animals trampling the clays. Certainly the published artifact illustration looks unconvincing. And, for a variety of technical reasons, the dates are considered much too old. MacNeish, however, claims there was "at least one pebble or flake-chopper and some worked bone from good context" at El Bosque. Even the excavators, most of them firm believers in pre-15,000-year-old Americans, seem unhappy with this site.

MacNeish's second phase is characterized by "bone tools and a unifacial industry." He dates this to between 30,000 and 15,000 years ago. One of his key group of sites lies near Valsequillo, 9 miles (14.5 km) south of Pueblo in central Mexico. Here the archaeologists Juan Armenta Camacho and Cynthia Irwin-Williams found thirteen apparent unifacial stone implements, including "points," "burins," and "side scrapers," in association with the bones of extinct animals at five locations. The finds came from the lower deposits in some stratified gravels, the upper levels of which contained bifacial tools. Irwin-Williams also obtained a single radiocarbon date of 21,850 ± 850 years ago from a freshwater shell found near a stone flake at one of the sites – Caulapan. Camacho goes as far as to claim he found extinct animals and stone choppers, as well as worked bones, nearby. He dates these finds to between nearly 24,000 and over 35,000 years ago.

Although Irwin-Williams is satisfied with the single radiocarbon date from Valsequillo, other researchers raise questions about the stratigraphy of the lower levels, the associations of fauna and artifacts, and the nature of the tools themselves. Some geologists believe the gravels from which the flakes came may date to as early as 200,000 years – which would put the site in the Calico Hills class and call into question its authenticity as an early archaeological site in its lowest levels. Valsequillo may be a promising location, but more excavation is needed.

Not that these doubts stop MacNeish from further theorizing. "There is no denying the fact that this cultural complex [Valsequillo] existed at that time," he writes excitedly. The same types of artifacts are found at other Mexican sites, he claims. The most famous is Tlapacoya near Mexico City, where andesite and obsidian flakes have been found supposedly in association with mammoth bones. Unfortunately, most of the "artifacts" are simple, untrimmed flakes that cannot be classified as formal tools. The most publicized is an obsidian example, which was found not *in situ* but in one of the sifting screens used by the excavators. Two radiocarbon dates of 24,000 ± 4000 and 21,700 ± 500 years ago have been applied to the Tlapacoya finds. Again, serious doubts have been raised about whether or not the stone flakes and mammoth bones are genuinely associated, and about the dating and identification of the flakes. According to MacNeish, "There was indisputable association of man's unifacial tools with the bones of extinct animals such as the mammoth, mastodon, horse, etc." Most experts think this is much too confident a statement.

In addition to Tlapacoya, MacNeish points to at least two other sites, both rockshelters, where he claims tools are found in association with the bones of extinct animals, in chronological contexts earlier than 9,000 years ago. But in both cases, initial excavations were inconclusive, and further research has yet to begin. He also cites some isolated finds – among them a pointed horse-bone tool dated to 22,010 ± 540 years ago from San Luis Potosi. None of these finds are adequately documented, exhaustively excavated, or even thoroughly published. All must be regarded as highly questionable.

MacNeish is totally convinced that human occupation in Mexico dates to before 20,000 years ago. He admits that none of the early sites have yielded large artifact inventories and that larger-scale excavations are needed. He also recognizes that other scholars, such as Vance Haynes and Dennis Stanford, have their doubts, but he remarks tartly: "They cannot ignore the facts and wish these finds out of existence." To which comment the dispassionate observer feels compelled to ask, "What facts and what well-documented finds?" At present there are precious few "facts," if any, to ignore.

The more reliable archaeological record in Central America begins about 11,000 years ago, when isolated Paleo-Indian hunting groups are found south of the Rio Grande. A few finely made projectile points associated with big-game animals have been discovered in highland Mexico, at Iztapan and Tlapacoya, dating from around that time. Then there are the famous Lerma points, from the site of that name in Tamaulipas, radiocarbon-dated to about 9,270 years ago. Here extinct beaver and deer bones lie alongside stone projectile heads. A scatter of Clovis-and Folsom-like points are known from sites in northwest Mexico, and fish-tail-like projectile heads from Honduras, Guatemala, and Panama. These finds are all undated, which is a pity, for it would be interesting to compare their dates with those of Clovis finds in North America.

The First South Americans?

Supporters of pre-15,000-year settlement reserve their greatest enthusiasm for a series of possible early occupation sites from South America, scattered in locations as disparate as the Caribbean coast of Venezuela and northern Chile.

Until very recently, almost all the evidence for early human settlement in South America consisted of surface finds, scatters of simple stone tools, many of which could easily have been made by prehistoric peoples millennia later.

In 1971, Gordon Willey hypothesized that there was an "early Flake Tool Tradition" that had arrived sometime before 12,000 years ago. This simple stone technology of scrapers, knives, beaked tools, and snapped flakes had spread through South America, presumably from the north. There was also a "Chopper Tradition," which included crude, bifacially flaked chopping artifacts. Willey also argued for a later bifacial tradition that brought more-developed, better-finished large bifaces to South America. Whether these traditions represented successive migrations or the slow development of a single "flake-and-biface" kind of tradition, he was unable to tell. All these early technological traditions were, Willey argued, deceptively simple, used for fashioning wood and bone tools. After 12,000 years ago, wrote Willey, Paleo-Indian immigrants settled in South America, bringing with them the characteristic projectile points and more sophisticated stone technology found far to the north, in North America.

Willey's notion of a unifacial flake tradition as evidence for the first settlement of South America is by no means universally accepted. Thomas Lynch, a scholar long experienced in the study of early settlement in the Andes, rejects the idea altogether. He argues that all such isolated finds are in fact either inadequate samples – material collected uncritically from quarry sites, where ancient people roughed out more sophisticated artifacts – or collections from areas where the raw material was unsuitable for making fine, bifacially flaked projectile heads. Thus, he argues, the so-called Flake Tool Tradition is in fact part and parcel of a much more specialized big-game hunting tradition that utilized finely made projectile heads.

Lynch would be the first to accept an earlier cultural tradition, if such a tradition were documented in a reliably stratified and dated archaeological context. Surface collections are not an adequate way of defining any technological tradition, let alone one that is the earliest in a huge landmass, with a great diversity of later occupations. Since Willey wrote his great synthesis of South American archaeology in 1971, several early stratified sites have in fact been excavated, but their dating and interpretation are far from straightforward, as we shall see.

Alan Bryan, long an advocate of early settlement in South America, disagrees with Lynch. He believes there are major differences between Paleo-Indian sites in North America and those in the south. Very few big-game kill sites are known from South America. Thus, he argues, the archaeological record will be very different. Early South Americans had to adapt to diverse forest and open environments, using a "simple basic technology, composed of flakes and simple core tools which could be used to make useful objects from fiber, wood, sinew, skin, and bone." Some of these early settlers, he believes, did not even flake stone. The chances of finding sites where there are just flakes and no diagnostic tools like projectile heads seems high, Bryan says. He points to the early settlement of Australia, where human occupation was identified on the basis of simple flakes. If in Australia, why not in the Americas, he asks? "It is illogical to require the presence of diagnostic shaped tools in America and not to require their presence in Australia in order to prove that that continent was populated at least 40,000 years ago."

While Bryan is undoubtedly right in assuming that projectile points may not be found at every early South American site, he is still faced with the problem of distinguishing humanly made stone artifacts from those "manufactured" by natural phenomena. Several South American sites, among them Pikimachay in the Peruvian Andes and Monte Verde in Chile, which we discuss below, show how difficult this can be.

Over the years, Bryan has evolved a series of hypotheses for first settlement. One version imagines the hunter-gatherers "expanding their . . . territory through Panama . . . sometime before 20,000 years ago." These people settled in northwestern South America, retaining their "ancient unifacial Flake and Core Tool tradition for working stone and bone." Eventually, they spread throughout lowland South America.

Meanwhile, Bryan continues, other groups hunted large herbivores in arid thorn environments along the Caribbean coast. They developed more sophisticated hunting methods, using cylindrical stone points. Later, some of these groups expanded into the Venezuelan Andes and eventually south into northwest Argentina.

The Bryan hypothesis is based not only on his belief that human beings moved across the Isthmus of Panama long before 20,000 years ago, but on a scatter of archaeological sites throughout South America, most of them in actual fact considerably later than his hypothetical date of first settlement. For example, Bryan and his wife Ruth Gruhn excavated the skeleton of a young, partially butchered, mastodon at Taima-Taima in northern Venezuela. The bones lay near the base of some grey, clayey sands, part of an old spring deposit, sealed off about 10,000 years ago. A broken so-called "El Jobo" projectile point lay lodged in the mastodon's pelvic area. Four radiocarbon dates from a mass of sheared twigs that Bryan believes came from the mastodon's stomach "indicate a date of 13,000 years ago for the kill." El Jobo points are almost cylindrical, willow-leafed artifacts that clearly belong within the general Paleo-Indian tradition. Fifteen radiocarbon dates from the sand levels range between about 13,400 and 12,500 years ago.

The Taima-Taima mastodon kill comes from spring deposits that Bryan admits show "local convoluting and particle-sorting." Such geological layers are notoriously unreliable sources of dating information, because the upwelling spring water can shift and sort the deposits and their contents into stratigraphic confusion. The El Jobo point found with the skeleton is the sort of hunting weapon commonly used somewhat later, after 11,000 years ago. One suspects the Taima-Taima kill is therefore a little later than the radiocarbon

An "El Jobo" point of the type found by Alan Bryan at Taima Taima and elsewhere.

dates suggest, but there can be no doubt about the association between the mastodon and the artifact. Bryan himself argues for "the local development of a proboscidean [elephant]-hunting complex certainly by 13,000 years ago."

El Abra rockshelter near Bogota, Colombia, is another early site referred to by Bryan. Here a scatter of simple flakes and cores occurs in the lower levels of a rockshelter – levels that are thought to have been occupied before 12,500 years ago. The flakes and cores are generalized at best, the stratigraphy not studied in detail. At Tibito, in the suburbs of Bogota, mastodon, horse, and deer bones are associated with flakes, cores, and "simple bone tools." They are dated to about 11,750 years ago. No evidence of earlier occupation was forthcoming at this location.

Bryan claims these finds in the 13,500-to-11,700-year-old range are evidence that some of his early settlers "adapted themselves to the high-altitude open savannas." Not only are these sites much later than the pre-20,000-year date for first settlement he postulates, but he also has to explain how human settlers might have reached tropical latitudes over 20,000 years ago without leaving any convincing traces in North America.

A scatter of sites from Peru, Chile, and Brazil are claimed to date to much earlier millennia, closer to Bryan's hypothetical date.

Pikimachay Cave, Peru Richard MacNeish bases many of his ideas about early South American settlement on his excavations at Pikimachay Cave, high up in the foothills of the Andes in southern Peru. Pikimachay is a deep cave about 45 feet (13.7 m) high, with a lava-flow floor. Earth and disintegrating volcanic tuff from the cave walls overlie bedrock. MacNeish identified seven stratified zones at Pikimachay. He feels that the finds in the cave fall into two major groups, and a later third one that need not concern us here. The first, and earliest, found in earth and cemented soil, contained sloth and deer bones, as well as crude core tools. Two radiocarbon dates from bone assign these layers to 20,250-19,650 years ago, with large potential statistical errors. MacNeish argues from "microscopic study of wear patterns" that the artifacts were used as choppers and scrapers. The only people who doubt these tools, he says, are "those who have not studied all the artifacts in question."

The second group of artifacts comes from two overlying layers of yellow and orange-red soil, and includes large crude bifaces, some unifacial projectile points, scrapers, and choppers, as well as a bone tool. These artifacts and waste flakes were associated with over 500 animal bones, including sloth, horse, camel and puma. A single date from one of the bones gave a reading of $14,200 \pm 180$ years.

The 14,000-year-old artifacts at Pikimachay are undoubtedly tools, however crude, and many of them are choppers – perhaps used for butchery and woodworking. Although it is dangerous to rely on a single radiocarbon date, if the date and the stratigraphy are valid, then this level of Pikimachay is the earliest authentic post-glacial occupation in South America, and one of the earliest in the New World.

But was Pikimachay occupied in still earlier millennia, as MacNeish maintains? We cannot be sure. The jumbled stratigraphy gives cause for concern. The radiocarbon dates for the basal levels have very large statistical errors, errors that hint they may be completely inaccurate. Furthermore, the flakes and tools from the earlier horizons are very doubtful, made from rock spalls from the cave walls that could have received edge damage as they fell into the deposits. Indeed the Pikimachay flakes raise some fundamental issues about just how one does correctly identify very early tools.

Surmise versus Science Almost all claims of human colonization before 12,000 years ago are based on collections of stone artifacts, collections often as thin and inherently undiagnostic as those from the lowest levels of Pikimachay Cave. Are there, then, scientific criteria that can be used to distinguish humanly manufactured stone tools from "artifacts" fabricated by natural geological causes, like water movement, soil creep, or stones falling off a cliff? Can one use stone artifacts unassociated with fossil animal bones or human remains to prove the existence of the first Americans? The problem has exasperated and fascinated archaeologists for generations, going back to Charles Abbott and his so-called "palaeoliths." So absurd were some of the early European claims that the famous French palaeontologist Marcelin Boule threw flint cobbles into a cement mixer. He soon had a collection of superb prehistoric "artifacts."

In the 1920s and 1930s, immensely old and extremely primitive chopping tools came to light in East African river valleys, "Oldowan" artifacts that were found in association with the bones of long-extinct animals in 1.75-million-year-old lake beds at Olduvai Gorge, Tanzania, and elsewhere. Even with these tools, however, the context of the discovery and its association had to be examined very carefully. For example, African archaeologist J. Desmond Clark showed that beautiful "tools" identical to East African choppers resulted from basalt cobbles falling off a 300-foot (91-m) high cliff into the deep Zambezi River gorge.

Since then, the identification of stone tools has become ever more sophisticated, partly because we know a great deal more about stone technology, and also because of pioneering microscopic studies of edge wear on prehistoric artifacts. Unfortunately, relatively few American archaeologists have good training in prehistoric stone technology, unlike their Old World counterparts. Even fewer of them have handled very early stone artifacts from places like Olduvai Gorge. Although they talk of "primitive" technology and simple artifacts, they have, in fact, never seen a truly ancient, extremely simple artifact, let alone a good assemblage of Upper Palaeolithic tools from, say, western Europe. Many purported early artifact collections from American sites like El Bosque have been claimed as being human on completely subjective grounds, on identifications that rely heavily on the instincts or biases of the investigator.

For instance, Richard MacNeish says that several lithic experts have absolutely no doubts about the "artifacts" from the basal Pikimachay levels in Peru. This sweeping statement falls far short of the kind of rigorous technological analysis that is needed to establish the authenticity of the tools. Any scientific analysis of early artifacts must take into account the whole range of natural conditions at the site that could produce human-like fractures, as well as the geological context of the finds. What is striking about humanly made artifacts is that the stoneworkers scatter waste flakes and cores where they work. This type of scatter is distinctive, and quite different from the random patterning that usually results from natural fracturing. Even then, flake concentrations that look like humanly generated scatters can occur. This raises another question. Do these concentrations repeat themselves and form a coherent pattern that reflects deliberate human activity rather than fortuitous occurrence?

The tools themselves can only be approached from a number of investigative angles. The first is, of course, the close examination of the percussion scars. An expert eye can distinguish humanly applied percussion force from fractures caused by soil pressure and other natural factors, but the differences are subtle, often misleading. The flake angle is also a useful attribute, for experiments by modern stoneworkers have shown that *controlled* flaking cannot be achieved with striking platforms greater than 90 degrees. Nature can also produce flakes with angles less than 90 degrees, but she does not do so in a controlled manner. Nor does she prepare striking platforms, or systematically remove more than one flake from a core.

Many of the "artifacts" found in early South American sites are unifacial flakes that have been "retouched" into scrapers and other "tools." Few of the experts who pronounce judgment on these "artifacts" look closely at the retouch patterns on their edges. Hoofed animals and human feet can cause accidental "retouch" on the edge of a flake. Experience has shown that natural and chance edge wear usually consists of short, steep, uneven, and random flake scars. Humanly manufactured retouch is much more regular, unidirectional, and controlled. By looking at the retouch with a 10-power magnifying glass, any experienced stoneworker can detect unifacial tools from chance "artifacts." It is also almost impossible for natural forces to produce patterned bifacial flaking. Many of the early "bifaces" claimed from early sites are in fact random, amorphous objects produced by random forces rather than by controlled flaking.

Few scientific studies that included microscopic examination of retouch and wear patterns have ever been conducted on American sites claimed to be earlier than 10,000 years old. Until proven otherwise, we must assume the Pikimachay flakes are natural rock spalls.

New Sites in Brazil Brazil has long been famous for its wealth of archaeological sites, many of them finely painted rockshelters, others early hunting sites. Most belong to the period after 10,000 years ago, certainly after Clovis occupation far to the north.

Wesley Hurd of Indiana University has recently reexamined alleged early artifacts from the Alice Böer site in south-central Brazil. This multi-level site was excavated in the early 1960s, and contains well-documented Paleo-Indian occupation, including stemmed and leaf-shaped projectile points. These come from Level III, for the lower part of which the Brazilian archaeologist Maria Beltrão obtained a single radiocarbon date of 14,200 ± 1150 years – the high potential statistical error of 1150 years making it a somewhat suspect reading. A date obtained from slightly higher in the same level (using a technique called thermoluminescence)* came out at 11,000 years ago, with about a 10 percent potential error. While one may agree with Hurd, Bryan, and others that a date in the 14,000-year-range is not out of the question, much more work is needed to verify the age of Level III.

As with Pikimachay, there are far more dubious claims made by Beltrão for stone tools dating to between 20,000 and 40,000 years old in Level V at Alice Böer. Level V, an ancient river bed, is separated from Level III by a layer of

---

* Thermoluminescence is an important method of dating that measures the amount of energy (in the form of trapped alpha particles) left in clay or stones that have been heated at a specific time in the past.

sterile sand. Hurd himself cautions against uncritical acceptance of the "tools" from Level V (unifacial objects and battered cobbles) as humanly manufactured. He does claim, however, that some show multiple and secondary flaking, as well as striking platforms and flake scars. He believes that the objects include human artifacts, among them a blade scraper. Unfortunately, however, the geological circumstances of these objects and the uncertain date of Level V make any claims for human manufacture dubious at best. Certainly, the few illustrated specimens from the early layer are unconvincing.

The site called Boqueirão of Pedra Furada is one of more than 200 painted rockshelters known from the remote northeast Brazilian plateau. A scientific paper published in 1986 about the site and the finds there caused widespread international excitement. *The New York Times* ran a long article on the rockshelter under the banner headline, "New Finds Challenge Ideas on First Americans," and left the reader with the impression that Pedra Furada might even imply South America had been colonized first, before North America. So what was it that archaeologists found at this evidently important new site in the depths of Brazil?

Pedra Furada was first discovered in 1973 and lies on the steep bank of a sandstone cliff 65.6 feet (20 m) above the bottom of the Pedra Furada valley. French archaeologist Niède Guidon subsequently excavated the rockshelter in an attempt to date the cave art in the region and obtained dates in the order of 7,600 to 8,000 years ago. She dug deeper into the rockshelter deposits and reached bedrock at a depth of more than 9.8 feet (3 m). "Traces of human occupations succeed one another throughout the stratigraphic sequence," she writes. "Based upon the distribution and number of artifacts which were . . . associated with the hearths, it appears that the site was occupied only by a small human group on a temporary basis."

There were five distinct sedimentological layers in the rockshelter, all with a high sand component, some with pebbles and gravel beds in them. Layers B, C, D, and E contained lens-shaped "hearths," heavy concentrations of ash and charcoal. Guidon claims that each layer contains quartz and quartzite artifacts. She used the tools and hearth structures to classify the site into two stages, "Pedra Furada" and "Serra Talhada." The Pedra Furada stage is in turn divided into four subdivisions on the basis of its stone artifacts. The earliest is characterized by large circular hearths formed of fallen blocks, and identified by 560 stone pebbles, "principally pieces with blunt points obtained by two, three, or four convergent flakings." There are also "pebble tools (chopping tools and choppers) . . . denticulates, burins, notched pieces, retouched flakes, and double-edged flakes." The excavator also states that there are fragments of painted rock from the walls within the Pedra Furada deposits. The earliest hearth at the site produced two radiocarbon dates of 31,700 ± 830 and 32,160 ± 1,000 years ago.

The later stages of "Pedra Furada" are dated from about 30,000 to 21,000 years ago, by which time the stone artifacts include "side-scrapers and blunt points" as well as "small bifaces." A radiocarbon date of 17,000 ± 400 years ago comes from a slightly higher hearth containing "a piece of rock with two red painted lines." This Guidon believes to represent the earliest art in the Americas.

The upper layers of the site yielded "Serra Talhada" implements, better retouched tools, some made of flint and other fine-grained rocks. No hearths came from the early stages of this occupation, but Guidon estimates it is between 12,000 and 10,000 years old. The occupation becomes denser higher up the sequence, with hearths being used more than once and more varied stone artifacts, including blades. There is abundant ocher in these levels, which have been radiocarbon-dated to about 8,500 to 6,000 years ago. By this time the hearths are much larger and often elliptical, containing bone, wood, and leaf fragments, as well as stone tools.

Guidon claims her finds are evidence for human occupation of northeastern Brazil from before 31,500 years ago right up until Paleo-Indian times – by people using quartz and quartzite pebble cores and flakes with limited retouch. What are we to make of this discovery? We have but preliminary reports of the excavations to work with, and these do not present the detailed analyses of hearths, artifacts, or painted rock spalls. While the radiocarbon dates for the deposits are internally consistent, many questions remain unanswered. How were the geological layers of the rockshelter formed? Were the "hearths" formed by human activity, or by natural depositional processes? I was fortunate to hear Nièle Guidon describe her researches at a conference in 1985. Her slides showed she had uncovered a large area of the deposits, a welcome approach in an era of small test holes and extravagant claims. The shelter's early occupants are said to have camped alongside a stream, which seems to have flowed through the site. Judging from slides of the excavations, some parts of the deposits are stream-bed formations. Others have a high density of quartzite fragments from the walls and ceiling. Clearly, any scientific evaluation of the dates and context of the artifacts must await detailed description of the geology of the rockshelter layers.

Pedra Furada has yielded no animal bones earlier than about 17,000 years old. Nor have the artifacts, their stratigraphy, or the pigments on the alleged rock painting spall, yet been subjected to rigorous scientific description and analysis. The few artifacts illustrated at the conference looked unconvincing, as are the drawings and photographs in a recent preliminary publication. With quartzite spalling off the rockshelter walls and ceiling, a rigorous analysis of edge wear, flake scars, and every facet of the alleged artifacts is in order. Until it is completed, and the geological context of both hearths and strata are described in detail, Pedra Furada's earlier occupation levels must remain a question mark. That human settlement dates back to Paleo-Indian times in this area seems certain. What remains in doubt is the precise age of that first settlement.

Monte Verde, Chile Hunter-gatherer bands reached the southern latitudes of South America at least as early as 11,000 years ago, pursuing such varied animals as the guanaco and perhaps the now-extinct ground sloth. The most intriguing site in the region is Monte Verde, an open settlement on the banks of a small creek 9.3 miles (15 km) from the Pacific in south-central Chile. The stream drains a wet boggy area in a humid sub-antarctic forest that has flourished in the area since the Ice Age. Preservation is so good at this site that not only stones and bone fragments survive, but wooden objects as well.

Tom Dillehay of the University of Kentucky has excavated Monte Verde with a team of students from the Universidad Austral de Chile. He found traces of several activity areas on the north side of the creek, a settlement occupied when low sandy knolls and bogs bordered the stream. The excavations revealed what Dillehay calls twelve wooden dwellings on the bank, joined together to form two rows. Several huts were furnished with shallow, clay-lined braziers, with two large fireplaces outside, adjacent to the modern creek. The people spread their activities over a 1312-foot (400-m) long stretch of the stream bank. In one place they erected a wishbone-shaped wooden structure, perhaps with side walls made of branches. One support pole had been sharpened before being set in the ground.

The Monte Verde people exploited mammoth, for the modified bones of five to six individuals came from the site. It is possible they were scavenging rather than hunting, for no signs of the butchery sites were found. Large quantities of edible fruit and plants were recovered from the site as well. The artifacts include two wooden hafts for fractured stone pebbles, also modified branches that may have been used as curved "handles."

The more than 200 stones from Monte Verde show an absolute minimum of modification, but include an obviously man-made biface fashioned of quartzite from the Coastal Range some 37 miles (60 km) away. There is a chopper, a core, some grooved and spherical stones, as well as a miscellany of edge-battered and multifaceted pebbles. Such an ill-defined collection of broken stones almost defies conventional archaeological classification. The excavators subjected the collection to edge-wear analysis, in the hope that they could establish the ways in which the specimens were used, if at all. Michael Collins and Tom Dillehay admit that some of Monte Verde's so-called tools may not have been humanly made at all. The preliminary wear studies suggest that many of the edge-battered stones were used for woodworking, not for the hunt, or for butchery.

Dillehay estimates on the basis of radiocarbon dates that Monte Verde is between 12,000 and 14,000 years old, an age that is not out of line with those reported for Pikimachay and other locations. If the dates are correct, then this remarkable site may be evidence for very diversified hunting and foraging strategies in the Americas at the beginning of post-glacial times. Dillehay is also excavating in lower levels at the site, where radiocarbon dates in the 33,000-year range have been reported. Dillehay claims he has found a split basalt pebble, wood fragments, and some modified stones in his small trenches, but – as with the lowest levels at Pikimachay and Alice Böer – verification of these finds as being of human origin has not so far been forthcoming.

Did People Live in the Americas Before 15,000 Years Ago?

The proposition that human beings lived in the Americas during the Wisconsin glaciation does not appear to match the reliable archaeological record. None of the claims for 25,000-15,000-year-old "generalized hunting, fishing, and gathering economies," or "basic unifacial flaked-stone technologies," or "chopper-tool industries" have stood up to rigorous scientific dissection. There is not even general agreement as to the type of people being sought, largely because the artifacts, or alleged artifacts, that have come to light are very difficult to authenticate.

Most archaeologists tend to believe the first settlers were relatively sophisticated, highly adaptable people. However, Alan Bryan states that the Monte Verde discoveries in all their simplicity will cause scholars to rethink their conceptions of the first Americans. These people, with their simple wooden artifacts and minimal stone industry found in "carefully observed cultural contexts," make Bryan feel that we should be looking for "generalized foragers," who might occasionally kill a large animal if conditions were propitious. They were, he writes, "always looking for sharp-edged pieces of bone, tusk, or stone to use in the procurement and preparation of plant and animal remains."

Bryan may be right that one should be looking for simple stone, and indeed wood and bone, artifacts. But the problem is to know when one has found them, even when the stratigraphic context is well established and securely dated by radiocarbon readings. In this context, it is refreshing to see the careful edge-use studies and experiments being undertaken with the Monte Verde material, where classification of artifacts is almost impossible. Hopefully, similar studies will be carried out on the Pikimachay artifacts, and the finds from Boqueirão of Pedra Furada. At present, both these sites are haunted by the specter of "artifacts" created by wall and ceiling spalling, or other causes. It is certainly not enough to claim "possibilities" for early settlement on the basis of intuitive judgments. Scientific verification replaced instinct in these matters a long time ago.

The Wisconsin-period occupation of the Americas remains a *possibility*, nothing more. It is a possibility that many scientists would be happy to live with *if* adequate archaeological documentation were forthcoming. Given the great sophistication of late-twentieth-century archaeology, and the intense search for pre-Clovis settlement that is underway, the question of Wisconsin settlement is now closer to resolution than ever before, and may even be solved in our lifetimes.

At present, the earliest human occupation in the Americas that is widely accepted appears to date to between 15,000 years ago (or less) in the extreme north and 14,000-12,000 years ago farther south. Bluefish Caves in the Yukon Territory, Meadowcroft, Fort Rock, and Wilson Butte Cave in North America, Taima-Taima, Pikimachay, perhaps some Brazilian sites such as Pedra Furada, and Monte Verde in the south – all are possibilities. What is striking and perhaps highly significant is the immediate appearance of isolated traces of human settlement directly at the very end of the Wisconsin glaciation. None of the earliest locations dating to about 14,000-12,000 years ago is without its problems, but they may be legitimate predecessors to the numerous Paleo-Indian sites found throughout North America and further afield after 11,500 years ago. The few artifacts and broken animal bones from these pre-Clovis locations may signal the very beginnings of human settlement in the New World, settlement that perhaps involved just a few families who moved slowly into the heart of an uninhabited continent as the Ice Age ended.

As we move from the era of possibilities to one of probabilities, we now turn to the Paleo-Indian Clovis people as they open up vast new hunting and foraging territories in the North American heartland.

CHAPTER NINE

The Clovis People and their Forebears

ACT 3, SCENE 2
North America at the End of the Ice Age

About 11,500 years ago, the highly distinctive Clovis culture appeared on the Great Plains of North America, a culture documented from dozens of sites where stone artifacts have been found in direct association with the bones of large, extinct Ice Age mammals like the mammoth, mastodon, and extinct bison. Most Clovis sites are radiocarbon-dated to the five centuries after 11,500 years ago. The dating is so precise that twenty-one dates from the Lehner and Murray Springs kill sites in Arizona give a mean reading of $11,000 \pm 200$ years ago, a remarkably consistent result by radiocarbon standards.

This was a dramatic period in American prehistory. There was a veritable explosion in the number of archaeological sites everywhere from the California deserts to the Eastern Woodlands. From nothing, the archaeological record mushrooms into a well-documented scatter of locations, then, after 11,000 years ago, proliferates even further, evolving continuously from then on right into modern times. At this watershed in America's past we emerge from the shadows into the sunlight, for every scholar, whatever his or her views on the dating of first settlement, agrees that Clovis people flourished over wide areas of North America after 11,500 years ago. But there is still considerable argument over the origins of Clovis.

The Clovis Way of Life

At the end of the Wisconsin glaciation, the areas in the rainshadow of the western mountains of North America were dominated throughout the year by the dry mid-Pacific air mass. Most rain fell, and still falls, in spring and early summer, supporting short grasses that keep much of their biomass beneath the soil. This helped retain moisture at the roots, providing mammoths, bison, and other ruminants with high-quality nutrients in the dry fall and into the winter. These grasslands expanded at the end of the Wisconsin and were colonized by herds of ruminants who were selective feeders. They were also home for scattered bands of Clovis people. Within a few centuries, small groups of Clovis hunters had spread to both North American coasts and as far south as Guadalajara, Mexico – perhaps, also, deep into South America.

The bands were constantly on the move, following migrating game. Many of the hunters camped on low terraces along rivers and streams. Their abandoned settlements were soon buried by thunderstorms and torrential downpours that eroded clayey silts from adjacent slopes. Several thousand years later, downcutting streams have exposed Clovis sites for archaeologists to examine.

According to the palaeontologist Vance Haynes, some Clovis people favored perennial springs and waterholes, places where mammoth and other big game came regularly to drink. The hunters also visited caves and rockshelters, some of which may have served as winter encampments.

Everything points to a very small and scattered Clovis population. Their sites are relatively small compared with those of later Paleo-Indian locations. At Murray Springs, Arizona, for example, there are three different activity areas – a mammoth kill of some 10,600 square feet (986 sq. m), a bison kill area covering about 15,900 square feet (1479 sq. m), and a camp site nearby that spread over some 7060 square feet (657 sq. m). That the camp was associated with the kills is certain. Mammoth bones were found there, also a damaged Clovis point, an impact flake from which was discovered among the bison bones. A few projectile points and other tools, and thousands of thinning and sharpening flakes, lay among the dismembered carcasses. The ratio between tools and waste flakes was 6:10,000. Only 36 finished tools came from the entire site, presumably because the hunters conserved their best artifacts and took them away for reuse.

Eleven bison died at Murray Springs, yielding enough meat to support as many as 50 to 100 people, perhaps many fewer. A single mammoth found by archaeologist Emil Haury at Naco, Arizona, had no less than 8 Clovis points in its carcass, four times more than any other known kill. Perhaps it escaped wounded, only to die later. If each point belonged to an individual hunter, then at least 8 men attacked the beast – 4 if each fired off 2 spears. Haynes believes the actual figure may lie between these two extremes, with hunters representing a fifth of a band of about 20 to 40 men, women, and children. Not that the Clovis people used all the meat they killed. Wherever they butchered mammoth, the hunters only partially dismembered the carcasses, taking some choice parts away with them. The rest they abandoned – presumably for reasons of size and weight. At Clovis itself, Murray Springs, and the Colby site in Wyoming, they created piles of disarticulated bones, perhaps as winter caches. Bison carcasses were more heavily utilized, and less was left at the kill site.

Clovis hunting methods Everyone agrees that the Clovis people hunted both big game and smaller animals as well, besides collecting wild vegetable foods during spring, summer, and fall. However, preservation conditions are such that it is the animal bones that have survived, so much so that there has been a tendency to overemphasize the meat element in the diet. But the Clovis folk were opportunists, like all hunters and foragers, and we can safely assume that they took big game whenever they could. They seem to have been especially fond of mammoth, for their bones are found at every site where bone survives. The hunters also favored now-extinct forms of bison, and on occasion they pursued horse, camel, tapir, bear, and rabbit.

Judging from modern African elephant-hunting societies, these large beasts were attractive quarry for many reasons. A single animal could provide a band with meat for weeks on end, and if dried, for much of the winter, too. Hides, tusks, bones, and pelts were used to make household possessions and weapons, for shelter, even clothing. Precious fat from the internal organs could be melted down and used for cooking and burning in lamps.

We do not know whether the hunters attacked mammoth individually or in groups. Most Clovis mammoth kills lie on low ground, near creeks, springs, or ponds. They may have ambushed the animals at watering places, spots where the soft ground restricted their movements. Modern field research into African and Asian elephants show they are not restricted to a rigid annual cycle. They are highly mobile and can respond quickly to fluctuations in food availability due to rainfall, fire, or flooding. Modern elephants have a matriarchal social organization, wandering in family units of a matriarch and one or two mature daughters and their immature offspring. Bulls leave their parental units when they reach sexual maturity. They tend to lead solitary lives. Ice Age mammoth may have had the same form of social organization. Such an organization allows the development of traditions among family groups for resource-oriented movements. Generation after generation, mammoth would return to the same salt licks, waterholes, trails, and favored patches of vegetation. It is hardly surprising to find hunting sites close to permanent water supplies dotted over a dry landscape.

While males lead more solitary lives, there are advantages for female elephants in associating with others. Their young develop slowly, so each female may have as many as two or three dependents at one time. The elephants cooperate in defending their young, in the care and nursing of offspring, and in rescuing members from danger or natural mishaps. Palaeontologist Jeffrey Saunders examined the mammoth bones from the Lehner site. He believes the hunters dispatched an entire family of 13 mammoth in a single hunt, a group ranging from 2 to 30 years of age. When threatened in open country, elephants cluster together for defense. Thus, they are vulnerable to nimble hunters, who drive them into swamps or narrow defiles, where they are killed with spearthrusts to the soft abdomen.

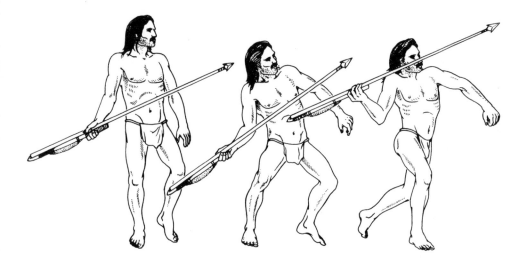

The atlatl, or spear-thrower, in action. Such weapons were a vital part of the armory of Clovis hunters. The increased power and thrust provided by the atlatl made it easier to bring down or wound game animals.

Vance Haynes questions Saunders' findings, arguing that the task might have been beyond the capabilities of Clovis technology. He believes the hunters were obviously shrewd observers of elephant behavior. They must have followed matriarchal groups for weeks on end, and observed the behavior of individual beasts with sedulous care. By watching closely, and attacking each animal at a moment when they could catch it off guard and apart from the herd, they could, over a period of years, accumulate carcasses of varying ages, in what would appear to be a family group. Thus, Lehner was not a mass kill site, but a place where solitary beasts were taken regularly.

Haynes' interpretation receives some support from modern experiments. Archaeologist George Frison of the University of Wyoming has recently experimented with replicas of stone-tipped Clovis spears using dead modern African elephants in Zimbabwe, Central Africa. His research was designed to see whether Clovis weaponry could deliver a missile of such velocity that it could lethally wound elephants of all ages and both sexes. He found the greatest accuracy was achieved by standing still and aiming carefully. So he

argues that the hunters worked in pairs, with one man getting the mammoth's attention while the other took a shot with a spear and atlatl, a wooden throwing stick that increased the velocity of the spear.

Clovis weapons could indeed have inflicted severe wounds on mammoth, Frison believes, but were not capable of dropping an animal in its tracks like a high-powered rifle can. In all probability, the hunters stalked herds, then concentrated their efforts on animals that strayed from the matriarch. They would then maneuver themselves into the right spot for a wounding shot that would eventually kill the solitary beast. By using both a spear and a throwing stick and a simple thrusting spear, a team of hunters could play a waiting game and kill their quarry at their leisure. Perhaps the Clovis people did occasionally drive a mammoth herd into a swamp and dispatch several beasts at once. More often, however, they probably concentrated on single animals.

The view that Clovis hunters were not quite so effective as their later counterparts is borne out by other research. James Judge, a distinguished Southwestern archaeologist, has studied hunting and living patterns on Paleo-Indian sites using the frequencies of projectile points and scraping tools, the mean number of artifacts per site, the completeness of the points recovered, and the presence of animal bones. His ingenious typology enabled him to distinguish between camp sites, kill sites, food processing sites, and quarries where the hunters obtained fine-grained rock. He found that most reported Clovis kill sites did not conform to the type of site inventories found in later Paleo-Indian cultures. Judge feels many of them were in fact places where mammoth wounded by projectile points finally died. The carcass was never butchered by the hunters, who lost track of the animal. Judge bases his argument on the rarity of all artifacts, the relative absence of butchering tools, and the unusual frequency of complete projectile points, normally artifacts that the hunters would have carried away with them.

But what exactly was the nature of the Clovis toolkit?

A portable toolkit The Clovis people used a range of tools and weapons well suited to their mobile life. Most Clovis sites contain relatively few artifacts, but there can be no question they are of human manufacture. The Clovis point itself is often, but by no means always, fluted and varies considerably in size and shape. The most famous points are the eight from the Naco mammoth site. The largest is 4.5 in. (11.4 cm) long.

Clovis stoneworkers were expert at their craft. They frequently selected the finest of exotic materials from which to fashion beautiful points, materials selected for their translucency, color, or smooth texture. By the same token, Clovis artisans were perfectly capable of producing a bifacial point from intractable quartz. Their skill contrasts dramatically with the irregular "tools" alleged to have been made by earlier American stoneworkers. Why did the Clovis workmen deliberately select fine materials? Perhaps it was easier to make good projectile heads, perhaps the material was more economical in use. Conceivably, beautiful weapons were thought pleasing to the hunter's prey, or they were buried with the dead – as may be the case with two children deposited in the Anzick site near Wilsall, Montana.

Clovis stone technology was based in part on precious, fine-grained rock that came from widely separated outcrops. The hunters used many of the finest siliceous rock sources in North America, aboriginal quarries that were exploited for thousands of years by their successors. They utilized not only local material, but stone from prized outcrops up to 186 miles (299 km) away. These included alibates, a form of banded, agatized dolomite from the Canadian River area of Texas. Translucent dark brown chalcedony came from the Knife River Valley of North Dakota and Manitoba. There was chalcedony from Ohio, volcanic obsidian from the Yellowstone Park region. The hunters traveled great distances for their stone, and traded it from band to band over many miles. Effective procurement of other raw materials – bone, hide, sinews, even wood – depended on an adequate supply of fine-grained rock to kill and process big game and cut down trees.

Clovis stoneworkers used a careful reduction process that started with large bifaces and branched out into smaller artifacts made with maximum economy and logical efficiency. Step-by-step, the stoneworker fashioned a projectile head by trimming a flake on both faces to the required shape. The fluting flake was struck off with a punch placed on the carefully beveled and pressure-flaked base. The heads were time-consuming to manufacture, so the hunters resharpened the tips when they were damaged on impact. Some Clovis points display high burnish on their faces, as if they were bound tightly onto a shaft, the working of the binding causing a gloss to develop on the stone. Exactly how the points were hafted is unknown but they may have been mounted in a foreshaft that worked loose from the shaft itself once the head had penetrated its quarry. Frison's recent African experiments were based on this assumption.

Besides the projectile heads there were bifacially trimmed points and other woodworking and butchering artifacts, as well as flakes used simply as sharp-edged, convenient tools in their struck-off form. The large biface from which the flakes came served not only as a source of raw material but also as a butchery knife and chopper itself. You can see the process at the Murray Springs kill site in Arizona. This yielded the carcasses of both mammoth and bison in an astonishingly undisturbed state. Hundreds of bifacial trimming flakes came from the ancient land surfaces covered by overburden for thousands of years. Bruce Huckell of the Arizona State Museum pieced together clusters of thin flakes to reconstruct the bifaces that produced them.

Bifaces and butchery One way we can understand how stone tools were used is by experimenting with modern replicas. Huckell was lucky enough to be able to supervise the skinning and dismemberment of a twenty-four-year-old Indian elephant that had died suddenly while performing in a circus in Tucson, Arizona. When delivered, the carcass lay on its right side, so Huckell skinned the left flank, comparing the performances of modern steel knives and chipped stone replicas modeled after tools found on Clovis sites. Huckell and his assistants used bifaces for every type of butchering task, from skinning to muscle stripping. The large biface used to make the initial cut through the skin had to be sharpened five times to make a single cut through the tough epidermis, from the pubis up the flank to the backbone. The sides of the cut had to be held open while the biface was sawed backward and forward in the incision. It took only a few seconds to remove small sharpening flakes from the dulled edge, so the work could continue. The modern steel knives stayed sharper longer, but were more time-consuming to sharpen.

The bifaces were highly effective for meat cutting and muscle stripping, but the butchers soon realized that it paid to keep the tools sharp. Otherwise, they expended too much effort to cut meat. By using the whole working edge, too, they could extend its longevity. As the butchering proceeded, the edges of the stone tools soon became clogged with muscle fiber and tissue. They had to be wiped frequently. Blood accumulated on the hands and artifacts and had to be washed off. While butchering Plains bison, George Frison solved the problem by wrapping bison hair around the part of the tool he held in his hand. Grass would have served just as well.

By far the most effective way to butcher a large animal like an elephant or a bison was for two people to work together – the one cutting, the other maintaining a constant tension on the piece being cut. Perhaps as many as four hunters would butcher very large animals, especially when removing limbs or other large parts.

The butchery experiment gave Huckell a chance to examine the tough elephant skin close up. Where would a hunter on foot and armed with a spear be able to penetrate the hide? The thinnest spot appeared to be along the middle of the chest and stomach, the very place where Bambule pygmies of Zaire in central Africa aim their thrusting spears. The elephant's foot-long heart lies in this area, as do the vulnerable lungs, the stomach, and the intestines.

Huckell found the meat extremely lean, if somewhat gristly in parts. Since the circus animal had died of unknown causes and had been on medication, he made no attempt to eat the flesh. So much meat came from the one flank of the elephant that he wondered if the Clovis hunters would have done anything more than selectively butcher a mammoth or mastodon. One calculation based on African elephants suggests that an 11,990-pound (5431-kg) individual fully dressed could yield as much as 4,565 pounds (2068 kg) of edible products, a vast amount of meat for a small band. San hunters from the Kalahari Desert of southern Africa are able to consume up to 10 pounds (4.5 kg) of meat at a kill, but even if Clovis people ate this amount of fresh meat, they would still have had a great deal of surplus flesh to hand. Another strong argument for selective butchering is the sheer weight of the carcass. It took a pickup truck, a tow chain, and two people standing on the legs to turn over the dead elephant. Even a large number of adults would have had trouble performing this task. They probably never tried it.

Few bone tools have come from Clovis sites, but such artifacts were clearly much more important than is apparent to us now. They included foreshafts and points with beveled ends, awls, punches, and fleshers. The basal levels were scored, as if to increase friction where the join meant another bevel on the shaft. A similar artifice was used on European Upper Palaeolithic bone points. The Murray Springs site has also yielded a mammoth bone "shaft wrench," a form of artifact used for straightening wooden shafts and polishing sinews also found on Old World Upper Palaeolithic sites.

Where Did Clovis Come From?

There are, as we have seen, isolated hints of occupation in North America before 11,500 years ago, at places like Wilson Butte Cave and Meadowcroft

Rockshelter, but none of this yet proves that there were indigenous ancestors for Clovis south of the ice sheets. The evidence is simply too sparse and the range of tools too inadequate to suggest a local origin for the highly developed Clovis technology. With the "indigenous" hypothesis so far unsupported by archaeology, we should consider Vance Haynes' proposition: that the Clovis people came originally from north of the ice sheets and migrated south in pursuit of big game at the very end of the Wisconsin as the glaciers melted and retreated.

Is there any evidence for widespread population movements in the far north at the end of the Ice Age and before the full flowering of Clovis 11,500 years ago? This is where dental and genetic research can be called in again to provide vital clues.

As we saw, Christy Turner is an expert on the study of changing physical characteristics in prehistoric teeth, features of tooth crowns and roots that are stable enough in evolutionary terms to give clues about the relationships between prehistoric peoples. Turner points out that prehistoric Americans share the constellation of dental traits known as "Sinodonty" with northern Asians. He believes Sinodonty emerged at least 20,000 years ago in Asia, and that Asians colonized the New World.

Dental morphology does more than provide a basis for theorizing about evolutionary changes. It can also provide clues to the time it has taken for such divergence to take place. Turner applied the mean measure of divergence statistic to isolated Aleut populations that were cut off from any connection with Asia as sea levels rose at the end of the Ice Age. The changes in the teeth of these populations gave him an overall rate of dental microevolution of 0.0964/Mean Measure of Divergence/1,000 years. This he then applied to Paleo-Indian and Asian samples, an experiment that gave a reading of 14,000 years ago for the first crossing of the Bering land bridge and the earliest penetration of Alaska.

The Paleo-Indians were then followed a few thousand years later, Turner says, by two successive waves of later immigrants from Siberia: "Na-Dene" folk, the ancestors of modern Athabaskan Indians and some Northwest Coast peoples; and "Ancestral Aleut-Eskimo."

This hypothesis receives some support from the distribution of genetic markers (Gm allotypes) in modern American populations. This long-term research project led by physical anthropologist Robert Williams has accumulated enormous samples of genetic typings, including over 5,400 from people in western cultural groups. The typing divides this western sample into two, distinct, pre-European groupings. The first includes Pimans, Pueblans, and Pai, the second the Apache and Navajo, both Athabaskan-speakers. A third group includes the Eskimo, who were not part of this particular study. The groupings that emerged from the typing led Williams and his colleagues to agree with Christy Turner: the first Americans were Paleo-Indians, followed by Athabaskan-speakers (the Apache and Navajo part of the western sample) and, later, the ancestors of the Aleuts and Eskimos.

Neither of the latter two groups penetrated deep into the Americas, for the more than 14,000 Central and South American Indians typed fell into the Paleo-Indian category, people with the two Gm typings Gm 1;21 and Gm 1,2;21. The Williams team believes that their three populations originated in a northeastern Siberian population with Gm types Gm 1;21, Gm 1,2;21, and Gm 11,13 in polymorphic frequencies. The genetic differences between the groups could have arisen as a result of genetic drift, natural selection, or some other mechanism.

Dental morphology and genetic research thus hint strongly at a relatively late settlement date. Support for the Turner hypothesis also comes from the linguistic researches of Joseph Greenberg. Back in 1956, Greenberg proposed that most North American and all South American languages were part of one large Amerind family. Aleut-Eskimo and Na-Dene were quite separate linguistic groups, making a total of three for the whole of the Americas. Greenberg then began compiling a vast database on the vocabulary and grammar of American Indian languages, the salient features of which he published in 1986. This massive study confirms his belief that there were three linguistic groups that correspond to migrations into the Americas. The first and earliest was what Greenberg calls "Amerind." This centers far to the south of the others and shows much greater internal differentiation. The northern groups show much less variation, as if they are more recent and had less time to develop internal differences. Na-Dene, says Greenberg, shows deeper internal divisions than Aleut-Eskimo and perhaps arrived earlier. So great are the differences between the three groups that there is little likelihood that they are branches of a single linguistic stock. Greenberg believes that his Amerind group arrived before 11,000 years ago, Na-Denes around 9,000 years ago, and that Aleuts and Eskimos diverged about 4,000 years ago.

By no means all American Indian linguists accept Greenberg's classifications, especially his assumption that there are three linguistic stocks that correspond to three basic migrations. Another school of thought argues there are numerous such stocks, with few relationships between them. To accept this viewpoint means either thinking in terms of dozens of migrations across the Bering Strait, or saying that the time elapsed since a few primeval migrations is so vast that all traces of similarities between different languages have vanished without trace. Neither argument seems convincing.

There are other disagreements, too. Richard Rogers of the University of Kansas has studied the distribution and differentiation of American Indian languages relative to the distribution of Wisconsin ice sheets. He points out that the areas that were never glaciated during the Wisconsin glacial maximum contain 93 percent of the native North American languages. The areas that were once glaciated are overwhelmingly dominated by languages also present in the non-glaciated areas. So languages may have spread from ice-free North American areas into regions deglaciated after 12,000 years ago. They would not have had sufficient time to differentiate into local languages. In contrast, there is much greater linguistic differentiation in the non-glaciated areas. Rogers believes this is a function of the greater length of occupation in these regions, and suggests that human occupation of North America occurred *prior* to the Wisconsin maximum. He also studied the distribution of Eskimo-Aleut, Na-Dene, and Algonquian languages, and hypothesizes that they spread from the periphery of the ice sheets into newly unglaciated lands.

The prehistory of languages is at best a controversial subject. We may know, for example, that antique Egyptian, now a liturgical language, is at least 5,000 years old, but beyond the frontiers of written records, the early evolution of this tongue, like all prehistoric dialects, is almost a complete mystery. Thus, while Rogers has documented sharp contrasts in linguistic differentiation, his date for early settlement is little more than a rough guess – and one that flies in the face of reliable archaeological evidence. It can be argued that the great diversity of American Indian languages in more temperate areas developed as a result of the great variety of environments to which the inhabitants had to adapt in post-glacial times. It is interesting to note, for example, that there is far more linguistic diversity in extreme north-west America where there are many contrasting local environments than occur in the relatively recently deglaciated northeast where diversity is minimal.

What, then, is the archaeological evidence to support the dental morphology, genetics and Greenberg's linguistic theories?

Northern Connections?

If Haynes and Turner are right, and the Clovis people or their immediate forebears are the first settlers, the archaeological problem is easily posed. Are there technological links between Clovis artifacts and late Palaeolithic tools made in the far north earlier than 11,500 years ago?

Distinctive Clovis points with or without fluted bases are found in all the Canadian provinces, on the Great Plains and in much of North America, as well as in Mexico, Guatemala, Costa Rica, and Panama, perhaps even further south. However, no securely dated prototypes that are widely accepted as such have come to light in Alaska or the Yukon, except in later sites or in poorly documented circumstances. Most Alaskan projectile heads are small with multiple fluting scars, somewhat different from classic Clovis points to the south. Many scholars believe the Clovis point was an indigenous development, first fabricated on the Great Plains and not in the arctic at all.

As we saw in Chapter 6, the microblade and core traditions of Alaska are really no earlier than Clovis itself, and at many sites perhaps a millennium or so later. Only Bluefish Caves and Dry Creek 1 offer hints as to an ancestral occupation in eastern Beringia. Dry Creek 1 did yield triangular bifacial points, what Vance Haynes calls "Paleo-Indian style" scrapers, and flake tools in a context dating to about 11,170 years ago. Microblades are absent, as they are apparently in some Dyukhtai sites in Siberia too. It is probably pointless to speculate further about connections between Clovis technology and that of the far north until we have access to many more dated sites.

Vance Haynes and Hansjürgen Müller-Beck argue that the mammoth was to the late Palaeolithic hunter what the reindeer is to the Lapplander or the caribou to the inland Eskimo. They both believe that general similarities between Clovis stone and bone tools and those from classic mammoth hunting sites in eastern Europe and the Ukraine mean that the first settlement of the New World was part of a big-game hunting tradition that spread across Russia into northeast Asia. Ultimately descendants of the big-game hunters crossed to Alaska.

This line of thinking agrees well with Turner's dental calculations for the land-bridge crossing. However, Turner points out that the child found buried at Mal'ta and other European specimens do not display Sinodonty, an Asian as well as Paleo-Indian trait. Did, then, the ancestral populations come from the south in Asia? The inconsistency between the two points of view may not be important, for northeast Asia was environmentally highly diverse, a region that may have supported a far more varied population than just big-game hunters, peoples with distant cultural roots in the far east as well as in the west. It is therefore not illogical to argue that Clovis derived ultimately from late Palaeolithic cultural roots, even if the details of their technological ancestry remain enigmatic.

After 14,000 years ago, the ice sheets began to melt, removing natural barriers for humans and big-game animals to move south between the Laurentide and Cordilleran ice masses. Haynes believes that Ice Age animals were becoming extinct in Alaska as early as 13,000 years ago. He hypothesizes that the ancestors of the Clovis people wandered further south pursuing their favorite quarry, the woolly mammoth. Eventually they reached the Canadian prairies where they encountered new mammoth species and a greater bounty of other big-game species.

This scenario is almost as inadequately documented as some of the hypotheses that espouse much earlier dates for first settlement. However, it enjoys one major advantage. The cumulative sum of the limited data that can be brought to bear on it seems to support rather than undermine it.

*   *   *

Extinctions

The Clovis people flourished on the Great Plains for about 500 years and then, around 11,000 years ago, they abruptly vanished, to be replaced by a multitude of different hunting-and-gathering cultures in the millennia that followed. Quite what happened is one of the mysteries of modern archaeology. By an intriguing coincidence – if coincidence it be – the disappearance of Clovis coincides with one of the great mysteries of vertebrate palaeontology too – the mass extinction of Ice Age big-game animals, the megafauna. Inevitably, scholars have theorized that the Clovis people overhunted these creatures and drove them into extinction. But what evidence is there that human beings were the culprits?

Everywhere in the world, the end of the Ice Age saw massive, even catastrophic, extinctions of big-game species. The mammoth, mastodon, giant sloth, and many camel species were just a few of the casualties. In Australia, another continent that was peopled by human beings late in prehistory, two genera of kangaroo, a large flightless bird named *Genyornis*, and several forms of wombat were among the animals that vanished after 30,000 years ago. Other species like the famous koala bear evolved into smaller forms. With bewildering rapidity, too, North America's big game vanished soon after the retreat of the ice sheets, most of them by about 11,000 years ago, although some species lingered on in the east to perhaps as late as 9,000. "We live in a zoologically impoverished world," wrote the famous biologist Alfred Wallace in 1876, "from which all the hugest, and fiercest, and strange forms have recently disappeared . . . yet it is surely a marvelous fact, and one that has hardly been sufficiently dwelt upon, this sudden dying out of so many large Mammalia, not in one place only, but over half the land surface of the globe." Wallace thought the extinctions were the result of worldwide deglaciation, but later he changed his mind. Humans, he wrote, were the cause. The extinctions controversy has raged since Wallace's day.

Thirty-one genera of large, North American herbivores became extinct, mainly big-game animals weighing over 110 pounds (50 kg) adult body weight. There were mass extinctions at the end of earlier geological epochs and Ice Age glaciations, but these affected small mammal and other animal populations as well. This time amphibians, reptiles, and freshwater molluscs, even ocean fish populations, remained relatively unchanged, with the loss of only a few species. The late Ice Age extinction left glaringly empty niches in the terrestrial ecosystem of the Americas. Something catastrophic affected only a relatively small segment of America's animal population.

Paul Martin of the University of Arizona spent his early career studying prehistoric climatic change in the Southwest. This research took him to Clovis sites in Arizona where he collected fossil pollens associated with mammoth bones. His samples were supposed to demonstrate that climatic change had driven Ice Age big game from the region. Instead, he found that the climate had not altered very much, indeed that climatic change and mammalian extinctions seemed to be out of phase. Then he thought about the mastodons of the northeastern states, elephants that were greater browsers than mammoths. They had adapted to more temperate conditions, then become extinct later, just as their range was expanding, as was that of the human beings who hunted them. Could humans, rather than climatic changes, have driven the Ice Age megafauna into extinction?

Martin remembered New Zealand, where twenty-seven species of Moa, flightless birds up to 10 feet (3 m) tall, flourished at the end of the last glaciation. Some Moa populations had reached a density of 800 to the acre, perhaps even more. When the first human colonists arrived about 1,000 years ago, they favored Moa over almost any other food source. The flightless birds were sitting targets for even a moderately skilled hunter. Evidence of no fewer than twenty-three Moa species has come from early settlements, but they soon vanished. Archaeologists believe that human exploitation drove the Moa into extinction in a few centuries. Could the Clovis people have done the same with the mammoth and the mastodon?

Until Martin came along, archaeologists thought in terms of a slow, almost imperceptible, human population growth between first settlement and European contact 500 years ago, on the order of 0.1 percent annually. Martin disagreed, claiming the big-game hunters found themselves in an exceptionally favorable environment, peopled by herds of unsuspicious mammoth and other herbivores, not wary of humans like their arctic relatives. As a result, the human population exploded.

Population densities are almost impossible to detect from early sites, so Martin indulged in intelligent speculation. He pointed to figures of 3.4 percent a year for population growth among mutineers from the British ship *H.M.S. Bounty* after they landed on Pitcairn Island during the late eighteenth century. An island is a small area. What would happen if big-game hunters had an entire continent at their disposal, a continent with diverse environments and well populated with large mammals?

Martin took the Pitcairn Island figure and calculated the time that it would have taken human populations to cover the unglaciated areas of the Americas with a population of one person per square mile (a maximum figure for prime hunting territory in many parts of the world). This would have involved a doubling of population every 20 years. Seventeen generations of a band of 100 hunters would have needed 340 years to cover the continent. Even at a population increase of 1.4 percent a year, and a doubling every 50 years, saturation would require only 800 years.

No one suggests that population growth maintained such rates for a long time, or that the Paleo-Indian population ever reached saturation. The point that Martin makes is that the advancing front of the human invasion was the

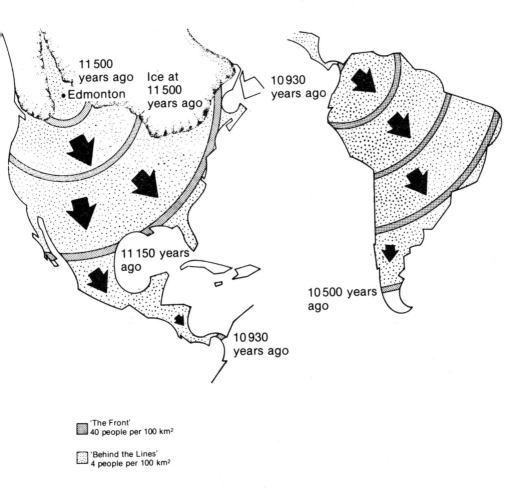

Paul Martin's hypothetical scheme for the rapid progress of the first hunters through the Americas. As local extinctions occurred at the "front," so the hunters moved on.

critical element in the megafaunal equation. He looked into studies of animal invasions, of new species of giant snails in Africa, and of exotic animals introduced into New Zealand. In each case, a high population density occurred early on, then declined. Not only that, but the highest populations were along the advancing "front" of the new species. Martin believes the first Americans would have been no different. Like their arctic ancestors, their lives were adapted to the habits of the big game they exploited. Their advance into new territory was determined partly by the distribution of game resources within the front, as well as by the internal dynamics of hunting groups, the distribution of waterholes, and other variables. Whatever factors affected band movement, a rapidly expanding hunter population would soon deplete the slow-breeding mammoth and mastodon groups. As big game became scarcer, many hunters would move on. The bands that stayed on had brutal options: survive off the decimated biomass, exploit new food resources, or perish.

Martin applied some tantalizing figures to North America. He assumed that a band of 100 hunters arrived in the Edmonton area of Canada, and allowed them a 10-mile (16-km) a year southward movement, a by-no-means excessive figure. With high population growth, 100 people could have expanded 397 miles (639 km) southward over a front 100 miles (161 km) wide with a population of one person per square mile. He estimated a maximum hunter population of 600,000, with half that number still at the "front" as it reached the Gulf of Mexico, 2,050 miles (3,299 km) south of Edmonton. Martin developed computer projections that had Paleo-Indians in Panama by 10,930 years ago, and within sight of Tierra del Fuego by 10,500 years ago. Thus, he believes, the population of the entire continent south of the ice sheets took a mere 1,000 years. Monte Verde and other early sites may push back these dates, but the principle remains the same.

This dramatic population explosion had a momentous effect on the Ice Age megafauna, Martin argued. Again, he made some hypothetical calculations. With a density of one hunter per square mile, and 50 "animal units" per square mile (an animal unit is 1,000 pounds (453 kg), or about 0.2 mammoth – the weight of a horse or five sheep), and a 10-year period, what would the "removal rate" be? Wolves on Isle Royale in Lake Superior annually cull 18 percent of the moose herd there, mainly older and young beasts. The herd survives, but a slower-breeding, large mammal like a mammoth is far more vulnerable to such a removal rate by predators, even in danger of eventual extinction.

Martin estimated that a 30 percent removal rate of the megafauna biomass by hunters would have exceeded normal reproduction replacement rates for all extinct late Ice Age mammals. If one person in four did all the hunting, destroying one animal unit a week from an animal population on the "front" averaging 50 animal units per section, one individual would destroy 26 percent of the biomass in a single year.

This is very wasteful hunting. Martin estimates that only 5 percent of the assumed animal units per square mile would be needed, provided the carcasses were carefully butchered and utilized. But the Clovis situation was an unusual one, for the colonists arrived in an uninhabited continent. They could apparently afford to be wasteful, for game seemed plentiful. However, they achieved high population densities for only a few generations, when large animals were abundant. Martin believes they destroyed 26 percent of the mammal biomass on the "front" every year, under conditions of explosive

The Clovis People and their Forebears 193

population growth. "There was insufficient time for the fauna to learn defensive behaviors," says Martin, "or for more than a few kill sites to be buried and preserved for the archaeologist." The result was a human population crash following the big-game extinctions.

Vance Haynes, like many other scientists, has no problems with a rapid rate of human movement through the Americas, for, as he says, 1,000 years is about 40 generations. The immigrants were people who were accustomed to pursuing big-game species that had a low density per square mile, and covered large distances each year. The land was virgin; there were few, if any, human competitors.

However, Haynes modifies the Martin hypothesis with a climatic overlay. As the transition to post-glacial climate progressed, water-table levels fell over much of North America. Many streams ceased to be perennial, reliable waterholes were in shorter supply. The large mammals suffered increased stress and were far more vulnerable to hunting, for they clustered at the few remaining springs. Mammoth were still to be found, but the hunters had to cover far greater distances to take their prey. This would have accelerated the southward movement through Central and South America.

Haynes disagrees with Martin about the dramatic population explosion that accompanied these movements. He believes the human density at the "front" was always low. Instead of a population explosion, then a crash, there was a slow growth of human populations, one that brought neighboring bands together in cooperative hunts and led to far greater cultural diversity in later centuries.

Other scientists take the climatic argument even further. They believe that the much drier conditions at the end of the Ice Age led to mass starvations in game populations and eventual extinction. Gary Haynes of the Smithsonian Institution has studied the composition of modern African elephant populations relative to mammoth-bone assemblages dating to the very end of the Ice Age in North America. He argues that some sites, such as Lamb Springs, Colorado, where humans did not kill the mammoths unearthed at such sites, contain a higher proportion of younger beasts. This may superficially reflect a vigorous population. In fact, says Haynes, the Lamb Springs mammoths were probably under severe stress from harsh droughts, which led to the deaths of prime animals if modern analogies from Africa are anything to judge by.

The debate over extinctions will be difficult to resolve, largely because we lack what one might call the "smoking gun," the archaeological culprit in the form of kill sites with varied animals represented, or the geological or palaeontological evidence of devastating environmental change. Martin's only approach is to produce more and more evidence of the contemporaneous disappearance of ecologically different animals, from precisely dated sites. Fortunately, so-called "tandem accelerator mass spectrometers" have made radiocarbon dating less destructive by requiring less than a gram of test material. This has enabled Martin and others to date prized fossil finds, including some horns of the now-extinct Harrington mountain goat from caves in the Grand Canyon to a little more than 11,000 years ago. These goats were found in association with the bones of the likewise extinct Shasta ground sloth. Martin believes that these very different creatures vanished at the same time, animals that could be expected to have responded quite differently to climatic stress, if any had occurred. Indeed, a change that was unfavorable to goats might have favored the sloth and vice versa. Thus, he argues, big-game hunters caused both species to disappear from the Grand Canyon simultaneously.

The mountain goat dates do not prove that humans decimated the Ice Age megafauna, but they are significant because they are a first step in dating the changeover precisely. Once dozens of such occurrences are documented, we may have a clearer perspective on Martin's hypothesis.

In New Zealand, human predators clearly decimated the population of vulnerable birds in historical times. The mass extinctions of big game in late Ice Age Australia, on the other hand, have thrown up as many possible explanations as the American megafaunal collapse. But there is a growing consensus that Australian extinctions resulted from a combination of new ecological conditions and human predators, who hunted big game in an opportunistic way, taking animals that offered the best short-term yield. In time, the combination of both agencies, and other factors, caused impoverishment of the Australian fauna – and a greater diversity of human subsistence activities. It is likely that just as complicated a set of circumstances spelled the extinction of the American megafauna. Perhaps humans were involved. They

Australian extinctions: Sthenurus *is one of several species of kangaroo that died out at the end of the Ice Age in a megafaunal collapse comparable with the demise of American big-game animals.*

may well have accelerated the disappearance of the great Ice Age animals of the Americas. They may even have delivered the final *coup-de-grâce*, setting the stage for a new chapter in prehistory that saw people adapt to the full diversity of arctic, temperate, and tropical environments in the Americas.

The First Americans

Human beings had colonized vast areas of the Americas by the time the big game vanished, perhaps helped on their way by Clovis hunters. This was the closing episode in a grand Ice Age drama that had begun hundreds of thousands of years earlier, and tens of thousands of miles from the Great Plains of North America.

The question of the first peopling of the Americas remains one of the burning issues in modern archaeology. Any attempt to find a consensus among practitioners is fruitless; there are too many competing points of view, based as much on gut feelings as on hard scientific facts. But it is possible, as we have shown, to build up a broad picture that accommodates the most reliable evidence, and casts doubt on the wilder theories and more dubious sites.

The peopling of America was part of a long, complex process that started in Africa. Here humankind emerged in the tropical savannas, then spread into more temperate latitudes perhaps as early as a million years ago. These *Homo erectus* people used fire, and adapted to quite severe winter conditions. But neither they, nor early *Homo sapiens*, nor the Neanderthals, appear to have settled in extreme arctic environments – the chilly plains of Siberia and northern Asia that were the gateway to the New World.

About 40,000 to 35,000 years ago, fully modern humans – *Homo sapiens sapiens* – emerged. These were people with vastly enhanced intellectual skills and the technology and ability to communicate that were needed to conquer the arctic. They soon hunted their way north and east into Siberia and northwest Asia, onto the lowlying, dry steppe-tundra of Beringia. They crossed the Bering land bridge on foot, perhaps during the last cold snap of the Wisconsin glaciation between 25,000 and 15,000 years ago. Judging from the Bluefish Caves finds, they may have reached Alaska by 15,000 years ago.

Archaeology gives no firm answer as to exactly when human beings then spread south of the Wisconsin ice sheets. But it is likely that, as the glaciers retreated, hunters pursued big-game animals along the ever-widening corridor between the Cordilleran and Laurentide ice caps to reach the North American plains sometime between 14,000 and 12,000 years ago. There are even hints of human settlement as far south as Brazil and the Andes by the same period – a possibility that fits in with Paul Martin's hypothesis of a rapid, 1,000-year colonization of the Americas from north to south (although the older data he worked from suggested that colonization began somewhat later).

The Clovis people appear 11,500 years ago and are the first securely dated Americans. But their origins remain something of a mystery. If their advanced big-game hunting culture evolved indigenously on the Great Plains, then we have still to find the earlier Plains sites that will demonstrate the link. In the meantime it seems plausible enough to suppose that their skills had been honed by millennia of living in the extremes of the arctic north. Unleashed in an unpopulated, but game-rich, continent, the new settlers may have become superpredators. At first the hunters prospered in a land of unsuspecting mammals. The bands proliferated. But then game became scarcer. The superpredators accelerated the process of extinction, allowing the megafauna no evolutionary time to adjust to warmer conditions. Within a few centuries, most large mammals had vanished for ever, leaving only the bison for the American Indians to prey on.

PART FIVE

THE GREAT DIVERSITY

"For a long time everyone spoke the same language, but suddenly people began to speak in different tongues. Kulsu [the Creator], however, could speak all of the languages, so he called his people together and told them the names of the animals in their own language, taught them to get food, and gave them their laws and rituals. Then he sent each tribe to a different place to live . . ."

Maidu Indian Creation Myth from California

ARCTIC OCEAN

SIBERIA

CHUKCHI
SEA

BERING
SEA

BEAUFORT
SEA

GREENLAND

BAFFIN
LAND

Ipiutak

Norton
Bay

ALASKA

Yukon R.

Mackenzie R.

HUDSON
BAY

LABRADOR

NEWFOUNDLAND

ALEUTIAN
ISLANDS

Anangula

QUEEN CHARLOTTE
ISLANDS

CANADA

N. Saskatchewan R.

NORTHWEST

Prince Rupert

Namu

ROCKY

Head-Smashed-In

COAST

Ozette

Seattle

Columbia R.

Hanson

Casper

Agate Basin

Hell Gap

Scottsbluff

Lindenmeier

GREAT

MOUNTAINS

PLAINS

Missouri R.

Koster

Serpent
Mound

Ohio R.

Cahokia

PACIFIC

CALIFORNIA

Hogup Cave

Danger Cave

Lovelock Cave

Gatecliff Rockshelter

Olsen-Chubbock

Arkansas R.

Folsom

Arkansas R.

Tennessee R.

EASTERN

WOODLANDS

Spiro

Mississippi R.

OCEAN

Santa Barbara
Channel

Mesa Verde

Chaco Canyon
(Pueblo Bonito)

Colorado R.

Garnsey

Crooks Mound

Moundville

FLORIDA

ATLANTIC

OCEAN

Rio Grande

GULF OF

MEXICO

MEXICO

GULF OF
MEXICO

Mexico City

*North America after the Ice Age. The Great Diversity included bison hunters on
the Great Plains, the complex societies of the Northwest Coast (a high-ranking
Tlingit is shown wearing ceremonial robe and headdress), kayak-paddling Eskimos
of the far north, and farmers of the East (a tattooed Virginia Indian of the
Carolina Sounds; compare plate 6).*

CHAPTER TEN

The Bison Hunters

Our original journey may be over, but the story of the prehistoric Americans continues for many thousands of years, raising further intriguing questions. What happened to the first settlers? How did they adapt to environments where Ice Age mammals were no longer to be found? Did the huge variety of human societies found in the Americas by European settlers evolve from Paleo-Indian roots alone? "The Great Diversity" is the sequel of first settlement, the story of how the native Americans built on the achievement of their ancestors.

The Clovis people may have helped to bring about the demise of the mammoth and many other Ice Age beasts, but they did not kill off all the big animal species. A handful survived to provide quarry for future hunters, and the largest and most plentiful of these was the bison. For over 10,000 years the successors of Clovis pursued these magnificent animals on the Great Plains, creating in the process a culture that gives us our closest insight into the big-game-hunting way of life. First-hand accounts by European settlers of Plains bison hunters in historic times help to fill out the picture conveyed by archaeology.

But what was it that enabled the bison to escape the fate of so many other big-game animals at the close of the Ice Age?

Why Did the Bison Survive?

The steppe bison, *Bison priscus*, flourished widely in northern Eurasia during the later Ice Age. This long-horned beast was well adapted to the arid continental steppe with its seasonal extremes. It had evolved so that it grew to the utmost during the short spring and summer, and relatively little in winter when food was scarce. Compared with, say, the domestic ox, the steppe bison's modern descendants have increased digestive efficiency to cope with the high-fiber, low-nutrient dead grass of winter. They are also efficient at grazing even in deep snow.

Bison colonized central North America long before the Wisconsin glaciation. The primeval forms reached enormous sizes, with horns spanning 6 feet

(2m) from tip to tip. The smaller Wisconsin long-horned form, *Bison antiquus*, was distributed mostly between Alberta and Texas, but also as far afield as California and Florida.

After the Ice Age, European bison decreased rapidly in body size as well as in numbers. In North America, bison became more abundant, although also decreasing in body size. A northern post-glacial type, *Bison occidentalis*, invaded the Great Plains and came into contact with the much larger *antiquus* form. From their genetic mixing evolved the Plains bison, *Bison bison*.

Bison succeeded where other animals failed because they adapted to become short-grass feeders as this type of grassland expanded in post-glacial times. When the Ice Age megafauna vanished about 11,000 years ago, a vast tract of arid grassland extended from the frontiers of Alaska to the shores of the Gulf of Mexico. This was the "Great Bison Belt," which lay in the rainshadow of the western mountains. It was dominated throughout the year by the dry mid-Pacific air mass. Most rain fell, and still falls, in spring and early summer, supporting short grasses that keep much of their biomass beneath the soil. This retains moisture at the roots, providing high-quality nutrients in the dry autumn and into the winter. The short grasses made the Great Bison Belt the optimum bison habitat in North America.

It was not only in their diet that the bison adapted to the expansion of the short-grass belt. Northern ungulates like *Bison priscus* had a very short spring calving season, for the young had to be reared before the next harsh winter. *Bison bison* has a much longer rutting season that covers several months. There is no climatic vice to constrain them, for the short-grass range is quite nutritious even in severe winters. As bison adapted to the short grasslands, their winter mortality declined, the breeding season lengthened, and they became much less selective eaters. So they flourished while other large mammals came under increasing stress. The people who preyed on the mammoth and other Ice Age species turned to bison hunting instead. By 10,500 years ago, these animals are the dominant species in all archaeological sites throughout the Bison Belt.

North America's Great Plains cover an enormous area, from the Rockies in the west to the Eastern Woodlands near the Mississippi. They stretch from Canada in the north to Mexico's Rio Grande in the south. People tend to think of the Great Plains as a homogeneous area, but a closer examination reveals many subtle differences. Rainfall patterns vary greatly, increasing as you move eastwards. The short grasses of the west give way to taller species, then to lusher vegetation as you approach the Eastern Woodlands. The landscape seems drab and monotonous to the traveler, until one comes across a stream bed or waterhole. They are like desert oases, totally changing the aspect of the country. These microenvironments were vital to both animals and humans. Here bison and other game rolled in dirt wallows and drank from perennial springs. Here they sought shade under trees on hot summer days, and shelter from winter blizzards in February. The hunters who preyed on the bison could only survive by a careful, planned utilization of the Plains' complex ecosystem.

The Plains supported a sparse population of hunters and gatherers, some of them probably only seasonal visitors. Judging from analogies with historic Plains Indian societies, each band had a well-defined hunting territory, where the hunters knew their plant and animal resources intimately. These prehistoric peoples occupied thousands of temporary camps through the generations. A single band would leave hundreds of "archaeological sites" behind them in the course of a generation of constant movement. Only a tiny fraction have survived for archaeologists to probe, and only a handful of those provide detailed information about the bison hunters, let alone diagnostic artifacts. Perhaps the best-known sites come from the Northwestern Plains, a huge area covering parts of southern Montana, Wyoming, western South Dakota, Nebraska, and northern Colorado. They provide the best insight into prehistoric Plains life.

The Archaeology of the Plains Hunters

The bison hunters had to carry everything with them: food supplies, dwellings, infants – and weapons. The most important weapons were wooden spears tipped with detachable foreshafts and stone projectile points. The hunters used atlatls – the throwing sticks – to increase the velocity and range of their spears. The stone projectile heads were flaked on both faces, and carefully thinned and ground at the base for ease of hafting and to prevent wear on the haft binding. Such projectile points have become the hallmark of the prehistoric Plains. At least seven major forms are known, with names like Folsom, Scottsbluff and Hell Gap after the places where they were first identified, and all of them are apparently descended from the fluted Clovis

Three of the major types of Paleo-Indian projectile head that succeeded the Clovis point: left to right, Folsom, Scottsbluff, and Hell Gap. The largest shown is about 4 in. (10 cm) tall.

point. The number of head types and sites proliferate after 10,000 years ago, perhaps reflecting increasingly specialized bison hunting, or more diverse hunting and gathering activities in mountain and foothill areas.

Do the various point types relate to separate Paleo-Indian cultures, as some archaeologists believe? George Frison's experiments with replicas suggest not. He has shown that each weapon outfit was a very individual thing. The relationship between arm length, throwing stick length, and the length of the foreshaft was one that varied from hunter to hunter. Presumably the weight and shape of the projectile head varied in the same way.

Lithic expert Jeffrey Flenniken likewise maintains that the "archaeological point types" are meaningless in cultural terms. He has manufactured thousands of Paleo-Indian point replicas of every known form. He has also conducted controlled experiments with live feral goats to test the effectiveness of the "archaeological" types used to classify the stone heads as indicators of different Paleo-Indian cultures. His "hunters" used wooden spears with three different forms of stone head hafted with sinew and pitch into hardwood foreshafts. These were mounted in turn into softwood spear shafts 6.56 feet (2 m) long. The "hunters" separated two large adult male goats from a winter herd and trapped them in the snow. They were quickly killed by five assailants using hand-thrown spears. As the animals moved, foreshafts broke off, points snapped inside the moving body. Quickly, the hunters "reloaded" their wooden spear shafts with new heads mounted in hardwood foreshafts slung from their wrists. This meant they were not encumbered with a handful of long spears as they hunted their quarry.

After the hunt, the salvagable points were rejuvenated by pressure flaking. Flenniken tried to replicate the same shape as before. In most cases, the repaired head was transformed from one "archaeological" type to another during repair, showing the "cause" of the variations in form. Some were turned from points into knives by systematic resharpening and shaping, too. What is important, he believes, is not the finished points, but the stoneworking techniques used to make them. These technologies changed slowly over the millennia, and are likely to be a far more accurate reflection of changing Plains cultures than mere projectile points.

One way archaeologists can reconstruct this technology is through controlled replication of ancient artifacts. Every year, Flenniken runs a lithic technology school, at which he teaches students to make a wide range of stone artifacts, including Clovis and Folsom points. Flenniken can turn out a complete Folsom replica in forty minutes. He teaches his students that flint knappers have a language of their own, a language that revolves around the raw material and the techniques they use, not the ultimate uses of the artifact. He teaches them pressure flaking in such a way that "you have to feel when it's [the flake] going to come off." "Get that topography down and they run," he says of his delicately fashioned projectile point blanks. Flenniken's experiments bring us about as close as we will ever get to the way prehistoric stoneworkers operated.

Both Flenniken's researches and formal artifact classifications by veteran researchers like Marie Wormington confirm that Paleo-Indian artifacts, whether bifaces, projectile heads, scrapers, or simple knives, were versatile tools used for a wide variety of basic tasks. Another line of research has focussed on such phenomena as the angles of working edges on stone tools, as well as the edge wear resulting from prehistoric use. One good example of this approach comes from George Frison and Bruce Bradley's excavations at the Hanson site in northeast Wyoming. This Folsom location was unusual, for it was a living site rather than a bison kill, although Frison believes that the kill site lay close by. Excavations in the 1970s revealed three hard-packed areas that could be circular lodge structures, radiocarbon-dated to at least 10,000 years ago. Hanson yielded a highly informative collection of stone tools. These Folsom stoneworkers used disc cores and bifaces as the basis for most of their tools. Although they made projectile heads, scrapers, and other finished artifacts, they made much use of unretouched flakes. Hundreds of these bear signs of edge wear resulting from momentary, very specialized use. They were just the most convenient pieces of stone around.

The Hanson stone artifacts represent only a tiny part of what must have been a highly varied technology. Frison believes that the inhabitants had butchered their bison into very small parts. They ate some of the meat fresh, dried much of the rest, extracted oil and marrow from the carcasses. Then they used their stone scrapers for hide preparation – fleshing, rubbing, and smoothing. These hides were vital – as clothing, containers, lodge covers, perishable aspects of their material culture that never appear in archaeological sites. Sewn clothing was important during the cold months. The people may have used sharp-edged stone flakes to cut out clothing, also to fashion bone needles like the one that came from the Hanson site.

Stone choppers, notched flakes, coarse saw-edged artifacts and sharp-edged scrapers were essential for removing bark, trimming branches, and other rough woodworking. The hunters undoubtedly fashioned spear shafts and foreshafts with much more delicate stone tools. Their projectile heads were ineffective without secure foreshafts and finely balanced wooden shafts.

Frison speculates that the Hanson Folsom site was occupied by a band of several families for a short period of time. Judging from much later, 1,800-year-old prehistoric occupations from caves in the area, the Folsom people, living in a basically similar environment, made use of a wide range of woods. These may have included pine, willow, chokecherry, and box elder, all of them requiring different woodworking techniques, and used for different purposes.

Plains material culture evolved slowly over thousands of years, and eventually changed beyond superficial recognition. The many forms it took are a reflection of ever-more effective ways of driving and hunting bison in a dry plains environment.

Bison Hunting

Our knowledge of Paleo-Indian life is a matter of archaeological shreds and patches, of clues obtained from excavations all over the Plains. Folsom, Midland, Plainsview – the cultural names proliferate, warning us that generalization is dangerous. Nevertheless, there are certain broad similarities between Paleo-Indian bison hunters throughout the Plains, and between these people and their successors, which enable us to capture some of the flavor of their nomadic way of life.

The Folsom site itself in New Mexico was a place where several bison were killed within a short period of time, probably in late fall or early winter. We still do not know whether the hunters at this classic location killed just individual beasts or cooperated with neighboring bands in mass hunts that netted many more animals. Most likely a combination of solo and cooperative hunting ensured a regular supply of bison flesh.

The Lindenmeier site 46 miles (74 km) north of Fort Collins, Colorado, was a favored Paleo-Indian camp site for generations about 9,000 years ago. It lay in a small, well-watered valley near the Plains grasslands. Archaeologist Ed Wilmsen believes Lindenmeier was visited by at least two semi-autonomous groups, who cooperated in bison hunts and regular social transactions. There are few other known Folsom kill sites. The best evidence for mass bison drives comes from later Paleo-Indian sites, but the methods used there were probably developed in earlier millennia.

Most excavated Paleo-Indian artifacts come from ancient bison kill sites that tell us much of the drama of the hunt. They may also give us a false impression of Plains life as a kind of macabre orgy of mass game drives. Such hunts sound like an easy way of obtaining meat supplies, but in fact driving bison is difficult, especially on foot. Left alone, the bison soon become less fearful of humans. Subjected continuously to pursuit, they become unpredictable. If Paleo-Indians were like historic bison hunters, then they must have watched the herds closely. They were probably careful to pursue them intermittently, giving them time to calm down. Modern bison can be driven short distances of a mile or so without trouble. Then they start to break and run. It is almost impossible to stop them. A skilled hunting band could subject a quarry herd to gentle influences by gradual movements over several days that brought them close to the selected trap or jump. The hunters were careful to "arrange" the topography of the approach to the trap in such a way that the animals would stampede in a predictable direction. Decoys were undoubtedly used. Men dressed in bison hides approached the unsuspecting animals within a few yards to drive them in the right direction. The hunters would run and shout, even wave skins, until the sheer weight and mass of the herd forced the leaders over a precipice to their deaths, or into a corral lying under a low cliff.

The hunters apparently returned to the same location repeatedly. At Agate Basin in eastern Wyoming, George Frison excavated a natural basin crossed by steep arroyos (gullies). One arroyo is about 10 feet (3 m) deep at the site, but gets deeper downstream. The hunters maneuvred groups of ten to twenty animals into the bottom of the arroyo several hundred yards below natural "knickpoints" in the gully, places with steep cliffs where bison could be trapped. They drove the frightened animals upstream towards the cliff face. The herd leaders balked and threw the other beasts into confusion. The hunters pressed close, setting about the trapped animals with spears as they tried to jump out of the arroyo. Once the killing was over, the Indians butchered their quarry. Some they cut up at the kill site. Others they dismembered at a processing site on a gentle slope nearby. Judging from the teeth in the bison jaws, most of the animals were mature females with younger animals. They were probably killed within a month or so of calving time, probably in late February or early March.

George Frison's excavations at the Casper site, also in Wyoming, showed how the hunters used a parabolic sand dune with steep, loose sides to trap a herd of about 100 bison during a late autumn hunt. They drove the animals into the curve of the steep-sided dune, animals that may have been grazing near a natural pond nearby. The bisons' hooves sank into the loose sand. As they panicked, the hunters moved in to kill them as fast as they could. They knew there was much more to trapping bison than just blindly shooting into the herd until the animals died. Each hunter, or group of hunters, would select a single animal, and aim deliberately to thrust their spears through the rib cage into the heart. If a cow or her calf were killed, chances were that the other animal could be bagged as it stampeded.

Frison found eighty-one fragmentary or complete projectile heads in the Casper site. Since he wanted to know how the hunters had used them, he took a typical Hell Gap projectile point that had been found on the surface and mounted it with a sinew binding in a slotted pine shaft, bonding the haft with pine pitch. Unlike Flenniken, Frison did not use a foreshaft in his experiment. He thrust and threw the 11-foot (3.3-m) long spear into the carcass of a domesticated ox. Frison found that an extremely hard thrust would penetrate the rib cage and hide, sometimes even reaching the heart, causing an extremely lethal wound. Sometimes the point would break, but it was easily sharpened for reuse later. The haft was strong enough not to break, even after the hardest thrust. A skilled hunter with a long spear that gave him some distance from his quarry could deliver very lethal blows in short order without endangering himself unduly.

The Olsen-Chubbock Hunt The famous Olsen-Chubbock site 16 miles (25.7 km) southeast of Kit Carson, Colorado, provides dramatic proof of the effectiveness of Paleo-Indian bison hunting about 8,500 years ago. In 1958 and 1960, University of Colorado archaeologist Joe Ben Wheat excavated a bone-filled dry gulch, where the carcasses of 152 bison lay in three buried layers. Wheat used the tightly wedged skeletons to reconstruct the hunt. The hunters had located a large herd and stalked them for several days. They stayed downwind, and slowly moved the bison into a strategic position at right angles to the arroyo. Then they stampeded them into the gully. The leaders arrived at the steep edge, hesitated, but were swept on by the animals behind them. They tumbled into the arroyo and were immobilized and trampled to death. Ten animals were pinned with their heads down and their rumps up. Two lay on their backs. Most of the skeletons lay where they had perished, facing south. Given Wheat's reasonable assumption that the hunters approached the herd from downwind, the wind would have been blowing from the south on the day of the hunt.

Once the stampede was over, the hunters faced many hours of arduous work. First, the Indians maneuvred the carcasses into a position where they could be cut up at the edge of the arroyo. The bison wedged at the bottom were butchered where they lay. The butchers worked in teams and cut up several animals at once. They rolled the animals on their bellies, slit the hide down the back, and pulled it down the flanks to form a carpet for the meat. Then they removed the blanket of prime flesh on the back, the forelimbs, shoulder blades, hump meat, and rib cage. They probably ate the tongues and some internal organs as they went along, piling the bones in the arroyo. Judging from historic Plains Indians practice, they dried the tough meat to make powdered pemmican.

Pemmican is a mixture of dried meat and fat, exactly what its Indian name signifies (*Pemmi* – meat, *kon* – fat). The artist Paul Kane saw Plains people make pemmican many times in the mid-nineteenth century. "The thin slices of dried meat are pounded between two stones until the fibres separate," he wrote. "About 50 lbs. of this are put in a bag of buffalo skin, with about 40 lbs. of melted fat, and mixed together while hot, and sewed up, forming a hard and compact mass." Pemmican was a highly effective way of storing food for use on the march and during the winter months. Bison drives were as important for their pemmican potential as they were for supplies of fresh meat.

The Olsen-Chubbock hunters butchered 75 percent of the animals they killed, acquiring about 54,640 lbs (24,752 kg) of meat in the process. They also obtained 5,400 lbs (2,449 kg) of fat and 4,000 lbs (1,812 kg) of edible internal organs as well. The meat from this particular hunt may have sustained over 100 Indians for a month or more.

*   *   *

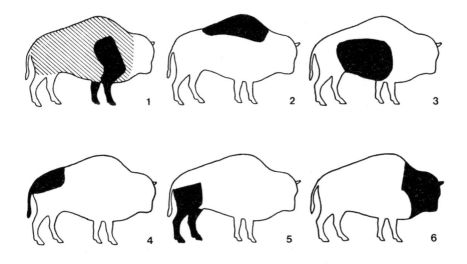

The archaeologist Joe Ben Wheat has reconstructed Paleo-Indian butchery methods on the basis of historic Plains Indian practice and his own excavations at the Olsen-Chubbock site. The hunters skinned the bison down the back to get at the layer of tender meat (hatched area) just beneath the surface. When this was removed, the bison's forelegs and shoulder blades could be cut free (1), exposing the much-prized hump meat (2) as well as the rib meat and inner organs (3). The next step was to sever the spine and take off the pelvis (4) and hind legs (5). Finally the neck and skull were cut away as a single unit (6), their tough meat being dried and converted into pemmican.

Bison Jumps Communal bison hunting on foot reached its greatest prehistoric intensity after 1,400 years ago, during a period that saw the bow and arrow reach the Plains, perhaps from the northwest. The bow had great value as a close-range weapon, but was probably little more effective than the spear unless driven through the ribs. It was apparently adopted quite quickly, but still did not solve the problem of driving and controlling the movement of the quarry. As time went on, the hunters made increasing use of bison jumps, high bluffs approached by long lines of stone piles, over which they could stampede large herds. These drive lines served as markers for the stalkers moving the herd into position.

The famous "Head-Smashed-In" buffalo jump in western Alberta was used for more than 7,000 years. Six streams feed into a shallow basin in the plains surrounded by high ground. A large creek forms the only entrance. More than 500 stone cairns up to a foot (0.33 m) high mark drive lines as much as 5 miles (8 km) long leading to the sandstone cliff that formed the jump. Deep deposits of bison bones lie below the cliff, dating back to as early as 7,400 years ago.

This type of bison drive was still in use when Hudson Bay Company trader Peter Fidler spent six weeks among the Piegan Indians in 1797. He witnessed many bison drives as he camped with them at one of their drive pounds. The hunters killed more than 250 beasts, and would have taken more. But "when the wind happened to blow from the pound in the direction of the tents, there was an intolerable stench of the large number of petrified [sic] carcasses, etc on which account the reason of our leaving it."

Sites like Olsen-Chubbock and Head-Smashed-In represent what must have been relatively infrequent events for Plains hunters. For such mass hunting strategies to be successful, the bison density would have had to reach a critical level, a density only reached at certain times of the year, when patterns of animal migration permitted it. Many communal hunts may have been annual affairs, or conducted after periods of higher rainfall, when the bison population increased. At the Vore site near Sundance, Wyoming, for example, five bison hunts took place between 400 and 410 years ago. If this was a typical experience, then the average hunter may have witnessed a large drive every couple of years or so. Smaller communal hunts may have gone on every year, perhaps conducted at the same spots year after year.

John Speth's excavations at Garnsey, New Mexico, chronicle one such kill. About 400 years ago, a group of hunters visited a small gully where they knew bison would congregate in late March or early April. Instead of just killing every animal on sight, they tended to concentrate on the male beasts.

Plains hunters disguised as wolves creep up on a bison herd in this sketch by the nineteenth-century artist George Catlin. By his day this age-old hunting method was being supplanted by direct assaults from gun-toting horse riders who massacred the animals wholesale.

51 **The Mammoth Hunters** Arizona State Museum's diorama reconstruction of a Paleo-Indian mammoth kill. The hunter on top of the cliff is casting a boulder down on a trapped mammoth, while another approaches the doomed beast. Most of our knowledge of early Paleo-Indian life comes from mammoth kills.

52–56 **Clovis Sites** Many famous scholars have worked on Paleo-Indian sites on the Plains. They include Paul Martin, seen with mammoth bones at Naco, Arizona (*left*), and archaeologist Emil Haury (*bottom*, right figure), working at the final clearance of the prehistoric beasts. Palaeontologist John Lance assists Haury. The Naco mammoth had 8 Clovis points (*center*) in its skeleton, four times the number found with any other such kill. This suggests the animal may have got away from its hunters only to die somewhat later. Vance Haynes (*opposite below*, right figure, with Emil Haury) argues that 4 hunters may have pursued the mammoth, perhaps a fifth of a band population of between 20 and 40 people.

The Lehner site in Arizona is exposed in an arroyo bank (*below*), and includes hearth areas, also the remains of what might be a family unit of 13 mammoths between 2 and 30 years of age, but is perhaps instead a series of individuals culled over a longer period of time. The black layer in the Lehner arroyo wall marks the stratum where the mammoth kills were made.

George Frison is another archaeologist who has excavated many Paleo-Indian sites, including Colby in Wyoming (*right*, Frison on the left, with Bruce Bradley). Here the mammoth hunters left piles of disarticulated bones, perhaps the remains of meat caches for the lean winter months.

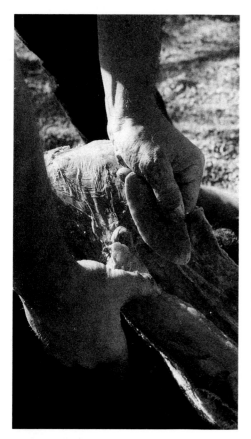

57, 58 How to Skin an Elephant Bruce Huckell of the Arizona State Museum in Tucson took advantage of the sudden death of a circus elephant to conduct some butchery experiments. Like a prehistoric kill, the elephant lay on its side, the right side in this case. The initial skin cut was made with a stone biface, a replica of those used by Paleo-Indians (*left*). Huckell has studied bifaces of equivalent type at the Murray Springs site in Arizona. Numerous clusters of Murray Springs stone flakes were fitted together to reconstruct biface sizes. Much of the stoneworking at that site was devoted to making and sharpening butchery tools. The bottom picture shows the elephant after the left foreleg and three sections of hide had been removed with stone artifacts. The butchery team found that the only way they could turn over the carcass was by using a pickup truck. This suggests that many prehistoric mammoths were only partially butchered, for the hunters would have been unable to turn them over to get at the meat on the other flank.

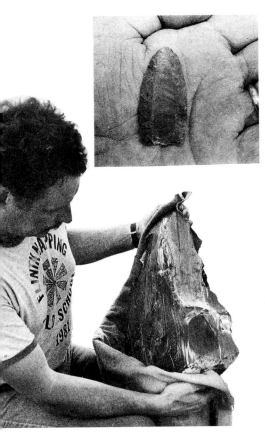

59–64 Making a Projectile Point Lithic expert Jeffrey Flenniken has been manufacturing stone tools since he was a child. Here he demonstrates the making of a Folsom point replica, complete with channel flake (*top left*). The process starts with an obsidian cobble (*top lower left*). This is reduced with the aid of a large hammerstone (*middle left*), the large flakes providing ideal raw material for point manufacture. The chosen flake is now turned into a projectile point blank, using careful percussion and pressure flaking (*middle right*). The final flaking is carried out in the palm of the hand, as the stoneworker removes shallow, parallel flakes from each side of the artifact (*bottom left*). Then the channel flake is removed with a fine punch centered on the base of the point (*bottom right*). This process requires fine judgment to produce a properly thinned point. Flenniken has produced thousands of Paleo-Indian points and believes that many distinctive forms identified by archaeologists are in fact the result of reuse of damaged artifacts.

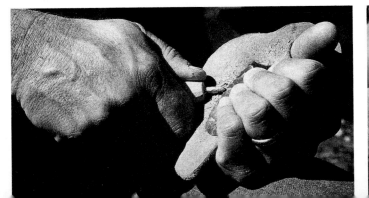

65, 66 **The Bison Jump** A stirring
reconstruction of a Paleo-Indian bison drive
(*left*), based on archaeological sites like the
Olsen-Chubbock location in Colorado
(*below*). Olsen-Chubbock provided minute
details of the drive such as the butchery
procedure used by the hunters, even the
wind direction on the day of the hunt.
Olsen-Chubbock and other sites show that
the hunters only butchered a small
proportion of driven herds, some of them
only for their hides which provided clothing
and shelter.

67, 68 Bison Hunt, Bison Dance The introduction of the horse by the Spanish ushered in a dramatic change in Plains life. By the late eighteenth century, Plains Indians were enjoying a flamboyant culture. Tribes such as the Sioux pursued bison on horseback (*left*, painted by the famous artist George Catlin). The young Swiss artist Karl Bodmer was one of the first to record the Mandan *Okipa* summer ceremony in the 1830s that acted out creation myths and celebrated the coming of the bison (*below*). The final stages of the ceremonial saw initiation rites, ordeals that hardened warriors for extreme trials of endurance.

Speth believes this was because males are in better condition in the spring, and their bone marrow has a higher fat content. Hunters everywhere prefer fattier meat, for it is an important source of energy and essential fatty acids. In spring, such flesh was hard to come by, for the herds were still recovering from the lean winter months. So the hunters selected male beasts at Garnsey, only consuming the choicest parts with higher fat content from the few cows they killed.

Everything depended on an intimate knowledge of the bison, and on the elaborate hunting magic associated with it. In later times, the entire hunt was surrounded by complex shamanistic rituals. These prepared both humans and bison for the hunt, and controlled the direction and conduct of the drive. Such controls were essential, for the success of the kill depended on the animals being kept together in tight formation, pushed at top speed, and headed in exactly the right direction. The hunters hid behind bushes, rocks, and stone piles. They would appear at just the right moment, to keep the panic going. Split-second timing was critical, right to the moment when the bison stampeded over the cliff or entered the corral. There the shaman presided over the slaughter and butchery that followed.

The Coming of the Horse and the Rifle

For more than 10,000 years, big-game hunting flourished on the Plains. The techniques of the chase evolved slowly, as new weapons or driving techniques came into use, or minor cycles of wet and dry weather altered both densities and distributions of bison herds. Human populations were never large. Farming gradually spread from Mexico and eventually came to sustain certain village groups that dwelt near the perennial rivers crossing the Plains. There was constant tension and rivalry between the settled people of the valleys and the nomadic bison hunters of the open plains. The farmers traded with the nomads, but both ways of life were relatively stable, even if there were constant adjustments in village size. This stability would probably have endured, had it not been for the arrival of Europeans and their horses.

In AD 1547, about the time hunters were killing bison at Garnsey, the Spaniard Pedro de Castañeda and his conquistadors reintroduced horses to the Plains. It took about a century for the "mystery dogs," as the Indians called them, to reach the northern Plains. The new animals brought drastic changes to Plains life. For a start, the horse enlarged the range of the hunter, and his ability to carry large quantities of meat. Many more hunters slaughtered many more bison every year. In time the herds moved west across the Plains away from the Missouri River as they were decimated. Their robes and hides were in demand, hunting became harder as the beasts became more wary of humans. The horse did enable the Indians to pursue solitary beasts with great efficiency, but food supplies were always chancy, even at the beginning of the nineteenth century when bison were still plentiful. With such precarious food supplies, the nomads relied on the sedentary villagers of the valleys for grain during the lean months. This in turn placed severe strain on the farmers, for the women were often diverted into preparation of bison hides, raids often depleted granaries, and crop failure brought a village perilously close to starvation.

The nomadic tribes were in a strong position. They could either live off their farming neighbors, or could trade bison meat and hides for grain when it suited them. The nomadic population of the Plains grew as the bison dwindled. Some formerly sedentary groups like the Dakota and Cheyenne became nomads, joining others like the Blackfoot and Comanche, who had been hunting for centuries. The bison belt became an economic battleground, as fierce war parties raided and counter-raided each other's camps, to seize horses and loot food stores in a constant cycle of attack and retaliation.

The changeover to horses, and to some extent to the rifle – a weapon that made people dependent on European traders – led to a chronically imbalanced and unstable way of life. Inevitably this created different cultural values, highly individualistic ones that pitted biological family against biological family, with little concern for the common welfare. Individual fortunes could change almost overnight as a result of a successful raid. The wealth obtained in battle could be used to promote family status. The ranks of individuals changed constantly, as hunter vied with hunter for the allegiance of followers and fellow warriors. A flamboyant, almost frenzied era of Plains life dawned, one where most nomadic tribes believed old age was evil, that it was better for a man to die in battle.

The combination of horses and firearms was a volatile mixture in the hands of ruthless leaders. The Blackfoot of the northern Plains were among the last hunters to receive the horse, in about 1740. They acquired guns from the Cree to the east at the same moment. Living as they did in a strategic position where they could control the spread of horses and guns, the Blackfoot took to the warpath. They became masters of the lightning raid. A war party would swoop down, drive away horses, slaughter people without pity and vanish over the horizon. By 1850, Blackfoot territory extended from the North Saskatchewan River to what is now Yellowstone Park.

The Blackfoot rose to prominence as European fur traders and settlers pressed onto the age-old Plains hunting grounds. But only a few European fur traders witnessed Plains life as it had been before the arrival of the horse and the rifle. Alexander Henry of the North West Company attended an Assiniboine Indian hunt in 1776, just before horses became commonplace. While the women pitched camp by a fenced pound, the chief sent out expert hunters on foot to decoy the animals into the corral. "They were dressed in ox-skins, with the hair and horns. Their faces were covered, and their gestures so closely resembled those of the animals themselves, that had I not been in the

George Catlin captured on canvas a way of life at its zenith. Lured westward by the desire "to rescue from oblivion" the Indians' "primitive looks and customs," in 1832 he traveled 2,000 miles up the Missouri and painted a staggering 135 pictures. Here he has sketched himself at his easel, painting a portrait of the Mandan chief Four Bears.

secret, I should have been as much deceived as the oxen," marveled Henry.

One of the decoyers slipped into camp to warn the waiting hunters. The dogs were muzzled. Men and women surrounded the pound. The herd was but half a mile away, moving slowly and pausing to feed. The decoyers bellowed like buffalo, stationing themselves between the pound and the curious animals. As the bison approached, the men fell back, repeating the call whenever the beasts stopped. The process continued until the leaders were inside the jaws of the pound. Then the hunters pounced as the decoys scrambled for safety. "The oxen made several attempts to force the fence; but the Indians stopped them . . . by shaking skins before their eyes. Skins were also . . . let down by strings, as soon as the oxen were inside. The slaughter was prolonged till the evening . . ." Next day, the chief was presented with seventy-two tongues, as was his ceremonial right.

Fur traders like Henry helped sow the seeds of wholesale slaughter, for they gladly exchanged firearms for beaver pelts. Indians mounted on horseback killed far more bison than they ever had on foot, with bows and arrows. Now white hunters joined the fray, leaving thousands of wasted carcasses rotting on the plains. Like the beaver, the bison began to dwindle. Then the railroads spread over the prairies. Special excursion trains took hunters into a sea of bison. The great herds of thundering animals, with their seemingly inexhaustible supplies of meat and hides, disappeared almost overnight. The last vestiges of the primeval big-game hunting life vanished in an orgy of nineteenth-century musketry. Fortunately, dedicated rescue efforts in the last fifty years have saved the bison from extinction, and now managed herds graze on the plains as their ancestors had done since the end of the Ice Age.

CHAPTER ELEVEN

The Northern World

In the far north, as on the Great Plains, late Ice Age hunting methods survived for thousands of years. But in this circumpolar zone, isolated from the south by dense boreal forests except in coastal regions, ideas and populations flowed freely from west to east, and sometimes back again, linking Eurasia with Alaska and arctic Canada and eventually bringing about long-term changes of great magnitude. Disentangling those changes has been the preoccupation of a dedicated band of scientists in recent decades.

Successors to the Paleo-Indians

The circumpolar zone was a mosaic of environments that could support only a small population of hunter-gatherers per square mile, even under the most favorable conditions. Hardly surprisingly, there were constant seasonal movements of human populations over large distances, of people following migrating caribou, establishing winter settlements in sheltered valleys, taking advantage of seasonal salmon runs. Most of these moves were cumulative, that is to say they brought families to new hunting or fishing grounds that extended ever further into new territory each year. These small-scale population shifts brought different linguistic groups and both terrestrial and maritime peoples to the far north for thousands of years after the arrival of the first settlers, peoples like the Aleuts, Eskimos, and Athabaskans.

Deciphering these prehistoric population movements is an intricate process. The controversies and speculations have continued for generations, and there is little general agreement. One way of highlighting the issues is to use Christy Turner's dental morphologies as a hypothetical framework. We have already discussed his argument that most native American societies are direct biological descendants of the Paleo-Indians, the primeval settlers from Siberia. Turner also believes there were two later migrations of Asian peoples into the New World, which by and large reached no further than the far north and Northwest Coast and never penetrated the rest of the Americas. As we have seen, this scenario receives some support from Gm allotyping which likewise divides American Indians into three groups.

The earlier of the two post-Paleo-Indian waves of immigration, Turner believes, introduced ancestral Na-Dene speakers to the eastern shores of the Bering Strait via the land bridge. These were forest hunter-gatherers from Siberia, perhaps people of the later Dyukhtai tradition. They used a toolkit that was effective against thin-skinned animals, one with microblades represented by Alaska's Paleo-Arctic tradition. Turner believes this crossing occurred at the very end of the Wisconsin glaciation, between 14,000 and 12,000 years ago, just before the land bridge was severed. According to his scheme, these ancestors of Na-Dene speakers spread south and west to Kodiak Island, to the Pacific Northwest coast (Tlingit Indians are part of the Na-Dene group of languages), and far into the interior, where they became the Athabaskans. Later, some of them split off and moved southward to become the modern-day Navajos and Apaches.

Turner argues that another migration brought the maritime "Aleut-Eskimo," the ancestors of the later Aleuts and Eskimos, to Alaska via the exposed continental shelf off the Kamchatka Peninsula, and the southern shores of the land bridge. Along the way they learnt how to hunt seal, otter, and other sea mammals. The "Aleut-Eskimo" may have arrived sometime after the Paleo-Indians, but before the land bridge was severed about 12,000 years ago. Unfortunately for Turner's theory, all traces of these people are submerged under modern high sea levels.

The Turner migrations have caused intense discussion among arctic archaeologists, who have raised all kinds of theoretical, and archaeological, objections to them. His population movements are just one of many competing models. The questions at issue are complex. How long ago did arctic maritime culture evolve, the kind of adaptation associated with the historic Aleuts and Eskimos? Did Aleuts and Eskimos originate separately from the Na-Dene, or did the latter evolve as a hybrid between Paleo-Indians and Aleuts and Eskimos? And can we be certain that these groups, starting with the Paleo-Indians, actually arrived at different times? No one can pretend that there are easy answers.

Aleuts and Eskimos*

If Turner is right, Na-Dene speakers spread widely through the interior and along the Northwest Coast early in post-glacial times, while the ancestors of the Aleuts and Eskimos arrived somewhat later. The origins of these last two distinctive peoples is one of the most controversial questions in arctic archaeology. Did they evolve in Alaska itself after the Ice Age, or are they descendants of much earlier maritime people, as Turner believes? And when did the two cultural groups split off from one another?

* The term *Inuit* is commonly used when referring to Eskimo peoples, especially in Canada. I have retained Eskimo here for clarity, and because most of the literature still uses the label.

Linguistically speaking, the Aleuts and Eskimos belong within a single Eskaleutian language group, divided into different groups about midway down the Alaskan Peninsula. The differences between Eskimo and Aleut are about as profound as those between Russian and English within the Indo-European language group. Eskimoan is spoken over a far wider area than Aleut dialects – from northeastern Siberia and the Alaskan Peninsula right across the northern latitudes of Canada into Greenland. There are several dialects, but linguists believe the differences between them are such that the settlement of the Arctic Ocean coast was a comparatively recent development.

Scholars unite in believing that the Aleuts and Eskimos are the most Asian of all native Americans. Their skeletons and genetic makeup are said to be readily distinguishable from those of more southerly native Americans, except where intermarriage has taken place. Eskaleutian languages have Siberian roots, too, and are related to the Chukchi language spoken in the far northeast of Siberia.

Despite Christy Turner and Nicholai Dikov's claims for the Ushki Lake sites on the Kamchatka Peninsula, thought to date to as early as 14,000 years ago, no specific archaeological ancestors for the Aleuts or Eskimos have been identified from Soviet territory. About the only candidates are tundra forest hunters like the little-known Sumniagin tradition of the Middle Lena Valley, who also hunted sea mammals, just like their Alaskan Paleo-Arctic cousins.

In all probability, the distinctive maritime Aleut and Eskimo cultures emerged from Paleo-Arctic roots on the islands and coasts of the Bering Strait, then spread far and wide.

Only a few sites provide some clues, including the famous Anangula village on an islet off Umnak Island in the eastern Aleutians. This coastal settlement was occupied about 8,800 years ago and in later millennia. Its inhabitants lived in elliptical houses about 15 feet (5m) long, fisherfolk and sea mammal hunters who spent much of their lives in boats. Anangula was probably like dozens of other coastal villages of the time, a more-or-less permanent base that was occupied for generations. The simple stone artifacts from the site seem to belong within the Paleo-Arctic tradition. Physical anthropologist William Laughlin claims that Anangula was the home of ancestral Aleuts. Unfortunately, the site was abandoned long before the first unmistakable traces of historic Aleuts of about 3,000 years ago and more recent centuries, so his claims have not been verified archaeologically.

The Aleutian Islands are situated in an area dominated by the Pacific maritime climate. Even the most sheltered bays rarely freeze, the climate is cool, and often cloudy and foggy, with few, if any, trees and only the open seas as a resource. The Aleuts were sea-mammal hunters in open water, expert boatmen from adolescence. They hunted in two-man kayaks, skin boats steered by one man while another speared the quarry. The Aleutian seas are rich in seals and sea lions, in sea otter that live off upwelling currents along the Aleutian Trough. Even short, fast-flowing streams support annual runs of sockeye and other salmon species. From earliest times, the inhabitants of this isolated island chain were expert maritime hunters and fisherfolk, people with ancestral connections with their Eskimo neighbors that weakened as each adapted to quite different ecological circumstances.

While the Aleuts developed from a cultural isolation in their remote archipelago, the Eskimos spread over thousands of miles of arctic mainland landscape. Aleut and Eskimo probably diverged before 4,000 years ago, by which time the Eskimo had developed a versatile culture supported by hunting of land and sea mammals, as well as both fresh and saltwater fish. This new culture existed on the coastlines that finally stabilized at broadly their modern configurations about 5,000 years ago.

The Qualities of the Arctic Hunter

Maritime hunting and foraging in the arctic required people to be as adept on water as they were on land. They needed bone, stone, and wood technologies not only to hunt caribou and moose, but to shoot down birds and venture offshore on ice and water. By the time sea-mammal hunting became important, Stone Age hunters were probably using small skin kayaks, which they literally wore like waterproof clothes, sealing themselves into the cockpit with their outer garments. Their canoes were made with the same technology that protected them from hypothermia. In summer, they may have carried heavier loads in larger skin boats, ancestors of the Eskimo *umiak*. When the ground froze, the dog sled became indispensable. This mobility on water and land turned the Bering Strait from a barrier into a natural highway on calm days when skies were clear and waters free of hazardous ice floes. It also meant that the maritime adaptation spread far and wide along arctic shores, then diffused eastward across the far north as far as Greenland.

We can gain some insights into how these arctic hunters survived by looking at modern Eskimo societies. Richard Nelson is a perceptive anthropologist who has spent years living among Eskimo and Athabaskan communities in Alaska. He studied the small village of Wainwright on the Bering Strait, a village where people still hunted sea mammals at all seasons of the year. Nelson found that the Eskimo had certain mental attitudes that were specifically adapted to the arctic hunt. After a year of traveling and hunting with the Wainwright people, he received an overwhelming impression of self-assurance and competence among the hunters. They knew their environment intimately, not only the resources, but a body of more arcane knowledge as well, knowledge that they might use only once in a lifetime, during an emergency. They were highly observant, and willingly shared knowledge with others. It followed that those with the most experience were the most respected, and those who listened to them rarely questioned what they were told.

Eskimos have to be in excellent physical condition, and have an impressive ability to withstand wet, cold, or arduous conditions for long periods of time. This mental and physical stamina makes the hunter persevere, even under conditions of extreme hardship. Self-sufficient, always equipped efficiently and lightly, and thorough about every task, the Eskimo is economic in expenditure of energy, always planning ahead. On his trip, Nelson observed the men pushing empty sleds in front of them over the ice when seal hunting. They knew that dragging a seal carcass over spring ice is an arduous task. Experience had shown a sled did the job with less effort.

The Wainwright people seemed to have what Nelson calls an "unspoken concept of percentage risk." They would not, for example, hunt walrus where there was a danger of being trapped by moving pack ice. By the same token, they were constantly alert – for polar bear while butchering meat, for an unexpected seal that could be shot as a bonus. In an environment where hypothermia and exposure can kill one in minutes, the Eskimo are adaptable, ready to improvise solutions with minimal resources. Several anthropologists have seen them build makeshift sleds of frozen meat to get them home. This adaptability includes an ethic of cooperation – assistance is readily given, meat is shared. Eskimo notions of obligation and reciprocity are entirely different from those of Europeans, for example. Gratitude is rarely expressed. There is an unspoken understanding that the giver will one day receive payment in kind.

Eskimos have adapted in other ways to the realities of their daily lives. They laugh at their own misfortunes, for humor seems to make it easier for them to overcome mishaps, certainly more effectively than anger. And by saying nothing, the Eskimo will go to extraordinary lengths to avoid conflict. In prehistoric times, they lived in small groups, in tiny winter dwellings where close contact was unavoidable. Aggressive behavior is self-destructive under these circumstances. So the Eskimo have learnt not to disagree with one another, to avoid conflict.

It makes no difference that Nelson lived among twentieth-century Eskimo using firearms. The methods of dispatching and transporting game may have changed, but the realities of the environment had not. We can be sure that prehistoric Eskimos and their predecessors displayed the same qualities.

Norton, Dorset, and Thule

For thousands of years, the predecessors of the modern Eskimo hunted caribou and musk ox, with apparently only occasional forays to the coast. Their prey was so dispersed that their hunting took them across the tundra shelf and ice of the Arctic Ocean as far as northern Greenland by 4,000 years ago. By this

The interior of an arctic winter dwelling on the Kamchatka peninsula, from Captain Cook's "Voyage to the Pacific" of 1784. Needing to live in close proximity for many months, the arctic peoples developed social patterns that avoided conflict.

time, the peoples of the Bering Strait far to the west were relying much more heavily on sea mammals. Many became skilled walrus and whale hunters, living in substantial, permanent settlements close to sea-mammal breeding grounds. The hunters lavished care on bone and ivory maritime hunting weapons like harpoon heads. By 2,000 years ago, the "Norton tradition," named after Norton Bay, where the first collections were made, flourished throughout the Bering Sea area, a culture that balanced hunting, fishing, and sea mammals. The Norton developed on both shores of the Bering and Chukchi Seas, some of the settlements reaching impressive size. Some 400 house sites survive near Cape Nome, Alaska, alone. Many people lived in square, permanent dwellings for much of the year. They excavated their houses as much as 20 in. (50 cm) into the soil, giving them short, sloping entryways and pole-and-sod roofs. These features provided much better insulation against the extremes of the arctic winter. Some communities erected larger ceremonial houses, the *kazigi* that doubled as a men's dwelling. It was here that the people carried on their discourse with the forces of the supernatural, with songs, recitations, sometimes with magic and mummery. The most adept among them were shamans, not only healers, but individuals capable of foretelling the future and interpreting the world around.

By the beginning of the Christian era, Norton people hunted over a enormous area from southern Cook Inlet to the Bering Sea and the Alaskan Peninsula, all the way to Canada's Firth River in the Yukon Territory. "Ipiutak" dwellings, named after the first site where they were found near Point Hope, document a highly developed version of the Norton tradition. They are famous for their elaborately decorated harpoon heads, antler arrow points, and knife handles. The artists fashioned not only utilitarian artifacts, but engraved ornamented beads, openwork carvings, animal figures, and miniature human figures.

In the early first millennium A D, "Thule tradition" peoples in the Bering Strait abandoned land mammal hunting and relied almost entirely on the ocean. ("Thule" is a Greek and Latin name for a distant land in the far north.) The coasts, islands, and waters of the area were far more productive than the land, once people had the technology to exploit them efficiently. Skilled boatmen, the Thule people became expert walrus and whale hunters and adopted a series of technological devices that greatly increased their ability to survive in the far north.

The Ipiutak culture, which evolved in northern Alaska around AD 350, is famous for its carvings on bone, ivory, and antler. This engraved ivory "mask" was found in a burial at Point Hope, and probably once had a wooden backing.

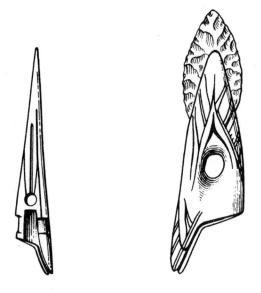

Ipiutak toggle harpoon heads, the largest about 4 in. (10 cm) tall.

Thule technology relied not only on bone and ivory, but on polished slate to make projectile heads, knives, and the *ulu*, a transverse-bladed knife often mounted in a carved ivory handle. The hunters refined a large skin boat known as the *umiak*, a vessel capable of carrying large numbers of people and their possessions to new villages or offshore to hunt. The captains of these vessels, the *umialiks*, acquired considerable social prestige in the large whaling settlements that now flourished by the coasts. They became what anthropologists call "big men," individuals respected for their hunting and leadership skills, as well as ritual prowess.

The *umiak* was a stable platform for harpooning whale and walrus offshore. The hunters used a new form of "toggling" harpoon, a weapon with a grooved base to which a line and foreshaft were attached. The harpoon would detach itself inside the body of the quarry and twist and turn at the end of the line, causing the animal to bleed, and keeping the head secure in the wound. The new design enabled the hunter not only to spear, but to retrieve, sea mammals away from the land. Using the new weapon, an ice hunter would secure his harpoon line to a convenient ice chunk. The boatman offshore would let out at least 180 feet (54 m) of line to allow the animal to run. The crew would hold on as the whale towed the boat and tired. Hunting walrus required great expertise. Fierce, young animals would approach the boat from beneath, turn on their backs, and rip out the bottom in a few seconds. So the paddlers had to be nimble and constantly alert. The walrus was often regarded by modern Eskimo as a mysterious, somehow malevolent animal. "Walruses are like people . . . they hear you when you talk," say the Eskimo. Nevertheless, the walrus was worth the risk. Like bison, they yield a great deal of meat and require two people to butcher them. They were of vital importance to the Thule people, who not only used the hide and meat, but fashioned artifacts and ornaments from their bone and ivory as well. Both fish and walrus meat were valued food for the dog teams that now pulled sturdy Thule sleds over the ice and snow even in the deepest snow. Thule housebuilders developed the cold trap door for their semi-subterranean dwellings, a real advance in permanent house construction that helped retain warmth even in the most savage sub-zero weather of midwinter.

The Thule people were active all year-round, and relied heavily on sewn clothes made with bone and antler needles. Ice-edge sealing goes on during the winter months to this day, on days when the thermometer may fall as low as -50 deg. F (-45.5 deg. C). The men remain by offshore ice leads for as long as eight hours on end. Although they keep warm by running and staying active, they wear layers of carefully tailored clothing. Some traditional garments are still in use and as effective, if not more so, as modern cold-weather clothing. The Eskimo hunter often still wears one or more hooded caribou-fur parkas, the inner one with the fur turned inwards. Two parkas are needed in very cold weather, but only then, for the well-fitted hide garments are both light and exceptionally warm. Wolverine fur around the hood forms a breathing tunnel of warm air that keeps frostbite at bay.

Efficient footwear is even more important, especially the *ugurulik*, a caribou and sealskin boot with a tough seal hide sole. The knee-length uppers are formed from caribou leg skin, carefully cut as far down the hooves as possible, then sewn to the sole with braided sinew and a strip of sealskin in between. Seal oil prolongs the life of the sole and keeps it waterproof, while a sinew drawstring round the uppers keeps snow out. Socks and caribou-skin liners keep the wearer warm.

All this clothing is not only carefully fitted, but dried out whenever the hunter returns home. Skin garments are liable to rot and shed their fur if not dried, and, in any case, the arctic hunter is well aware of the added safety of warm, dry clothes. We can be sure that the Thule people had clothing as effective as that worn before the advent of the European parka.

Thule was such a successful adaptation that it exploded across the north, reaching Greenland from the Bering Strait in little more than a hundred years, between the tenth and eleventh centuries A D. During these centuries, the climate warmed up considerably. There was less spring and autumn ice offshore. So migrating whales, as well as walrus and bearded seals, could move freely over a much wider path through the Bering and Chukchi Seas on their way to summer feeding grounds in the Beaufort Sea and Canadian archipelago. Many archaeologists believe the Thule tradition spread into the eastern arctic as fleets of kayaks and *umiaks* provisioned entire villages with a few kills, where hitherto land-based communities could barely make both ends meet. Archaeologist Moreau Maxwell says that one whale kill every two years would provide everyone in a small settlement of the time with about 8.8 lbs. (4 kg) of meat and blubber a day.

By the twelfth and thirteenth centuries A D, the Thule people had settled on the islands and coasts of the central Canadian arctic, along the north shores of Hudson Bay. They subsisted off seals, fish, and land mammals in Baffin Land, northern Greenland and Labrador. The sea-mammal hunters were not the first inhabitants of the eastern arctic. The descendants of much earlier caribou and musk-ox hunters had lived in the region for at least 2,000 years. They hunted sea mammals as well, subsisting in a harsh world beset by unpredictable supernatural forces. Their bone and wood carvings of sea mammals and bears reflect this world. The most respected and experienced hunters among these "Dorset" people were shamans, story-tellers and ritual leaders, who enlivened the long winter nights with magic, healing, and lengthy discourses.

The warmer, open-water conditions did not last long. Cooler temperatures about A D 1200 forced the Thule folk to demonstrate their remarkable capacity to adapt to radically new conditions. Many of the easterners moved onto the winter ice in snow houses and hunted seals at breathing holes through the pack ice. In summer, they pursued caribou and caught river fish. Some of them

A Greenland Eskimo clutching a seal – a nineteenth-century illustration.

The Norsemen (Vikings) reached Greenland a thousand years ago, but by the late fourteenth century their settlements had been abandoned in the face of a worsening climate and attacks from native Eskimos. This nineteenth-century woodcut of an Eskimo standing victorious over a dead Norse chieftain preserves a memory of conflicts from the long-distant past.

even moved onto the Barren Lands east of Hudson Bay to hunt caribou year-round and abandoned the ocean all together.

Conditions were better in the west, where the return of pack ice made whale hunting from ice loads viable once more. Great whaling villages flourished at places like Point Hope and Point Barrow, and other favored locations, some of which were to survive as settlements into the twentieth-century world. Meanwhile, other versatile Thule groups penetrated far inland, up the Yukon, Kuskokwim, and other great rivers.

As Thule culture was realizing its full potential, some eastern bands came in touch with strangers from without, rough seamen who arrived from over the eastern horizon in large wooden boats. These were the Norsemen, who had crossed to Greenland and then to Labrador and Newfoundland by AD 1000. They found the Eskimo tough, troublesome people – *skraelings*, "barbarians," they called them. For more than two centuries Eskimo and Norsemen traded iron for ivory and seal meat. Then the Norse settlements in Greenland collapsed in the face of the deteriorating climate, and perhaps attacks from the local people. The Eskimo were forgotten until the mid-sixteenth century, when new generations of Western explorers penetrated their arctic homeland.

The Northwest Coast

To the south, Alaska passes imperceptibly into the Pacific Northwest Coast. This is a shoreline built on vast proportions, with rows of mountains and foothills receding from the densely forested coast. Spruce, hemlock, and cedar cover the shore to within a few feet of the breakers. Even offshore islands are tree-covered. Only here and there are sheltered bays with shelving beaches and low rocky ledges, where prehistoric fisherfolk could settle and beach their canoes in sheltered water. The dense vegetation and ease of movement by water concentrated human populations by oceans and rivers, not so much inland.

The coast looked very different at the end of the Ice Age. In Wisconsin times, it was an icebound shore. As the Cordilleran ice cap retreated, mountain glaciers receded, snowlines climbed to higher elevations, and sea and land levels changed until they reached more-or-less modern heights by 5,000 years ago. The first vegetation to establish itself was open woodland, which flourished on the lowlands around Puget Sound, where the modern city of Seattle now stands. These woodlands lasted from about 10,000 to 5,500 years ago, when conditions may have been warmer and drier than today. Later, high rainfall brought closed spruce and cedar forest to the Northwest's islands and coasts. These changes had profound effects on human settlement.

The Pacific Northwest was, at best, very sparsely occupied during the first few millennia of post-glacial times, for much of it was still glaciated. We do not, of course, know anything of the coastal populations, for their homelands are long buried under the sea. It may be that the first settlement of the newly exposed coastal regions came from the north, originating from Paleo-Arctic peoples in southern Alaska. This hypothesis – it is nothing more – fits well with Christy Turner's dental morphologies. He claims the Pacific Northwest was settled by native peoples who were different from other American Indians. Turner identifies Northwest Indian dental characteristics in central British Columbia as early as 4,000 years ago, but believes the traits will be found in much earlier sites one day. The first Northwest people were forest hunter-gatherers, he believes, people quite distinct from the Aleuts and Eskimos, whose maritime adaptations developed in the north considerably later. Other scholars disagree and argue that both Eskimos and Northwest Indians had a common ancestor in Alaska, suggesting that the two groups branched off in the New World, instead of arriving at different times.

The Northwest Coast was an environment of relative plenty. More than 300 edible animal species populated the sea shore alone. Five species of salmon appeared in inshore waters each year, crowding upstream to spawn. With such a diversity of food supplies, even if there were occasional periods of scarcity, Northwest Coast societies evolved in elaborate and complex ways. With dense vegetation inland, the people chose sheltered coves for their villages. They spent most of the year in one spot, in places where canoes could land safely and food was abundant. Their houses reflected a new permanence, substantial rectangular plank dwellings with substantial log frames. Many families maintained frames at several locations. They simply moved their house planks from one place to the next on a pair of large canoes.

This type of more-or-less settled existence based on relatively predictable maritime food sources may have come into being about 5,000 years ago, perhaps much earlier. The earliest certain human camp site on the Queen Charlotte Islands dates to about 7,000 years ago (with hints at occupation several thousand years before that). It would have necessitated canoes, and it persisted for at least 2,000 years. A coastal site at Prince Rupert on the nearby mainland dating to about 5,000 years ago contains barbed bone harpoons that can only have been used against marine mammals. By 4,500 years ago, large shell middens had accumulated at Namu and elsewhere, a clear sign that people were exploiting the coasts. Bone projectile points, harpoon heads, and other artifacts characteristic of Northwest Coast sea-mammal hunters are now preserved in large numbers because of the alkaline content of the shell middens. The same trend toward coastal settlement is found along the shores of the Strait of Georgia.

By 3,000 years ago, rich sea-mammal and fishing cultures were flourishing all the way from the Kodiak area of southwest Alaska to southern British Columbia and northern Washington State, just as they were in Aleut and Eskimo country further north. The Northwest Coast societies were a new form of American Indian society, quite different from the scattered, egalitarian cultures of the resource-poor interior. They were ones in which wealth and social status assumed a vital importance.

The centuries around 5,000 years ago seem to have been of special significance, a catalytic moment in American Indian life. We can only speculate that stabilizing sea levels and post-glacial climate as well as population increases gave a sudden impetus to primeval hunting and gathering skills. In many areas – the arctic north, the Pacific Northwest, the California coast, the river bottoms of the Midwest, in Labrador and coastal New England, to mention only a few – much more elaborate hunting and foraging societies developed, in which individual wealth and prestige, and that of larger kin groups, were of paramount importance. These societies shared certain common features, which they evolved quite independently of one another. All flourished off a broad spectrum of foods, but exploited some (notably fish, sea mammals, waterfowl, or wild vegetable foods) very intensively. They were societies in which powerful individuals, ritual and political leaders, became respected chieftains, normally intermediaries with revered ancestors and the spiritual world. These were the people who controlled trade for essential commodities and prestige objects, those who redistributed vital resources throughout society, contracted alliances with neighbors and waged war. It was they who regulated ceremonial life, the rituals that assured the continuity of existence and the continued bounty of the environment.

The writings of early travelers like Captain James Cook tell us much about how later Northwest Coast societies were organized. The Indians enjoyed an elaborate ceremonial life and a rich material culture, based on a fundamentally simple technology. The damp, oceanic climate provided easily worked, softer woods like red and yellow cedar, fir and spruce. The woodworkers had no metal axes or saws, so they felled, split, and worked logs with polished stone, shell, and bone-edged adzes and chisels. Some of their finest woodworking artistry was reserved for their canoes. These craft had to be both seaworthy and strong load carriers, capable of moving house planks, heavy loads of salmon, or entire families. In time, the canoe builders, like whale hunters, became respected specialists in Northwest society. Renowned ancestors, mythical animals, and humans adorned the bowls, boxes, masks, and totem poles made by later Northwest peoples. The carvers emphasized themes that depicted family histories and genealogies, and incidents, both real and fictional, that enhanced the prestige of the ancestors. Perhaps the most famous art objects are the great totem poles, commemorative posts and portals that were once set up in front of their villages.

Few coastal villages have been excavated, with one notable exception – the Ozette site on the Olympia Peninsula of Washington State. About 500 years ago, a catastrophic mudslide buried a village of plank houses that nestled in the shelter of Ozette island on the Pacific coast. Everything was buried in a damp blanket: hearths, baskets, nets, fish hooks, wooden boxes, harpoons, even fragments of looms, ferns, and cedar leaves. Richard Daugherty of Washington State University spent over ten years excavating the remains of four cedarwood longhouses and their contents. He used high-pressure hoses and sprays to clear the mud away from the delicate woodwork and other waterlogged artifacts. One house was 68 feet (21 m) long and 46 feet (14 m) wide. Hanging mats and low walls divided the dwelling into small rooms, with separate hearths, cooking platforms, and sleeping benches. The inhabitants' possessions lay where they had been abandoned – bows and arrows, wooden bowls still impregnated with seal oil, even conical rain hats made of spruce roots. Daugherty found a cedar whalefin carving inlaid with 700 sea-otter teeth. No one had seen one of these objects since the time of Captain Cook.

The interior of a Northwest Coast Indian house on Nootka Sound in the eighteenth century, with elaborately carved supporting posts at the rear and racks overhead for drying salmon. Dried fish was one of the staple foods in winter.

The Makah Indians live in the Ozette area today. In the 1920s they abandoned the site where the prehistoric village was found. Tribal traditions go back some 200 years into the recent past. The Ozette excavations traced Makah history much further back into prehistoric times. The village lay close to a place where migrating whales came close inshore. Numerous whalebones from the excavation testify to the skill of the Makah canoe captains in pursuing these large mammals.

Many known nineteenth-century villages like the Haida settlement at Ninstints in the Queen Charlotte Islands were built atop much older middens. Victorian government surveyors took photographs of these villages before they were abandoned in the wake of a smallpox epidemic in the late nineteenth century. Many were veritable forests of carved totem poles. The genealogies depicted on these poles commemorated different kin groups and their ancestry. Northwest villages were inhabited by "privileged ones" and commoners, as well as war captives, slaves who were little more than chattels. Everyone was born a noble or a commoner, but there were subtle gradations within each broad social class. The noblest wore elaborate clothing and ornaments. They traditionally occupied a special place in the house, often close to the back wall. The social distinctions between nobles and commoners were modified by close kin ties that linked the highest and lowest members of society with common bonds. Everyone had a stake in the wealth and privileges of the kin group as a whole. Hereditary rank was important, but even the wealthiest and most important people had to share their riches with others.

Each village accumulated reserves of dried fish and sea-mammal meat as well as fish oil that tided it through the lean winter months. The people also spent a great deal of time accumulating wealth and social prestige. Individuals might acquire dozens of canoes and furs, but they, like houses, land, and prestige objects such as hammered copper ornaments, were actually group

A totemistic design from a ritual blanket given away at a Northwest Coast potlatch – the ceremonial feasts at which kin leaders reinforced their status by extravagant displays of wealth and generosity.

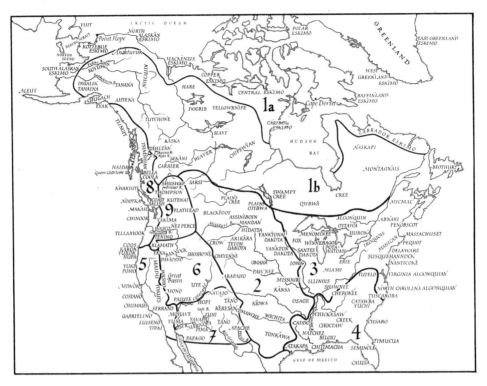

*The native tribes of North America, together with the main regions: 1a Arctic,
1b Subarctic, 2 Great Plains, 3 Eastern Woodlands, 4 Southeast, 5 California, 6
Great Basin, 7 Southwest, 8 Northwest Coast, 9 Plateau.*

property, a means of enhancing the prestige of the group among its neighbors.
The display and conspicuous consumption of this wealth was a primary
objective of Northwest society. These displays, commonly called "potlatches"
– a Chinook Indian slang word for "giving" – were dignified ceremonies held
by a kin leader and his fellow kinspeople. They invariably marked an
important event, like the marriage of a high-ranking person, the birth of a
noble heir, or the assumption of a right to a title or a crest. Speeches were
delivered, songs and dances enjoyed. Gifts were exchanged, perhaps a feast
was held. A potlatch was far more than a party. It was an official function,
where myths were reenacted, titles and ranks reinforced, and wealth
redistributed through society as a whole. Those who attended were expected
to reciprocate in the future. Everything reinforced not only the power of the
individual, but the power of competing kin groups, and the welfare of society
as a whole.

One finds many different social mechanisms with the same vital role in
many of the American Indian societies that developed in the temperate

latitudes south of the retreating Wisconsin ice sheets. This was a different world, one where periods of profound, broad environmental change led to a great variety of regional traditions, some of which reached remarkable levels of social complexity.

CHAPTER TWELVE

Epilog

The vast continent that lay south of the Wisconsin ice sheets was a world to itself, a magnificent diversity of environments populated by only a few thousand human beings 11,000 years ago. Today the five-hour flight from New York to California provides a lesson in the startling variety of temperate North America. You fly over rolling eastern woodlands, over the open patchwork of farm and grassland of the Plains; then comes the west – mountains, valleys, deserts, ancient lake beds, vast canyons, and rugged coasts. For nearly ten-and-a-half millennia, the successors of the first Americans prospered in this diverse continent without significant contact with the world without. By the time Europeans came, millions of native Americans occupied every conceivable form of landscape, from tropical rainforest to high desert, from grassland plain to boreal forest.

North American climate and sea levels seem to have stabilized close to their modern configurations after 8,000 years ago. Conditions became increasingly drier. The eastern United States was forested. Modern pine-oak vegetation moved into the southeast about 5,000 years ago. Desert scrub covered the Southwest by the same date, while chaparral and coastal brush flourished in the dry environments of California. This appears to have been the critical moment when human populations started to grow more rapidly. Almost everywhere in temperate North America the number of archaeological sites mushrooms within a millennium. The stage was set for rapid cultural, economic, and social change in many areas, change that was still climaxing as European explorers and colonists arrived in the New World.

Desert and Woodland Hunter-Gatherers

The disappearance of Ice Age animals made big-game hunting on any scale an impossibility outside the Great Bison Belt. The scattered human populations living to west and east of the Plains in desert and woodland environments learnt instead to hunt smaller, more solitary animals like the white-tailed deer and moose, and to exploit a broad spectrum of other foods, among them nuts, fish, and shellfish. The first human inhabitants lived in small, widely dispersed

239

bands, wandering over enormous tracts of relatively unproductive territory. They would sometimes congregate in large seasonal camps when local resources were plentiful.

In time, the richest areas filled up. No longer could families split off into new country with impunity when critical population densities were reached. They had no option but to settle down within restricted environmental zones and to make increasing use of local resources. More diversified and balanced diets developed out of necessity, making use of hitherto neglected or underexploited foods like shellfish or nuts. These new strategies spawned a battery of new artifacts: polished milling and nutting stones, steatite and clay containers, and fishing gear like harpoons, hooks, and net weights.

This more intensive foraging way of life developed from about 9,000 years ago to around 4,500 years ago, when post-glacial temperatures reached their maximum. The desert west saw people living a highly mobile life, returning to certain favored locations again and again for thousands of years.

The strategy worked well for the people who lived in Danger Cave, in Utah's eastern Great Basin. They occupied the cave from Paleo-Indian times, before 11,000 years ago, right up to the Christian era. Hogup Cave nearby was a base for desert hunter-gatherers from about 8,500 years ago to as recently as 500 years ago. Both sites flourished because the Great Salt Lake lay within easy reach. The dry deposits of each cave have yielded highly perishable artifacts, including sandals, baskets, netting fragments, and bone tools. At first the cave-dwellers exploited fish and waterfowl, but as the lake rose and flooded the marshlands after 3,000 years ago they turned increasingly to vegetable foods and small mammals.

Gatecliff Rockshelter in Nevada's Monitor Valley contains 40 feet (12.2 m) of habitation layers separated by zones of naturally deposited, sterile debris. David Hurst Thomas of the American Museum of Natural History dissected the site and found that it was occupied by small parties of visiting hunters as early as 9,000 years ago. There were temporary hunting camps in the shelter where people butchered game about 6,000 years ago. Three millennia later the inhabitants established a base camp at Gatecliff, from where they hunted mountain sheep and collected wild vegetable foods. Gatecliff was still in use 600 years ago, when ancestors of the present-day Shoshoni Indians were butchering mountain sheep in the shelter.

In western Nevada, Lovelock Cave provides a magnificent chronicle of lakeshore life in the Great Basin between about 4,500 and 150 years ago. The Lovelock people overlooked the Humboldt-Carson sink, a lake environment rich in fish and wildfowl. They hunted these with bows and spears, using extremely lifelike reed-duck decoys, some painted, some covered with fully feathered skins. Human coprolites show that over 90 percent of the foods consumed came from the lake area, including wetland grasses, fish such as chub, ducks, and mudhens. The plant remains come from every season, so

Lovelock, with its bird nets and basketry, was probably occupied year-round.

Some of North America's most favored environments lay in the bottomlands of the Mississippi River and its tributaries, where slow-moving rivers created a paradise for waterfowl and bottom fish. Nut-bearing deciduous trees like oak, hickory, beech, and chestnut abounded in and around the river valleys, which were exploited from as early as Paleo-Indian times.

Koster in the Illinois River Valley of the Midwest is one of the most famous archaeological sites in the New World. Stuart Struever of Northwestern University excavated the multi-level settlement with the aid not only of a multidisciplinary team of specialists, but of hundreds of volunteer undergraduates and high-school students, also enthusiastic amateur archaeologists from all over the world. Koster lies at the base of some 150-foot-high (45.7-m) bluffs overlooking the Illinois River, a place near to ancient Clovis hunting grounds, for their characteristic points have been found close by. People started living seasonally at Koster about 9,500 years ago. At least thirteen occupation levels representing more than twenty-six short and long occupations ensued in the millennia that followed.

The seasonal settlements prospered and the Indians stayed in larger numbers. By 7,500 years ago, a one-and-three-quarter-acre village flourished at the same site. The inhabitants erected much more substantial, rectangular huts, and exploited the floodplain more intensively. By this time, the Illinois River was a single main channel, whose natural levees ponded swamps and slowly drained backwater lakes. The Koster people could prey on thousands of migrating ducks each fall, spearing and netting bullfish and other sluggish fish in the shallow waterways all year. In late summer and fall, they collected tens of thousands of hickory nuts and acorns. They also harvested local plants, and perhaps even deliberately cultivated them, including such species as maygrass, and sumpweed, an edible swamp plant. By 6,000 years ago the Koster people had developed an extremely effective hunting and gathering economy. Their food yields rivaled those of agricultural villages in very fertile areas.

The act of deliberately planting, then harvesting, wild vegetable foods is often regarded as a very dramatic invention. It was not, for every hunting and gathering band is aware that seeds germinate and that wild vegetable foods have to be harvested during certain weeks of the year. The big step comes when people grow dependent on cultivated crops for most of their diet, a moment that came long after the first planting of wild foods to supplement natural yields.

Initially, then, cultivated plants were a very minor component of the diet. They had but limited nutritional value and required considerable energy to harvest and prepare. However, the new "gardens" were a source of easily stored commodities that could be used in lean times. Richard Ford of the University of Michigan believes that as populations rose and mobility declined, so people became more and more vulnerable to unpredictable nut harvests. Cultivated seeds could have made up the deficiency, a bank account, as it were, of edible foods that could be tended by child-bearing women, children, and old people, the most sedentary members of the community. Perhaps, too, the availability of such resources kicked off further population growth, especially when maize cultivation began some 1,500 years ago. Corn did not become a staple until much later, about 1,000 years ago.

Tending gardens and harvesting wild seeds drastically reduced people's mobility. Base camps became more permanent villages. The inhabitants also developed much more elaborate storage techniques to hoard vital stocks of dried fish and wild vegetable foods. At the same time, they fostered closer contacts with their neighbors through trade networks that handled foodstuffs and other commodities, items that compensated for local shortages. In time, these barter networks burgeoned into intricate social links that joined communities tens, if not hundreds, of miles apart. It may be that many trading links were not only those of economic need, but of social obligation as well, where distant chieftains, members of the same powerful clan, exchanged ceremonial gifts on a regular basis, the gestures of reciprocity between them assuming vital symbolic importance as the generations passed. Inevitably, perhaps, those who controlled trade networks became powerful economic, spiritual, and political figures. Just as in the Pacific Northwest, individual power and prestige melded with kin loyalties to produce more elaborate societies that were a far cry from the simple bands of Paleo-Indian times.

Farmers of the Eastern Woodlands

After 4,000 years ago, we find increasing signs of a preoccupation with burial and with life after death, of a new ideological foundation for local societies in the Eastern Woodlands. Between about 2,650 years ago and the beginning of the Christian era, a dynamic village culture flourished in the central Ohio Valley, that influenced communities as far northeast as New Brunswick in Canada and deep into the southeast. These "Adena" people lived in an egalitarian society, where some individuals achieved an enhanced social status. Perhaps these revered individuals were tribal shamans, who controlled long-distance trading networks that brought Yellowstone obsidian from the Rockies to the east and Midwest, Lake Superior copper into the southeast, and Gulf Coast shells to the Ohio Valley. The same networks handled everything from metals and shells to exotic objects used as status symbols for the living and the dead. Eastern peoples already enjoyed a longstanding tradition of burying personal possessions with the dead. As village life became more complex, so the number of individuals entitled to status symbols would increase, stimulating a constant and ever-increasing demand for more exotic artifacts to replace those buried with the dead.

Adena society, like its humbler predecessors, was built on a bedrock of kin loyalties. The people commemorated their dead not only with imposing burial mounds, but with extensive earthworks that follow the contours of flat-topped hills, enclosing areas as much as 350 feet (106 m) in diameter. These were probably ceremonial compounds rather than defensive earthworks, the "fortifications" so beloved of early "Moundbuilder" theorists. The nearby burial mounds were communal graves. The most important individuals lay in log-lined tombs, their corpses smeared with red ocher or graphite, and accompanied by finely carved soapstone pipes and tablets engraved with curving designs or kin symbols like birds of prey. Most other people were cremated, then buried in the mound.

About 2,400 years ago, a new, and very pervasive, "Hopewell" exchange system, known to archaeologists as the "Hopewell Interaction Sphere," emerged in the Midwest. We know nothing of the rituals that commemorated the dead, except that Hopewell-period burial mounds are much more elaborate than their Adena predecessors. Elaborate burial practices were widespread over the south and southeast, too, and persisted long after the Hopewell decline. For instance, Crook's Mound in Louisiana, far south of the Hopewell heartland, dating to between 1,500 and 1,000 years ago, rises 40 feet (12 m) high and is more than 98 feet (30 m) across. Over 165 people were buried within a large earthen platform before another 214 people were deposited on it and covered with a large mound. The new cultural patterns were so successful that they spread into Wisconsin, deep into Ohio, and to the edge of New York State, as well as to Louisiana. For nearly 1,000 years, the Midwest experienced a flowering of artistic traditions, revealed by the fine art objects buried with powerful Hopewell leaders. The living buried pipe bowls and axes as gifts to the dead. The deceased took cherished weapons with them, also clan symbols like thin copper sheets fashioned into head and breast ornaments, and mica sheets cut into striking, lustrous silhouettes of human figures, bird talons, and abstract designs. Most of these artifacts were manufactured by people working near major outcrops or raw material sources. They were distributed through the same centuries-old networks that carried foodstuffs and tools throughout Hopewell country.

After 600 years of brilliant efflorescence, the Hopewell societies went into decline. No one knows quite what happened, but population densities may have risen to the point that they strained the limits of the ancient economic system, causing competition between different trading networks. This ruptured long-established economic and political relationships.

Gradually, however, populations rose again and a new and spectacular culture took shape. The powerful successor to Hopewell was the so-called Mississippian culture. It began to emerge around AD 700 along the central Mississippi and the major floodplain corridors formed by its tributaries, into the Ohio, Tennessee, Arkansas, and Red Rivers, and their branches. These were areas of arable soil that were fertilized by spring floods just before planting season. The Mississippian people not only grew maize, beans, and squash, but relied heavily on hunting and gathering. Fish and migrating waterfowl may have formed over half the diet of many floodplain villages.

As long ago as 1818, a gentleman named Henry Brackenridge wrote a letter to Thomas Jefferson about the great earthworks in the Saint Louis area that we now know to have been built by the Mississippians. He suggested that a prehistoric population roughly the size of contemporary Philadelphia had lived in the area – some 54,000 people. They must have had a "powerful chief" and a highly structured society to be able to erect such mounds as those at Cahokia across the river from the city. But it was not until the 1920s that serious archaeological investigations began at Cahokia, excavations that caused part of the great site to be designated a state park in 1924. By the 1960s, Midwestern archaeologists from many universities had excavated at Cahokia. They calculated that perhaps 10,000 people had actually lived in and around Cahokia's more than 100 mounds. They established that the central area of the site was occupied from about AD 700 until 1300. The largest temple platform had been built in about fourteen stages between AD 900 and 1150-1250. This was "Monk's Mound," named after the community of Trappist monks who dwelt on its summit in the early days of white settlement. Today Monk's Mound rises dramatically 110 feet (33.5m) above the floodplain – as tall as a modern ten-story building – and covers 16 acres. Millions of basketfuls of earth went into the original construction of this gigantic mound. At the summit once stood a thatched temple, looking down on the east end of an enormous central plaza. Around the plaza rose other mounds, temples, storehouses, and the homes of the elite. The entire ceremonial area covered more than 200 acres and was stockaded with a log fence complete with gates and watchtowers. Numerous lesser communities lay outside the walled inner core of Cahokia, each with their own plazas and shrines. The pole-and-thatch houses of the residential areas extended over 2,000 acres, each cluster of houses surrounded by a patchwork of cultivated land.

Cahokia lay in the north of Mississippian territory, strategically placed to take advantage of local supplies of salt and fine grained cherts. Another great center lay at what is now Moundville, Alabama. Dozens of small centers and large villages existed between the two. More than just sacred places for annual ceremonies of planting and harvest, the major settlements were markets and political focal points, governed by small numbers of very powerful individuals, kin leaders turned chieftains, who owed their power not only to hereditary kin affiliations and control of lucrative trade routes, but to their religious associations as well.

The latest researches provide further hints as to the nature of Mississippian society. The most strongly centralized authority was found in small "core areas," where powerful chieftains ruled over single valleys or groups of

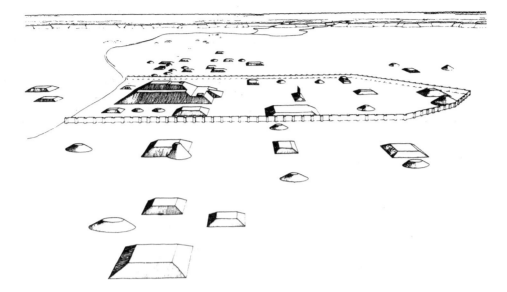

View of Cahokia, the great Mississippian stronghold in Illinois, as it might have appeared around AD 1300. At the center lay a palisaded main plaza with a giant temple platform ("Monk's Mound") and sixteen smaller earthworks. Outside the enclosure were 100 or more other mounds.

valleys, with, more controversially, some larger "provinces," presided over by much more important individuals. The political geography was rarely clearcut, as rival chieftains vied with one another for prestige and influence. Judging from later Spanish accounts, their successors lived in a state of chronic intergroup rivalry. The Mississippian world was one of constantly shifting alliances between neighbors, of short-lived wars and exchange of goods prestigious and utilitarian over short and long distances.

The elusive beliefs of the Mississippians were intimately entwined with the institution of chiefdomship. The architecture of both major and minor centers seems to have been laid out to instill in the beholder a sense of power and awe. Mississippian experts speculate that three separate, interlocking cult institutions with different artifacts and features supported chiefly power. One was a clan-based cult institution, associated with divine beings and warfare, represented by distinctive "effigy" pots and ritual motifs. Another was a communal cult associated with platform mounds that served the ritual needs of a broader social group. A third cult centered on a priesthood that had a responsibility for ancestor worship and burial rites. Perhaps these priests acted as mediators between the chiefly and community ritual affairs.

Our only clues to Mississippian religion come from surviving art objects, many of them from centers like Spiro in Oklahoma. Pots, large sea shells and other ceremonial artifacts display pervasive design motifs – human hands with an eye in the palm, sunbursts, or weeping eyes. Some experts believe that a distinctive "Southern Cult" associated with these motifs flourished throughout Mississippian territory. Perhaps the most famous Mississippian cult objects are the so-called effigy jars, which bear human faces, some with signs of face painting and tattoos. Others represent heads of sacrificial victims, their eyes closed and mouths tightly shut. Often the effigies are depicted weeping, perhaps denoting a connection between tears, rain, and water in Mississippian cosmology.

Whatever the origins of its theological beliefs, the Mississippian was an indigenous North American society conceived on a new, more grandiose, scale, in its way as spectacular as any of the magnificent Mexican civilizations that were its contemporaries. Its food supplies were diverse and stable enough for the new society to flourish until the sixteenth century. When Spanish conquistador Hernando de Soto journeyed from Florida to the Mississippi between 1539 and 1542, he encountered fortified communities with temple mounds and plazas. His plundering soldiers marveled at caches of copper-bladed weapons, battle axes, and clubs in chiefs' shrines. They watched "fine-looking" Indians in a fleet of Mississippi canoes that "appeared like a famous

Two conch shell engravings (left, from Spiro, Oklahoma; right, from Etowah, Georgia) portraying eagles in human form. Mississippian artists developed a style with common motifs that experts believe represents a widespread "Southern Cult" connected with ceremonies held on giant temple platforms.

armada of galleys." Unfortunately, the Spanish brought smallpox with them. The dread and unfamiliar disease decimated village after village and weakened Mississippian culture beyond recovery. Nevertheless, when Europeans colonized the south in the seventeenth century, they came up against a powerful alliance of fifty large Creek Indian settlements in what is now Alabama and Georgia. To the north lived the Cherokee, who still numbered more than 60,000 people, distributed in at least 100 settlements. The first European missionaries to work among them recorded dimly remembered folk memories of moundbuilding in earlier centuries.

Our last glimpse of the Mississippian comes from the writings of the French explorer Le Page du Pratz, who spent some time at the Great Village of the Natchez Indians in 1720. By chance Natchez Chief Tattooed-serpent died

The French explorer Le Page du Pratz gives us our last glimpse of the Mississippian culture. In 1720 he witnessed the funerary rite of the Natchez Indian Chief Tattooed-serpent. The dead man was carried on a litter to his temple high on an earthen mound. There he was buried with his wife and retainers, who had been strangled beforehand.

during his stay. Le Page describes the despair that gripped the Natchez. The chief's hearth was extinguished. He lay in state, dressed as for a long journey, his possessions placed by the bier. A solemn procession bore the corpse to his temple high on an earthen mound, followed by his wife and trusted counsellors with reddened heads and red feathers in their hair. They sat in assigned order on mats, their heads covered with skins, chewing tobacco pellets that served as stupefying drugs. Moments later, they were strangled to death. Tattooed-serpent was buried in a large trench with his wife as his house was burnt to the ground.

Nine years later the Natchez rose in bloody revolt against the French. Within a few years, however, the Indians were decimated, the Great Village deserted and forgotten. By this time Cahokia, Moundville, and other great Mississippian centers were long abandoned. Less than a century later, the myth of the moundbuilders was born, as European settlers cleared the rolling woodlands and found traces of earlier human settlement in the wilderness.

Pacific Fisherfolk and Southwestern Pueblos

Far to the west, the majority of Indian societies continued to live by hunting and foraging right up to European contact. The most prosperous were those in exceptionally favored areas of the southern California coast. In the Santa Barbara Channel area, for example, the people blended inshore and offshore fishing with marine mammal hunting as early as 8,000 years ago, as well as continuing the millennia-old hunting and gathering traditions. As time went on, this tradition evolved into the historic Chumash culture, one of the most elaborate societies in prehistoric California.

The Chumash congregated in large villages ruled by local chiefs, who maintained trading contacts over extensive areas of the west. The people lived off the ocean and the land. During the rainy season, from November to March, they subsisted on dried meat and stored vegetable foods. They also collected shellfish and caught fish from the dense kelp beds close offshore. In spring Chumash ranged far afield, collecting fresh plant growth and tubers. Summer brought tuna and other warm-water fish to Channel waters. The fishing season reached its peak at the end of the summer and in early fall, when the canoes caught enormous numbers of tuna. Pine nuts and acorns were gathered in the fall and stored for the leaner winter months. The Indians hunted sea mammals whenever the opportunity arose, and scavenged occasional whale carcasses that washed ashore on the beaches. This marine wealth resulted from the upwelling which replenishes the surface layers of the Santa Barbara Channel with nutrients and zooplankton. Billions of sardines feed here every spring. Larger fish and pelicans prey in turn on the sardines. The Chumash literally harvested the fish with hooks, nets, and spears. At least 125 fish species flourished in the thick kelp beds close offshore alone.

69 **Indians of the Northwest Coast** Northwest artisans were masters of all kinds of woodwork. The masks they fashioned served to link dancers with supernatural beings commemorated in clan myths. This Tsimshian mask of a girl with human hair and red facial paint has winged-bird pendants that can hinge open, as shown here.

70–72 **Peoples of the Far North** The Eskimos (Inuit) of the far north depended on an ingenious, well-developed technology to survive in their harsh arctic and subarctic environment. Skin boats like the kayak (*center*) were used for hunting in ice leads and open water. They were sealed by the paddlers' garments, so that one literally "wore" the canoe. If it capsized, the lower limbs stayed dry, the clothing seal protecting the paddler from hypothermia.

Eskimo hunting technology was based on spears (*below left*), bows and arrows, and harpoons. To be successful in the chase, Eskimos had to observe the habits of their prey extremely carefully, and develop an intimate knowledge of them, so they could spear or harpoon them from close quarters. It was no coincidence that the rapid spread eastward of Eskimo hunters across the far north from the Bering Strait coincided with major innovations in boat and hunting technology that enabled them to tackle whales and walrus with great consistency.

Prehistoric art from the far north reflects the artists' intimate knowledge of the animals in their environment. A 3-inch (7.5-cm) long walrus tusk fragment was fashioned into a realistic depiction of the real animal (*top*) by an Ipiutak artist at Point Hope, Alaska, some 1,500 years ago. The same artisans lavished their skill on the harpoons used to pursue a bounty of sea mammals. The rich hunting grounds enabled many groups living on the shores of the Bering Strait to occupy permanent settlements for generations.

73 To Catch a Water Bird A reconstruction of Archaic Indians pursuing duck with fiber decoys about 4,500 years ago, based on excavations at Lovelock Cave, Nevada, and

elsewhere. The hunter hid in the reeds and made dabbling noises in the water. He would then grab unsuspecting birds as they approached the floating decoy.

74–77 Artists of the Eastern Woodlands
The brilliant craftsmanship of Hopewell and Mississippian artists serves not only to distinguish individual cultures, but to provide valuable insights into prehistoric customs. The sealed eyelids and stitched mouth of a 1,000-year-old Mississippian effigy-head vessel from Arkansas (*right*) hint that it depicts a trophy head. Birds had deep symbolic significance, like a Hopewell silhouette of a raven or crow cut out and beaten from native sheet copper (*top left*), fashioned some 2,000 years ago. A Mississippian ceremonial stone effigy pipe shows a warrior decapitating a victim (*below left*). A shell ornament depicts a leaping man, perhaps a shaman, adorned with headdress and weeping eyes (*center*).

78 Architects of the Southwest The Cliff Palace in Mesa Verde, Colorado, an imposing Anasazi structure of some 900 years ago. Its rooms once housed more than 400 people.

The incredible bounty of Channel waters enabled the Chumash to live in more-or-less permanent villages. Population densities rose dramatically over the millennia. Anthropologists estimate that in historic times at least 15,000 Chumash were scattered over Ventura and Santa Barbara Counties, with perhaps as many as 3,000 people living on the offshore islands. This was one of the highest densities of hunter-gatherer populations in North America.

Directly one moved away from the coast, human populations tended to fall dramatically, on average to less than one person per square mile. But this was not true of one major region in later prehistory: the Southwest. This is the area of such famous Indian landmarks as Pueblo Bonito and Mesa Verde. Here human numbers eventually grew to the point where cultivated foods were introduced to supplement the diet. Maize, beans, and squash had been cultivated in northern Mexico for at least a thousand years before they spread into the Southwest. Not that the local people were unaware of agriculture. They simply had no need of it. However, wild food shortages may in time have caused the new crops to spread throughout the Southwest. By about AD 200 many local communities had settled in permanent villages. These varied greatly in size, depending on the abundance of local foods and the fertility of surrounding soils. Their descendants were the Southwest Indians of modern times.

Dry-land agriculture is always a risky business, a matter of careful soil selection and careful timing to ensure that planting coincides with an erratic

Two bowls painted with mythic human and animal figures. Potters 900 years ago in the Mimbres Valley, New Mexico, produced some of the finest ceramics made anywhere in the New World. Diameter of both about 7 in. (18 cm).

Zuñi Indians decorating pottery (above) and grinding corn (opposite) – illustrations from an account of these Pueblo Indians first published in the 1880s.

rainy season. Some Southwestern peoples in New Mexico relied wholly on dry farming, on annual rainfall which was erratic. The farmers of the Mogollon traditions of New Mexico, Arizona, and northern Mexico, subsisted not only off dry farming but hunting and collecting as well, between about 300 BC and AD 1350. There were many variants of Mogollon culture, perhaps the most famous centered on the Mimbres Valley in New Mexico, where skilled potters produced beautifully decorated ceramics about 900 years ago – among the finest painted wares to come from Pre-Columbian America.

In contrast, the Hohokam people of Arizona some 2,000 years ago began planting their crops to coincide with the biannual rainfall and flooding patterns. They dug canals and erected terraces and dams to catch runoff from streams and local storms. Their culture reached a peak between about AD 1100 and 1450, when they lived in large desert communities governed by chiefs. The longest-lived Southwestern farming tradition, however, was the Anasazi. This was, in general terms, the ancestor of modern Pueblo Indian culture – the Hopi, Zuñi, and others. It lasted for more than 2,000 years but had its roots in

much earlier cultural traditions. By AD 900, many Anasazi had shifted from small villages of pithouses to above-ground settlements composed of multi-room surface structures with mud or masonry walls. These "pueblos" made increasingly specialized use of space, especially for storage, food preparation, and for *kivas*, semi-subterranean rooms used in community rituals.

For reasons that are a mystery, perhaps in part because of drier conditions, the population congregated in fewer, but larger, pueblos after AD 1000. Some, like Pueblo Bonito in Chaco Canyon, New Mexico, were located in densely populated areas. Pueblo Bonito consisted of a huge D-shaped complex of no less than 800 rooms rising several stories high around the rim of the arc. The room complexes surrounded courts, with the highest stories at the back. Within the court lay the *kivas*, always one great *kiva* and several lesser ones. These were the subterranean rooms where secret societies met and clan rituals were celebrated. The great *kivas* were up to 60 feet (18.3 m) across, with wide masonry benches encircling the interior. A staircase leading from the floor of the *kiva* to the large floor above gave access to the sacred precinct.

Mesa Verde in Southwest Colorado was another center of Anasazi culture. In the late first millennium AD most Mesa Verde people lived in pit houses on mesa tops overlooking the canyon. Between AD 950 and 1000 the local population grew and the inhabitants congregated in larger pueblos, many of them built in rockshelters or the valley floor, like the famous Cliff Palace. After 1300 Mesa Verde was abandoned for reasons that are still a mystery.

In areas like Chaco Canyon the Anasazi Indians enjoyed roads and extensive irrigation systems, as well as widespread trading links. None of the great concentrations of population lasted long, for Southwestern society was in a constant state of flux. We do not understand why basically self-sufficient farming communities chose to congregate at such close quarters for centuries, then to abandon many of their large pueblos, like those in Chaco Canyon, between AD 1200 and 1300, in favor of more dispersed settlements. A combination of rainfall fluctuations, societal, and adaptive changes may have set in motion periods of turbulence, population dispersal, and culture change.

The pueblos were probably communities of closely knit clans that were run for the collective good with at least some ranking of society under community chieftains. In modern Hopi society, for example, clan superiority and kinship lineages play an important role in the election of such individuals. Thrust into close physical and spiritual intimacy by the nature of their architecture and environmental necessity, the Pueblo Indians developed well-integrated religious and ceremonial rituals to combat and defuse the tensions of close-quarters living. They survived because they learned how to conserve limited water supplies, and how to bring together water and soil by means of dams, canals, and other systems for distributing runoff. Like their hunter-gatherer predecessors, they exploited every type of food the desert offered, then added the fruits of their own gardens in a brilliant adaptation that lasted until European contact in the sixteenth century.

A Franciscan friar, Fray Marcos de Niza, was the first Spaniard to reach Pueblo country in 1538. He gazed secretly on the Zuñi pueblo known as Hawikuh. "It was a very fine appearance for a village," he reported, "the best I have seen in these parts . . . The houses, as the Indians had told me, are all of stone, built in stories, and with flat roofs." "The settlement is larger than the city of Mexico," he added inaccurately. Fray Marcos' exaggerated account, with its references to gold and great wealth, caused a sensation in Mexico City. Francisco Vasquez de Coronado arrived at the head of a party of gold-hungry conquistadors in July 1540. He expected the fabled Seven Lost Cities of Cibola. To his disgust, he saw a "little, crowded village looking as if it had been crumpled all up together . . . It is a village of about two hundred warriors, three or four stories high with the houses small and having only a few rooms." After an hour's fierce fighting, Hawikuh was in Spanish hands and the inhabitants melted into the mountains. The conquistadors found "much corn, beans, and fowl." But of gold there was no sign. It was fortunate for the Pueblo Indians that they lived in a land where gold was unknown. Many elements of their prehistoric culture were able to survive remarkably unscathed until the nineteenth century, and even later.

By the time Fray Marcos reached Zuñi country and Hernando de Soto the Mississippi, Europeans had been visiting the coasts of North America for five centuries. First Vikings, then Englishmen, Frenchmen, and Spaniards, probed the coasts of the continent, then settled there permanently. The long prehistory of the American Indian ended abruptly with the arrival of conquistadors and colonists, missionaries and explorers. A new chapter opened, one marked by genocide, endemic disease, constant social, economic, and cultural disruption, and the destruction of traditional ways of life that had been evolving without interruption from Clovis times. More than twelve millennia of cultural evolution were swept away in a few centuries. In the process, the great diversity was largely forgotten, jumbled together in the public mind in a ragbag of crude and inaccurate stereotypes – feathered braves, tepees, and noble savages. It is only now that modern science is restoring the balance, revealing the remarkable complexity of prehistoric American life in all its fascinating intricacy. The most telling conclusion of all from the researches of Samuel Haven and his successors is that human beings, even with the simplest of bone and stone technologies, are capable of colonizing, populating, and adapting successfully to a vast continent without all the elaborate artifices of modern industrial civilization. The minds of Haven's "learned and ingenious men" and their modern descendants have painted a brilliant picture of human cultural achievement, an achievement as momentous as the Industrial Revolution or the conquest of space. More's the pity that the forces of western history, and of long-nurtured ethnocentrism, have until now limited our awareness of the pre-Columbian triumph.

Further Reading

The literature on the peopling of America is so enormous and highly specialized that even experts have a hard time keeping up with the latest research. This book is based on thousands of different papers, monographs, reviews, and short reports in many languages. We can cite but a tiny number of them here. The guide to further reading is presented chapter by chapter, with an annotated list of major sources followed by further, more technical references. The reference lists are cumulative, so a citation in one chapter is not repeated in later ones.

Introduction An Archaeological Drama

This is a good moment to introduce the few general works that discuss the peopling of America. Robert Claiborne, *The First Americans* (Time-Life Books, New York and London, 1973) is a well illustrated summary for lay people that is very readable, if somewhat outdated. C.W. Ceram, *The First American* (Harcourt Brace Jovanovich, New York, 1971; Cape, London, 1976) ranges broadly and uncritically over the subject, but is widely read. Anyone interested in lost civilizations and what has been called "myth America" should read Robert Wauchope's *Lost Tribes and Sunken Continents* (University of Chicago Press, Chicago, 1962), which is truly witty and learned in a way that few academic authors can pull off.

General books on American archaeology as a whole are normally aimed at undergraduate audiences. Jesse D. Jennings has edited the two-volume *Ancient Native Americans* (W.H. Freeman, San Francisco, 1983). This contains authoritative articles on every major culture area of the Americas by acknowledged experts. Serious students will wish to consult Gordon R. Willey's magisterial two-volume *Introduction to American Archaeology* (Prentice-Hall, Englewood Cliffs, N.J., 1966 and 1971), although, inevitably, later research has refined much of his data and arguments.

This is not a book about archaeological methods and theories, but inevitably they impinge on the story told in these pages. Anyone interested in delving further into these subjects, and especially into the impact of science on archaeology, is best advised to start with a basic college textbook like James Deetz, *Invitation to Archaeology* (Natural History Press, Garden City, N.J., 1967) or my own *Archaeology: A Brief Introduction* (Little Brown, Boston, 3rd ed. 1987). Gordon R. Willey and Philip Phillips, *Method and Theory in American Archaeology* (University of Chicago Press, Chicago, 1958) is still a fundamental source on classificatory terms in New World prehistory. Lewis R. Binford, *In Pursuit of the Past* (Thames and Hudson, London and New York, 1983) summarizes some major theoretical and methodological trends of recent decades. David J. Meltzer, Don D. Fowler, and Jeremy A. Sabloff (eds.) *American Archaeology Past and Future* (Smithsonian Institution Press, Washington D.C., 1986) is a volume of essays that evaluates the current state, and prospects, of American archaeology.

Other References

Baudin, Henri. *Paradise on Earth*. Yale University Press, New Haven, 1969.

Brandon, William. *The American Heritage Book of Indians*. American Heritage, New York, 1961.

Brinton, Daniel G. *The Myths of the New World*. Henry Holt, New York, 2nd ed. 1876.

Coe, Michael D. *The Maya*. 4th ed. Thames and Hudson, London and New York, 1987.

——*Mexico*. 3rd ed. Thames and Hudson, London and New York, 1984.

Coe, Michael, Snow, Dean, and Benson, Elizabeth. *Atlas of Ancient America*. Facts on File, New York and London, 1986.

Fagan, Brian M. *The Aztecs*. W.H. Freeman, New York and Oxford, 1984.

——*Clash of Cultures*. W.H. Freeman, New York and Oxford, 1984.

Farb, Peter. *Man's Rise to Civilization as Shown by the Indians of North America from Primeval Times to the Coming of the Industrial State*. E.P. Dutton, New York, 1968.

Haven, Samuel. *Archaeology of the United States*. Smithsonian Institution, Washington D.C., 1856.

Josephy, Alvin. *The Indian Heritage of America*. Knopf, New York, 1968; London, 1972.

Lowie, Robert. *The Assiniboine*. Anthropological Papers of the American Museum of Natural History, New York, vol. 4, 1910, 1–270.

Chapter 1 Friars, Antiquarians, and Moundbuilders

Samuel Eliot Morison's *The European Discovery of America* (Oxford University Press, New York, vol. 1, 1971) provides a summary of Columbus that is more than adequate for our purposes. My *Clash of Cultures* (W.H. Freeman, New York and Oxford, 1984) treats of the controversies that followed European settlement. Hugh Honour, *The New Golden Land: European Images of America* (Putnam, New York, 1975) describes changing perceptions of the American Indian. So does Henry Savage's admirable *Discovering America 1700–1875* (Harper, New York, 1979). Gordon R. Willey and Jeremy A. Sabloff, *A History of American Archaeology* (W.H. Freeman, San Francisco, 2nd ed. 1980) is the definitive account of the subject. I have drawn on it heavily here. My *Elusive Treasure* (Charles Scribner, New York, 1977) covers some of the same ground for a general audience. Robert Silverberg, *The Mound Builders of Ancient America* (New York Graphic Society, Greenwich, 1968) describes the controversies surrounding Midwestern earthworks. Stephens and Catherwood speak for themselves. You only have to read Stephens' *Incidents of Travel in Central America, Chiapas, and Yucatan* (Harper, New York, 1841) and his *Incidents of Travel in Yucatan* (Harper, New York, 1843) to be captivated by these extraordinary men.

Other References

Anderson, Arthur O. and Dibble, Charles E. *The Florentine Codex*. University of Utah Press, Salt Lake City, 12 vols. 1971.

Atwater, Caleb. "Description of the Antiquities Discovered in the State of Ohio and Other Western States," *Transactions of the American Antiquarian Society*, vol. 1 (1820).

Bartram, William. *Travels through*

North and South Carolina, Georgia, east and west Florida. . . Philadelphia, 1791.

Duran, Diego. *The Aztec: The History of the Indies of New Spain* (translated by Doris Heyden and Fernando Horcasitas). Union Press, New York, 1964.

Hanke, Lewis. *The Struggle for Justice in the Conquest of America*. American Historical Society, New York, 1949.

Prescott, William. *The History of the Conquest of Mexico*. Harper, New York, 1843.

Robertson, William. *History of America*. London, 1877.

Squier, Ephraim, and Davis, Edwin. *Ancient Monuments of the Mississippi Valley*. Smithsonian Institution, Washington D.C., 1848.

Tozzer, Alfred M. *Diego de Landa's Relation de las Cosas de Yucatan*. Papers of the Peabody Museum of American Archaeology and Ethnology, no. 18 (1941).

von Hagen, Victor. *Maya Explorer*. University of Oklahoma Press, Norman, 1947.

Chapter 2 Palaeoliths and Extinct Animals

Donald L. Grayson, *The Establishment of Human Antiquity* (Academic Press, New York, 1983) is the definitive account of this major development in intellectual history. In addition to the sources cited for Chapter 2, any serious student should consult David J. Meltzer, "The Antiquity of Man and the Development of American Archaeology," *Advances in Archaeological Method and Theory*, vol. 6 (1983), 1–51, an account of the debates surrounding palaeoliths and early humans in the New World. I relied heavily on it here, also on Curtis M. Hinsley's *Savages and Scientists: The Smithsonian Institution and the Development of American Anthropology 1846–1910* (Smithsonian Institution Press, Washington D.C., 1981). C. Nelson, "William Henry Holmes: beginning a career in art and science," *Records of the Columbia Historical Society*, vol. 50 (1980), 252–278, provides an analysis of this complex man. Holmes' own views are well summarized in his "On the antiquity of man in America," *Science*, vol. 47 (1918), 561–562. Aleš Hrdlička made his position clear in a whole stream of authoritative papers. His "The origin and antiquity of man in America," *New York Academy of Medicine, Second Series, Bulletin* vol. 4(7) (1928), 802–816, is a typical statement. Jesse Figgins' classic paper on Folsom is "The antiquity of man in America," *Natural History*, vol. 27 (1927), 229–239. The later history of early human studies is well summarized by Willey and Sabloff in their *History of American Archaeology* (1980).

Other References

Abbott, C.C. "The stone age in New Jersey," *Smithsonian Institution Annual Report* (1875), 246–380.
———*Primitive Industry*. G.A. Bates, Salem, Mass., 1881.
———"Paleolithic man in North America," *Science*, vol. 20 (1892), 270–271.

Bada, Jeffrey L. and Hoffman, Patricia M. "Amino Acid Racemization Dating of Fossil Bones," *World Archaeology*, vol. 7(2) (1975), 160–173.

Binford, Lewis R. *In Pursuit of the Past*. Thames and Hudson, London and New York, 1983.

Brown, Barnum. "Recent finds relating to prehistoric man in North America," *Bulletin, New York Academy of Medicine* vol. 47, second series (1928), 824–828.

Clewlow, C. "Some thoughts on the background of early man, Hrdlička and Folsom," *Kroeber Anthropological Series Papers*, vol. 42 (1970), 26–46.

Dana, J. "On Dr. Koch's evidence with regard to the contemporaneity of man and the mastodon in Missouri." *American Journal of Science and Arts*, vol. 9 (1875), 335–346, 398.

Darrah, W. *Powell of the Colorado*. Princeton University Press, Princeton, 1951.

Gibbs, G. "Instructions for archaeological investigations in the United States," *Smithsonian Institution Annual Report* (1862), 392–396.

Grayson, Donald. "Eoliths, Archaeological Ambiguity, and the Generation of 'Middle-Range' research," in David J. Meltzer, Don D. Fowler, and Jeremy A. Sabloff (eds.), *American Archaeology Present and Future*. Smithsonian Institution Press, Washington D.C., 1986.

Gruber, Jacob W. "Archaeology, History, and Culture," in David J. Meltzer, Don D. Fowler, and Jeremy A. Sabloff (eds.) *American Archaeology Present and Future*. Smithsonian Institution Press, Washington D.C., 1986.

Harris, Marvin. *The Rise of Anthropological Theory*. Crowell, New York, 1968.

Holmes, W.H. "A quarry workshop of the flaked stone implement makers in the District of Columbia," *American Anthropologist*, vol. 3 (1890), 1–26.

——"Man and the glacial period," *The American Antiquarian*, vol. 15 (1893), 34–36.

——"Contributions of American archaeology to human history," *Smithsonian Institution Annual Report* (1904), 551–558.

——"The antiquity phantom in American archaeology," *Science*, vol. 62 (1925), 256–258.

Hrdlička, Aleš. "Skeletal remains suggesting or attributed to early man in North America," *Bureau of American Ethnology, Bulletin*, vol. 33 (1907).

Huxley, Thomas H. *Science and Christian tradition*. Appleton, New York, 1898.

Libby, Willard. *Radiocarbon Dating*. University of Chicago Press, Chicago, 1955.

MacCurdy, G.G. (ed.). *Early Man*. Lippincott, Philadelphia, 1937.

Meltzer, David J. "W.H. Holmes and the Folsom Finds," *History of Anthropology Newsletter*, vol. 8(2) (1981), 6–8.

Morgan, Lewis. *Ancient Society*. World Publishing, New York, 1877.

Putnam, F.W. "Comparison of Paleolithic implements," *Proceedings of the Boston Society of Natural History*, vol. 23 (1888), 421–424.

Roberts, F. "The Folsom problem in American Archaeology," in G.G. MacCurdy (ed.), *Early Man*, Lippincott, Philadelphia, 1937, 153–162.

Taylor, R.E. and others, "Spectrometry: None Older than 11,000 years," *American Antiquity*, vol. 50(1) (1985), 136–140.

Willey, Gordon R. and Phillips, P. *Method and Theory in American Archaeology*. University of Chicago Press, Chicago, 1958.

Wilmsen, E. "An outline of early man studies in the United States," *American Antiquity*, vol. 31 (1965), 172–192.

Wilson, David. *Prehistoric Man*. 2 vols. Macmillan, Cambridge, 1863.

Wright, G.F. *The Ice Age in North America and its Bearing upon the Antiquity of Man*. Appleton, New York, 1889.

——*Man and the Glacial Period*. Appleton, New York, 1892.

Chapter 3 **In the Beginning**

This chapter ranges so widely over world prehistory that it is difficult to give specific references. My own *People of the Earth* (Little Brown, Boston, 5th ed. 1986) summarizes the salient features of prehistoric times for beginners. So does Robert Wenke's *Patterns in Prehistory* (Oxford University Press, New York, 2nd ed. 1985). E. Delson (ed.) *Ancestors: The Hard Evidence* (Alan Liss, New York, 1985) gives much background on early human evolution, while Roger Lewin's *Human Evolution* (W.H. Freeman, New York, 1984) summarizes the subject for beginners. F. Smith and F. Spencer (eds.) *The Origins of Modern Humans* (Alan Liss, New York, 1984) describes early *Homo sapiens*. A good summary of early human occupation of Central Europe is Hansjurgen Müller-Beck, "Late Pleistocene Man in Northern Alaska and the Mammoth-Steppe Biome," *in* David M. Hopkins and others (eds.) *Paleoecology of Beringia* (Academic Press, New York, 1982, 329–352). Erik Trinkaus and W.W. Howell, "The Neanderthals," *Scientific American*, no. 241 (1979), 118–133, is an excellent summary of the subject.

Other References

Adam, K.D. "Der Waldelefant von Lehringen," *Quartär*, vol. 5 (1951), 79–92.

Binford, Lewis R. *Bones*. Academic Press, New York, 1981.

Bordes, François. *The Old Stone Age*. Weidenfeld, London, McGraw-Hill, New York, 1968.

Freeman, L.G. "The analysis of some occupation floor distributions from earlier and middle Palaeolithic sites in Spain," *in* L.G. Freeman (ed.), *View of the Past*, Mouton, The Hague, 1978, 57–116.

Haynes, C. Vance. "The Calico Site: Artifacts or Geofacts?" *Science*, vol. 181 (1973), 305–311.

Howell, F. Clark. "Observations on the earlier phases of the European Lower Paleolithic," *American Anthropologist*, vol. 68 (1966), 88–201.

————*Early Man*. Time-Life Books, New York and London, 1975.

Isaac, Glynn Ll. "The Food-Sharing Behavior of Protohuman hominids," *Scientific American*, vol. 238 (1978), 90–108.

Klein, Richard. "Mousterian cultures in European Russia," *Science*, vol. 165 (1969), 257–267.

————*Man and Culture in the Late Pleistocene*. Chandler Publishing, San Francisco, 1969.

Odladnikov, A.P. and Pospelova, G.A. "Ulalinka, the Oldest Palaeolithic Site in Siberia," *Current Anthropology* (1972), 710–712.

Pfeiffer, John. *The Emergence of Man*. Harper and Row, New York, 2nd ed. 1973.

Schuiling, W.C. (ed.) *Pleistocene Man at Calico: A Report on the Calico Mountains Excavations*. San Bernardino County Museum Association, Redlands, California, 1979.

Tode, A. and others. "Die Untersuchung der paläolithischen Freilandstation von Salzgitter-Lebenstedt," *Eiszeitalter und Gegenwart*, vol. 3 (1953), 114–220.

Yi, Seonbok, and Clark, G.A. "Observations on the Lower Palaeolithic of Northeast Asia," *Current Anthropology* (1983), 181–202.

Zamyatin, S.N. "The Paleolithic Station of Stalingrad," *Kratkie Soobshcheniya Instituta Istorii Material'noy Kul'tury*, vol. 82 (1961), 5–36 (English summary).

Chapter 4 **Modern Humans Take the Stage**

Olga Soffer, *The Upper Paleolithic of the Central Russian Plain* (Academic Press, New York, 1985) provides a valuable synthesis of the mammoth-hunting cultures of the Soviet Union. See also, Richard Klein, *Ice-age Hunters of the Ukraine* (University of Chicago Press, Chicago, 1973). Australian prehistory, briefly discussed here and in Chapter 5, is superbly summarized by J. Peter White and

James O'Connell, *A Prehistory of Australia, New Guinea, and Sahul* (Academic Press, Sydney, 1982). Siberian prehistory is virtually inaccessible to non-Russian speakers, but Chester S. Chard, *Northeast Asia in Prehistory* (University of Wisconsin Press, Madison, 1971) gives a general, if somewhat outdated, summary. Richard Klein, "The Pleistocene Prehistory of Siberia," *Quaternary Research*, vol. 2(1) (1971), 131–161, talks much commonsense about the region. N.N. Dikov, *Ancient Cultures of Northeastern Asia. Asia Joining America in Ancient Times* (Nauka Publishing House, Moscow, 1979) offers a Soviet perspective. So does Yuri A. Mochanov, *The Most Ancient Stages of the Human Settlement of Northeast Asia* (Science Press Siberian Division, Novosibirsk, 1977). Both are in Russian. Christy Turner summarizes his dental research in "Advances in the Dental Search for Native American Origins," *Acta Anthropogenetica*, vol. 8(1&2) (1984), 23–78.

Other References

Aigner, J.S. "The Paleolithic of China," in Alan L. Bryan (ed.), *Early Man in America from a Circum-Pacific Perspective*. University of Alberta, Edmonton, 1978.

Chung, Tang, and Pei, Gai, "Upper Paleolithic Cultural Traditions in North China," *Advances in World Archaeology*, 5 (1986), 339–364.

Dikov, Nikolai N. "The Stages and Routes of Human Occupation of the Beringian Land Bridge Based on Archaeological Data," in N.C. Flemming and others (eds.) *Quaternary Coastlines*, Academic Press, London, 1983, 347–364.

Gerasimov, M.M. "Excavations of the Palaeolithic site of Mal'ta," *Izvestia Gosudarstvennoy Akademii Istorii Materal'noy Kultury*, vol. 118 (1935), 78–115 (in Russian).

——"Worked bones from the Palaeolithic site of Mal'ta,"

Materialy i Issedovanii po Arskheologii SSSR, vol. 2 (1941), 65–85 (in Russian).

Klima, B. *Dolni Vestonice*. Monumenta Archaeologica, Prague, 1963.

——"Das Pavlovien in den Weinbergöhlen von Mauren," *Quartar*, vol. 19 (1968), 263–273.

Kozlowski, Janusz K. "The Gravettian in Central and Eastern Europe," *Advances in World Archaeology*, 5 (1986), 131–200.

Mochanov, Yuri. "The Paleolithic of NE Asia and the problem of the first peopling of America," in Alan L. Bryan (ed.), *Early Man etc.*, Edmonton, 1978, 67.

——"Stratigraphy and absolute chronology of the Paleolithic of Northeast Asia," in Alan L. Bryan (ed.), *Early Man etc.*, Edmonton, 1978, 54–66.

——"Early migrations to America in the light of a study of the Dyukhtai Paleolithic culture in North-east Asia," in David L. Browman (ed.) *Early Native Americans*, Mouton, The Hague, 1980.

Turner, Christy, Gai, P., and Stanford, D.J. *The North China Origin of American Indians* (in preparation).

Williams, Robert C. and others. "Gm allotypes in Native Americans: Evidence for Three Distinct Migrations Across the Bering Land Bridge," *American Journal of Physical Anthropology*, vol. 66 (1985), 1–19.

Chapter 5 Beringia

This chapter was written with the help of two seminal works: D.M. Hopkins (ed.) *The Bering Land Bridge* (Stanford University Press, Palo Alto, 1967), and David M. Hopkins, John V. Matthews, Charles E. Schweger, and Steven B. Young (eds.) *Paleoecology of Beringia* (Academic Press, New York, 1982). They are by far the best basic, even encyclopaedic, sources on the subject.

Other References

Bliss, L.C. "Productivity and nutrient content of tundra ecosystems," *Handbook of Nutrition and Food.* CRC Press, West Palm Beach, Florida, 1981.

Colinvaux, Paul. "The environment of the Bering Land Bridge," *Ecological Monographs*, vol. 34 (1964), 297–329.

——"Vegetation of the Bering Land Bridge revisited," *Quaternary Review of Archaeology*, vol. 1 (1980), 18–36.

——Historical ecology in Beringia: The south coast land bridge at St. Paul Island," *Quaternary Research*, vol. 16 (1981), 18–36.

Farrand, W.R. "Frozen mammoths and modern science," *Science*, vol. 133 (1961), 729–735.

Hopkins, David M. "Sea level history in Beringia during the last 250,000 years," *Quaternary Research*, vol. 3 (1973), 520–540.

——"Landscape and climate of Beringia during Late Pleistocene and Holocene time," *in* W.S. Laughlin and A.B. Harper (eds.) *The First Americans: origins, affinities, and adaptations*, Gustav Fischer, New York, 1979, 15–41.

Hulten, E. *Outline of the history of Arctic and Boreal biota during the Quaternary Period.* Bokforlagsaktiebolaget, Stockholm, 1937.

Matthews, J.V. "Beringia during the late Pleistocene: Arctic-steppe or discontinuous herb-tundra?" *Geological Survey of Canada Open File Report 649* (1979).

——"Quaternary vegetational history and the Arctic-steppe in Beringia," *Proceedings of the 4th International Palynological Conference*, vol. 3 (1980), 82–91.

Vereshchagin, N.K. "The mammoth 'cemeteries' of North-East Siberia," *Polar Record*, vol. 17 (106) (1974), 3–12.

——and Baryshnikov, G.F. "Range of the ungulate fauna of the U.S.S.R. in the Anthropogene," O.A. Scarlato (ed.) *Mlekopitayuskche Vostochnnoy Europy v Antropogene.* Zoologischeskogo Instituta, SSSR, 1980 (in Russian).

Yurtsev, B.A., and others. "The floristic delimitation and subdivision of the Arctic," *in* B. Yurtsev (ed.) *Arkicheskaya floristicheskaya oblast'*, Nautka Press, Leningrad, 9–104 (in Russian).

Chapter 6 **Alaska and the Yukon Territory**

The literature on this vast area can only be described as a confusing morass of conflicting data and opinions. There are almost more summaries than excavation reports. Frederick Hadleigh West, *The Archaeology of Beringia* (Columbia University Press, New York, 1981) offers a synthesis reviewed by Don E. Dumond, "Colonization of the American Arctic and the New World," *American Antiquity*, vol. 47 (4) (1982), 885–895. William S. Laughlin, G.H. Marsh, and Albert B. Harper (eds.) *The First Americans: Origins, Affinities, and Adaptations* (Gustav Fischer, New York, 1979) provides a more biological overview. Two monographs give invaluable perspectives on the problems of interpreting bone fractures: Richard E. Morlan, *Taphonomy and Archaeology in the Upper Pleistocene of the Northern Yukon Territory: A Glimpse into the Peopling of the New World* (National Museum of Man, Ottawa, 1980) and Robson Bonnichsen, *Pleistocene Bone Technology in the Beringian Refugium* (National Museum of Man, Ottawa, 1979). Other major summaries include Richard Morlan, "Pre-Clovis Occupation North of the Ice Sheets," *in* Richard Shutler (ed.) *Early Man in the New World* (Sage Publications, Beverly Hills, 1983), 47–64. Also Jesse D. Jennings, "Origins," *in* his edited *Ancient Native Americans* (W.H. Freeman, San Francisco, vol. 1,

1983), 1–41, and Don E. Dumond's closely and logically argued "The archaeology of Alaska and the peopling of America," *Science*, vol. 209 (1980), 984–991. Lewis R. Binford's *Nunamiut Ethnoarchaeology* (Academic Press, New York, 1978) and *Bones* (Academic Press, New York, 1983) provide both ancient and modern perspectives on the interpretation of ancient food remains that are relevant to an understanding of Alaskan and Yukon archaeology.

Other References

Anderson, D.D. "Akmak: An early archaeological assemblage from Onion Portage, northwest Alaska," *Acta Arctica*, vol. 16 (1970).
——"Microblade Traditions in Northwestern Alaska," *Arctic Anthropology*, vol. 7 (1970) 2–19.
Cinq-Mars, Jacques. "Bluefish Cave 1: a late Pleistocene eastern Beringian cave deposit in the northern Yukon," *Canadian Journal of Archaeology*, vol. 3 (1979), 1–32.
Clark, Donald W. and Morlan, Richard E. "Western Subarctic Prehistory: Twenty Years Later," *Canadian Journal of Archaeology*, vol. 6 (1982), 79–93.
Guthrie, R.D. "Paleoecology of the large-mammal community in interior Alaska during the Late Pleistocene," *American Midland Naturalist*, vol. 79 (1968), 346–363.
Ikawa-Smith, F. "The early prehistory of the Americas as seen from northeast Asia," *in* J.E. Ericson and others, *Peopling of the New World*, Ballena Press, Los Altos, California, 1982, 15–33.
Larsen, Helge. "Trail Creek: Final report on the excavations of two caves on Seward Peninsula, Alaska," *Acta Arctica*, vol. 15 (1968).
Morlan, Richard E. "Wedge-shaped core technology in northern North America," *Arctic Anthropology*, vol. 7 (1970), 17–37.
——"Fluted point makers and the extinction of the Arctic-Steppe Biome in eastern Beringia," *Canadian Journal of Archaeology*, vol. 1 (1977), 95–108.
——"Toward the Definition of Criteria for the Recognition of Artificial Bone Alterations," *Quaternary Research*, vol. 22, (1984), 160–171.
——and others. "Upper Pleistocene Stratigraphy, Paleoecology, and Archaeology of the Northern Yukon Interior, Eastern Beringia. I. Bonnet Plume Basin," *Arctic*, vol. 34(4) (1981), 329–365.
——and others. "New Radiocarbon Dates on Artifacts from the Northern Yukon Territory: Holocene not Upper Pleistocene in Age," *Science*, in press (1986).
Powers, W.R. and Hamilton, T.D. "Dry Creek: A Late Pleistocene human occupation in central Alaska," *in* Alan L. Bryan (ed.) *Early Man etc.*, Edmonton, 1978, 72–77.
West, F.H. "The Donnelly Ridge site and the definition of an early core and blade complex in central Alaska," *American Antiquity*, vol. 32 (1967), 360–382.
——"Dating the Denali Complex," *Arctic Anthropology*, vol. 2 (1975), 6–81.
——"Reflections on Beringian Prehistory and Early Man in America," *Geoscience and Man*, vol. 22 (1981), 103–114.
Workman, W.B. "Holocene peopling of the New World: Implications of the Arctic and Subarctic area," *Canadian Journal of Archaeology*, vol. 1 (1980), 129–139.

Chapter 7 **The Ice-Free Corridor?**

The best summary of the scattered literature is a series of papers grouped under the general title "The Ice-Free Corridor and Peopling the New World" in the *Canadian Journal of Anthropology*, vol. 1 (1980). They

David M. Hopkins and others (eds.), *Paleoecology of Beringia* (Academic Press, New York, 1982), 383–398. E.N. Wilmsen, *Lindenmeier: A Pleistocene hunting society* (Harper and Row, New York, 1974) describes excavations at one Paleo-Indian site. George Frison, *Prehistoric Hunters of the High Plains* (Academic Press, New York, 1978) is a definitive work on prehistoric plains hunting. The extinctions controversy has generated an enormous literature. Paul S. Martin and Henry Wright (eds.) *Pleistocene Extinctions: Search for a Cause* (Yale University Press, New Haven, 1967) and Paul S. Martin and Richard Klein (eds.) *A Pleistocene Revolution* (University of Arizona Press, Tucson, 1974) cover most bases. Joseph Greenberg's *Language in the Americas* (Stanford University Press, Palo Alto, 1987) will be the definitive statement on American Indian languages for a long time. For a summary of the major implications of his work, see Joseph Greenberg, Christy Turner, and Stephen Zegura, "The Settlement of the Americas: A Comparison of the Linguistic, Dental, and Genetic Evidence," *Current Anthropology*, 27(5) (1986), 477–497.

Other References
Douglas-Hamilton, I. and O. *Among the Elephants*. Viking Press, New York, 1975.
Frison, George C. and Bradley, Bruce A. *Folsom Tools and Technology of the Hanson Site, Wyoming.* University of New Mexico Press, Albuquerque, 1980.
Haury, E.W., and others. "Artifacts with mammoth remains, Naco, Arizona," *American Antiquity*, vol. 19 (1953), 1–14.
Haynes, C. Vance. "Fluted projectile points: Their age and dispersal," *Science*, vol. 145 (1964), 1408–1413.
Huckell, B.B. "Of chipped stone tools, elephants, and the Clovis hunters: an experiment," *Plains Anthropologist*, vol. 24 (1979), 177–189.

Johnson, D.L. and others. "Clovis Strategies of Hunting Mammoth (*Mammuthus columbi*)," *Canadian Journal of Anthropology*, vol. 1 (1980), 107–114.
MacDonald, George. "Eastern North America," in Richard Shutler Jr. (ed.) *Early Man in the New World*, Sage Publications, Beverly Hills, 1983, 97–108.
Martin, P.S. "The Discovery of America," *Science*, vol. 179 (1973), 969–974.
Sikes, S.K. *The Natural History of the African Elephant*. Weidenfeld, London, 1971.
Wormington, H.M. *Ancient Man in North America*. Denver Natural History Museum, Denver, 1957.

Chapter 10 **The Bison Hunters**

The literature on prehistoric bison hunting is enormous, but the best guide is George Frison's *Prehistoric Hunters of the High Plains* (Academic Press, New York, 1978). This describes many key sites and was the major source for this chapter. You can combine this with his essay on "The Western Plains and the Mountain Region," in Richard Shutler (ed.), *Early Man in the New World* (Sage Publications, Beverly Hills, California, 1983), 109–124. Joe Ben Wheat, "The Olsen-Chubbock Site: A Paleo-Indian Bison Kill," *Memoirs of the Society for American Archaeology*, no. 26 (1972), is a magnificent account of a kill site that has been a model for much subsequent work. Preston Holder's *The Hoe and the Horse on the Plains* (University of Nebraska Press, Lincoln, 1970) is a fascinating and sophisticated essay on the impact of European culture on the Plains Indians.

Other References
Frison, George C. *The Casper Site: A Hell Gap Bison Kill on the High Plains*. Academic Press, New York, 1974.

————"Man's interaction with Holocene environments on the Plains," *Quaternary Research*, vol. 5 (1975), 289–300.

Irwin, H.T. and Wormington, H.M. "Paleo-Indian tool types in the Great Plains," *American Antiquity*, vol. 325 (1970), 24–34.

Speth, John D. *Bison Kills and Bone Counts*. University of Chicago Press, Chicago, 1983.

Wedel, W.R. "The prehistoric Plains," *in* Jesse D. Jennings (ed.) *Ancient Native Americans*, vol. 1, W.H. Freeman, San Francisco, 1983, 183–220.

Chapter 11 **The Northern World**

Don Dumond, *The Eskimos and Aleuts* (Thames and Hudson, London and New York, revised ed., 1987) is a readily accessible guide to arctic archaeology. J.L. Giddings, *Ancient Men of the Arctic* (Knopf, New York, 1967) describes working conditions in the far north and work on the shores of the Bering Strait. Hans-Georg Bandi, *Eskimo Prehistory* (University of Alaska Press, College, Alaska, 1969) is still a basic source. Moreau S. Maxwell, *Prehistory of the Eastern Arctic* (Academic Press, New York, 1985) is the authoritative summary on the subject. William Laughlin, *Aleuts: survivors of the Bering Land Bridge* (Holt Rinehart and Winston, New York, 1980) describes Aleut life and some of the controversies over their ancestry. William Workman, "Holocene Peopling of the New World: Implications of the Arctic and Subarctic Data," *Canadian Journal of Anthropology*, vol. 1 (1980), 129–139, is an admirable discussion. The Northwest Coast is well summarized by Don Dumond, "Alaska and the Northwest Coast," *in* Jesse D. Jennings (ed.), *Ancient Native Americans* (W.H. Freeman, San Francisco, vol. 1, 1983), 43–93.

Other References

Aigner, Jean S. 1970. "The Unifacial, Core, and Blade Site on Anangula Island, Aleutians," *Arctic Anthropology*, vol. 7(2) (1970), 59–88.

Borden, C.E. "Origins and Development of Early Northwest Coast Culture to About 3000 B.C.," *Archaeological Survey of Canada Paper*, no. 45 (1975).

Collins, H.B. "Archaeology of St. Lawrence Island, Alaska," *Smithsonian Miscellaneous Collections*, vol. 96(1) (1936).

Cook, J.P. "Archaeology of interior Alaska," *The Western Canadian Journal of Anthropology*, vol. 5 (1975), 125–133.

Dumond, Don E. "On Eskaleutian Linguistics, Archaeology, and Prehistory," *American Anthropologist*, vol. 67 (1965), 1231–57.

————"Eskimo-Indian relationships: a view from prehistory," *Arctic Anthropology*, vol. 16(2) (1979), 3–21.

————"A Reexamination of Eskimo-Aleut Prehistory," *American Anthropologist*, vol. 89 (1987), 1–25.

Fladmark, K.R. "A Paleocological Model for Northwest Coast Prehistory," *Archaeological Survey of Canada Paper*, no. 43 (1975).

————*British Columbia Prehistory*. Canadian Prehistory Series, National Museum of Man, Canada, 1986.

Giddings, J.L. *The Archaeology of Cape Denbigh*. Brown University Press, Providence, Rhode Island, 1964.

Kirk, Ruth. *Hunters of the Whale*. Morrow, New York, 1975.

Larsen, H. and Rainey, F. "Ipiutak and the Arctic Whale Hunting Culture." *Anthropological Papers of the American Museum of Natural History*, vol. 42 (1948).

McGhee, Robert. *Copper Eskimo Prehistory*. National Museums of Canada, Publications in Archaeology, no. 2, 1972.

————*Canadian Arctic Prehistory*.

Toronto and New York, 1978.
Rainey, F. "Eskimo Prehistory: the Okvik site in the Punuk Islands. *Anthropological Papers of the American Museum of Natural History*, vol. 37(4) (1941), 443–569.
Rudenko, Sergei. *The Ancient Culture of the Bering Sea and the Eskimo Problem*. Arctic Institute of North America, Toronto, 1961. (Translated from the original Russian by Paul Tolstoy.)
Wahlgren, Erik. *The Vikings and America*. Thames and Hudson, London and New York, 1986.

Chapter 12 **Epilog**

The Epilog is a superficial glance at later cultural developments south of the Wisconsin ice sheets. Fortunately, a few key references provide an admirable guide for the beginning reader. A good starting point on the climatic background is H.E. Wright (ed.) *Late-Quaternary Environments of the United States, vol. 2: The Holocene* (University of Minnesota Press, Minneapolis, 1983), which contains essays on many aspects of the post-glacial. Two essays are of special interest to archaeologists: C.M. Aikens, "Environmental archaeology of the western United States," 239–251, and J.B. Stoltman and D.A. Barreis, "The Evolution of human ecosystems in the eastern and central United States," 252–268. Two recent books add a great deal to Aiken's summary: Michael J. Moratto, *California Archaeology* (Academic Press, New York, 1984) and Linda S. Cordell, *Prehistory of the Southwest* (Academic Press, New York, 1984). The Eastern Woodlands are summarized in two long papers in Jesse D. Jennings' edited *Ancient Native Americans* (W.H. Freeman, San Francisco, 1983): James Griffin, "The Midlands and Northeastern United States," 221–280, and Jon D. Muller, "The Southeast," 281–326. Stuart

Struever and Gail Holton, F.A. *Koster* (Anchor Press/Doubleday, New York, 1979) is a popular account of this famous site for general readers. Bruce Smith, "The archaeology of the Southeastern United States: From Dalton to de Soto, 10,500–500 B.P.," *Advances in World Archaeology*, 5 (1986), 1–92, covers much of the ground in this chapter in sophisticated detail.

Other References
Aikens, C.M. "Hogup Cave," *University of Utah Anthropological Papers*, no. 93 (1970).
Brose, D.S. and Greber, N. (eds.) *Hopewell Archaeology*. Kent State University Press, Kent, Ohio, 1979.
Caldwell, J.R. *Trend and Tradition in the Prehistory of the Eastern United States*. American Anthropological Association Memoir, no. 88, 1958.
Fowler, M.L. *Summary Report of Modoc Rockshelter*. Illinois State Museum, Springfield, 1959.
———(ed.) *Investigations in Cahokia Archaeology*. University of Illinois Press, Urbana, 1978.
———"Cahokia and the American Bottom: Settlement Archaeology," *in* Bruce C. Smith (ed.) *Mississippian Settlement Patterns*. Academic Press, New York, 1978.
Heizer, R.F. and Krieger, A.D. "The Archaeology of Humboldt Cave, Churchill County, Nevada," *University of California Publications in American Archaeology and Ethnology*, vol. 47 (1956), 1–190.
———and Napton, L.K. "Archaeology and the Prehistoric Great Basin Lacustrine Subsistence Regime as Seen from Lovelock Cave, Nevada," *Contributions of the University of California Archaeological Research Facility*, no. 10 (1970).
Hudson, Travis, and others. *Tomol: Chumash Watercraft as described in the ethnographic notes of John Harrington*. Ballena Press, Socorro, 1979.

Jennings, Jesse D. *Danger Cave.* University of Utah Anthropological Papers, no. 27, 1957.

Phillips, James L. and Brown, James A. (eds.) *Archaic Hunters and Gatherers in the American Midwest.* Academic Press, New York, 1983.

Snow, Dean, *The Archaeology of North America*, Thames and Hudson, New York, 1980.

Struever, S. "The Hopewell interaction sphere in riverine-western Great Lakes culture history," *in* J.R. Caldwell and R.L. Hall (eds.) *Hopewellian Studies*, Illinois State Museum, Springfield, 1964, 86–106.

Acknowledgments

The research for *The Great Journey* took me to every corner of North America and much further afield. During the three years of the project, I read thousands of books and articles, examined dozens of collections large and small, and visited many sites both real and imagined. Above all, I talked to my colleagues, who were not only helpful and critical, but perceptive and encouraging as well. It is impossible to thank all those who discussed their finds and theories with me, offered hospitality, or reviewed portions of the manuscript. I hope they will take this collective word of thanks and the very existence of this book as a measure of my respect for their dedicated researches. Needless to say, the opinions expressed in this book are not necessarily shared by them.

Some friends and colleagues deserve special thanks. Bob Griffith and Jack Lobdell were a mine of hospitable and vital information on Alaska. I learnt a great deal from a memorable visit to Richard Morlan and Jacques Cinq-Mars at the Museum of Man, Ottawa. Jeff Flenniken and his colleagues at the Washington State University Lithic Field School transformed my understanding of Paleo-Indian stone technology in a few memorable days. Frederick Hadleigh West gave me insights into his Alaskan researches. James Adovasio, Roy Carlson, Dena Dincauze, Michael Glassow, Vance Haynes, Thomas Lynch, Robert McGhee, Jon Muller, Colin Ridler, Jeremy Sabloff, Olga Soffer, Andrew Stewart, and Chris Stringer were among those who provided critical comments. I owe a special debt of gratitude to Esmée Webb, who generously shared her own research on the first Americans with me, as well as tearing an early draft of the text to shreds, which it richly deserved. Kathleen Brandes breathed on the manuscript with great effect at a critical stage in its evolution.

Financial support for some of the travel in connection with this project was provided by ARCO Alaska, the National Endowment for the Humanities, the National Geographic Society, and the UCSB Academic Senate Faculty Research Fund.

List of Illustrations

Index

Page numbers in *italic* refer to maps and drawings; numerals in **bold** refer to numbered plates and their captions.